Samuel J. Kon

JOHN
MARSHALL
and
ALEXANDER
HAMILTON

Architects of the

American Constitution

THE MACMILLAN COMPANY, NEW YORK
COLLIER-MACMILLAN LIMITED, LONDON

Third Printing 1967

THE MACMILLAN COMPANY, NEW YORK
COLLIER-MACMILLAN CANADA, LTD., TORONTO, ONTARIO

Library of Congress catalog card number: 64-19672

Printed in the United States of America

For my daughter Margaret
Whose persistent but gentle prodding also
helped

Acknowledgments

The research for this book was begun in the fall of 1957 when I came to the Institute for Advanced Study as a Member of its School of Historical Studies. It did not take me long to discover just what Abraham Flexner, founder of the Institute, meant when he described it as "a scholar's paradise." I shall always remember with warm appreciation the many thoughtful and imaginative ways in which Dr. J. Robert Oppenheimer and his colleagues facilitated my work.

During my second year at the Institute, I also had the benefit of a Faculty Research Fellowship from the Social Science Research Council. To Mr. Elbridge Sibley, the Council's Executive Associate, I am indeed grateful for much kindness and good advice. But the book could not have been completed without the uncommonly generous aid of Mr. Paul Mellon. I cannot possibly thank him enough.

In the course of preparing the manuscript, I had the cooperation of a number of research institutions, and I wish to take this opportunity to express my gratitude to their splendid staffs. Several persons were unusually helpful to me, and I must record my special debt to them: Miss Judith E. Sachs, Librarian of the Institute for Advanced Study; William S. Dix, Librarian of Princeton University; Earl C. Borgeson, Librarian of the Harvard Law School; James A. Servies, Librarian of the College of William and Mary; Gordon A. Rowell, Chief of the Social Science Division, Brooklyn College Library; Miss Norma Cuthbert, Manuscript Department of the Huntington Library; Francis L. Berkeley, Jr., Curator of Manuscripts, Alderman Library of the University of Virginia; Miss Margaret E. Lough, Chief of the Social

Science Library at the Johns Hopkins University; Miss Winifred Collins of the Massachusetts Historical Society; Lionel J. Coen, Librarian of the New York Law Institute; Joseph L. Andrews, Reference Librarian of the Association of the Bar of the City of New York; and Miss Dorothy S. Eaton, Manuscript Division of the Library of Congress. For the fine arrangements which enabled me to carry on research at their respective Law Schools during the summer of 1958, I have reason to be grateful to Dean William L. Prosser of the University of California at Berkeley, Dean Carl B. Spaeth of Stanford University, and Professor James D. Sumner, Jr., of the University of California at Los Angeles.

My obligation to Mrs. Anne Ritter of the Brooklyn Braille Bindery is greater than ever. Not only has she continued to transcribe for me research materials not otherwise available in braille, but this time she also shared the burden of reading galleys and page proof—and with characteristic devotion and care. I am no less appreciative of Mrs. Helene Koppelson's meticulous and steady performance as "hand-braillist." For their remarkably prompt and genial response to my numerous requests, I am constantly indebted to Miss Dorothy S. Knight and Mr. Bernard M. Krebs, who direct the transcribing program at The Lighthouse and the New York Guild, respectively. Mrs. Carol Weinbaum has my sincere thanks for a superb job of typing the manuscript.

It is a pleasure to speak of my happy association with Mr. Cecil Scott, Editor in Chief at The Macmillan Company. He may not realize how highly I value his friendly interest and expert piloting.

I do not quite know how to acknowledge my wife's contribution to the writing of this book, except to say that it has been, as always before, uniquely indispensable. Our children—Fred and Margaret—helped make the final stages of publication a rewarding family experience.

S. J. K.

April, 1964

Contents

◆◆◆◆◆◆◆◆◆I◆I◆I◆I◆◆◆I◆I◆◆

Introduction:

The Supreme Court and America's "Constitutional Destiny"

◆◆◆◆◆◆◆◆◆◆◆◆◆◆◆◆◆◆◆◆◆◆◆

Soon after he had completed fifteen years as a member of the Supreme Court, Felix Frankfurter undertook to explain, at a meeting of the American Philosophical Society, the subtle and difficult work done by his Court. But before turning to his task as teacher, the Justice stressed the great importance of understanding the true character of that work:

> Broadly speaking, the chief reliance of law in a democracy is the habit of popular respect for law. Especially true is it that law as promulgated by the Supreme Court ultimately depends upon confidence of the people in the Supreme Court as an institution. Indispensable, therefore, for the country's welfare is an appreciation of what the nature of the enterprise is in which that Court is engaged—an understanding of what the task is that has been committed to the succession of nine men.[1]

Justice Frankfurter did not exaggerate the significance of his subject. Any light thrown on the fundamental nature of the function performed by the Supreme Court is bound also to illuminate the whole complex scheme of government contemplated

[1] Frankfurter, "Some observations on the nature of the Judicial Process of Supreme Court Litigation," a paper read before the American Philosophical Society, April 22, 1954; reprinted in *Of Law and Men*, Papers and Addresses of Felix Frankfurter, edited by Philip Elman (New York: Harcourt, Brace & Co., 1956), p. 31.

by the Constitution of the United States. Perhaps this is the underlying reason for the continuing concern shown by Americans over the role to be played by the judiciary—a concern which actually antedates the adoption of the Constitution.

Yet Americans have not been the only ones to be intrigued and baffled by the seemingly strange phenomenon of having judges exert a well-nigh absolute veto over decisions of the politically responsible units of government. "No feature of the government of the United States," observed Lord Bryce, "has awakened so much curiosity in the European mind, caused so much discussion, received so much admiration and been more frequently misunderstood than the duties assigned to the Supreme Court, and the functions which it discharges in guarding the Ark of the Constitution." [2] This intimate identification of the Court with the Constitution has been more than a popular cult; it is a good clue to both the historic roots and the power of the Supreme Court as a social institution. Nevertheless, not even the Justices themselves have been able to agree on the exact scope of the authority the Constitution has vested in them. As Carl Brent Swisher has recently written, "Throughout its entire history . . . the Supreme Court has been in search of the Constitution as the judges sitting were able to see and define the Constitution, and throughout its entire history the Court has been seeking to determine the character and dimensions of its own role in the government." [3]

One of the consequences of this unending quest has been the emergence of what might be called a philosophy of institutional self-justification. It would be a mistake, however, to suppose that the Court has been engaged in an endeavor to keep the document of 1787 in its pristine purity. The contrary is, of course, one of the cardinal truths about the Supreme Court as the ultimate interpreter of the Constitution.

Paradoxically, the very fact that it is a *court* which has been exercising the power of judicial review may help account for the

[2] James Bryce, *The American Commonwealth* (London: Macmillan and Company, 1888), I, 323.
[3] Swisher, *The Supreme Court in Modern Role* (New York: New York University Press, 1958), p. 6.

confusion and misunderstanding. Not even the framers of the Constitution appreciated the potential impact of their handiwork when they reposed the "judicial power of the United States" in "one Supreme Court, and in such inferior Courts as the Congress may from time to time ordain and establish." What Justice Holmes said about the Constitution generally applies with special aptness to the language of its judicial article: "When we are dealing with words that also are a constituent act, like the Constitution of the United States, we must realize that they have called into life a being the development of which could not have been foreseen completely by the most gifted of its begetters." [4] While some of the delegates at the Constitutional Convention of 1787 no doubt looked to an independent judiciary, serving for life, to protect the young Republic against the excesses of popular government, it is by no means clear that they foresaw or intended that the Supreme Court would become the final arbiter of our constitutional system. The essence of the matter has been put simply enough by Edward S. Corwin: "Though the idea that courts were entitled to pronounce on the constitutionality of legislative acts had received countenance in a few dicta in some of the States and perhaps in one or two decisions, this idea was still at best in 1787 but the germ of a possible institution." [5]

By the time John Marshall had put aside his labors as Chief Justice of the United States in 1835, the fledgling doctrine of 1787 had evolved into what is without doubt the single most significant gloss on the Constitution. Judicial review had indeed become an "institution," an instrument of government no less vital to the American people than the institutions explicitly created by the Constitution—and in some respects perhaps even more so. It is probably true, moreover, as Jefferson B. Fordham has pointed out, that a "major factor in the durability of the Constitution has been the role of the courts in giving it authoritative interpretation." Dean Fordham follows this observation with several others which are also worth recalling:

[4] *Missouri v. Holland,* 252 U.S. 416, 433 (1920).
[5] Corwin, *John Marshall and the Constitution* (New Haven: Yale University Press, 1919), pp. 7–8.

This is not to suggest that the same conception of the function of judicial review has prevailed throughout. To Marshall it was an instrument of national supremacy wielded by a national court. To his successor, Taney, the Court occupied a somewhat detached position as an arbiter of a federal system of dual sovereignties. Today the Court again employs judicial review to preserve the principles of national supremacy but it also, and very significantly, exercises it to assure to the individual the benefit of the rule of law under the safeguards of the Bill of Rights. . . . The great function of judicial review continues as the legitimate means of applying to the problems of today and tomorrow the principles of the Constitution which were so wisely couched in broad and general terms. That this involves a kind of constitutional evolution is not realistically to be denied.[6]

Dean Fordham's theory of "constitutional evolution" may be contrasted with the rather oversimplified picture of the Constitution which Franklin D. Roosevelt drew for the American people when he was seeking their support for his 1937 plan to "pack" the Supreme Court. "I hope," the President told them in one of his fireside chats, "that you have reread the Constitution of the United States in these past few weeks. Like the Bible, it ought to be read again and again. It is an easy document to understand when you remember that it was called into being because the Articles of Confederation under which the original thirteen States tried to operate after the Revolution showed the need of a National Government with power enough to handle national problems." [7] Roosevelt revealed, perhaps unwittingly, his own attitude toward the role of the judiciary when he went on to speak of the relations among the three departments of the government:

Last Thursday I described the American form of Government as a three-horse team provided by the Constitution to the American people so that their field might be plowed. The three horses are,

[6] Fordham, "The Legal Profession and American Constitutionalism," 16th Benjamin N. Cardozo Lecture, The Record of the Association of the Bar of the City of New York, vol. 12, no. 9 (Dec., 1957), pp. 518, 520–521.

[7] March 9, 1937. *The Public Papers and Addresses of Franklin D. Roosevelt,* edited by Samuel I. Rosenman, 1937 Volume—The Constitution Prevails (London, Macmillan and Company, 1941), p. 124.

of course, the three branches of government—the Congress, the Executive and the Courts. Two of the horses are pulling in unison today; the third is not. Those who have intimated that the President of the United States is trying to drive that team, overlook the simple fact that the President, as Chief Executive, is himself one of the three horses.

It is the American people themselves who are in the driver's seat.

It is the American people themselves who want the furrow plowed.

It is the American people themselves who expect the third horse to pull in unison with the other two.[8]

It is plain from something else Roosevelt said on that occasion that he did not wish the people to blame the troubles he was having with the judiciary on its function in applying the Constitution. He was in effect telling them that the Supreme Court's action in nullifying important measures of economic recovery was not an inevitable by-product of the Court's exercise of the power of judicial review. "Our difficulty with the Court today," the President insisted, "rises not from the Court as an institution, but from human beings within it. But we cannot yield our constitutional destiny to the personal judgment of a few men who, being fearful of the future, would deny us the necessary means of dealing with the present." He assured the country that his proposal for enlarging the membership of the Supreme Court was intended merely "to restore the Court to its rightful and historic place in our system of Constitutional Government." Its adoption, he believed, would give the Nation courts "willing to enforce the Constitution as written, and unwilling to assert legislative powers by writing into it their own political and economic policies."[9]

[8] *Ibid.,* pp. 123–124.
[9] *Ibid.,* pp. 130, 132. One comment by Roosevelt must have been particularly irritating to Chief Justice Hughes. After referring to recent dissents in which the majority had been accused of passing on the "wisdom" or "public policy" embodied in the laws being annulled, the President added: "In the face of such dissenting opinions, it is perfectly clear, that as Chief Justice Hughes has said: 'We are under a Constitution, but the Constitution is what the Judges say it is.'" *Ibid.,* p. 126.
Hughes seems to have despaired of ever seeing his original statement

There is a striking parallel between Franklin D. Roosevelt's indictment of the Supreme Court's behavior in the 1930s and the Southern attack on the Court which erupted two decades later. Compare, for instance, Roosevelt's argument that the invalidation of New Deal legislation was the work of "a few men" who had "abused" their power under the Constitution, with the position taken by the Southern members of Congress who signed the "Declaration of Constitutional Principles" in the spring of 1956. Protesting the Court's decisions in the *School Segregation* cases,[10] the so-called "Southern Manifesto" began with the following pronouncement:

> The unwarranted decision of the Supreme Court in the public school cases is now bearing the fruit always produced when men substitute naked power for established law.
>
> The Founding Fathers gave us a Constitution of checks and balances because they realized the inescapable lesson of history that no man or group of men can be safely entrusted with unlimited power. They framed this Constitution with its provisions for change by amendment in order to secure the fundamentals of government against the dangers of temporary popular passion or the personal predilections of public officeholders.
>
> We regard the decision of the Supreme Court in the school cases as clear abuse of judicial power. It climaxes a trend in the Federal judiciary undertaking to legislate, in derogation of the authority of Congress, and to encroach upon the reserved rights of the States and the people.[11]

The main charge implicit in the manifesto has been expressed somewhat more succinctly by James F. Byrnes, himself a former

quoted in full, but this is what the future Chief Justice actually said in 1907 while he was Governor of New York: "I have the highest regard for the courts. My whole life has been spent in work conditioned upon respect for the courts. I reckon him one of the worst enemies of the community who will talk lightly of the dignity of the bench. We are under a Constitution, but the Constitution is what the judges say it is, and the judiciary is the safeguard of our liberty and of our property under the Constitution." See Merlo J. Pusey, *Charles Evans Hughes* (New York: The Macmillan Company, 1951), I, 204.

[10] *Brown v. Board of Education of Topeka,* 347 U.S. 483 (1954); *Brown v. Board of Education of Topeka,* 349 U.S. 294 (1955).

[11] Issued on March 11, 1956, the manifesto was signed by nineteen Senators and seventy-seven Representatives, all from Southern States. *84 Cong. Rec.* 4460–4461.

member of the Supreme Court. "The Court did not interpret the Constitution—the Court amended it." [12]

But the right of the Supreme Court to control the other organs of government has not gone unchallenged. Its very credentials, as it were, have been questioned. Indeed, at times the attack has emanated from unexpected quarters. Probably the most notable instance in the recent past is to be found in Judge Learned Hand's Oliver Wendell Holmes Lectures at the Harvard Law School. Coming near the close of his long life and after almost a half century of distinguished service on federal courts, Judge Hand's sharp words have the ring of a swan song inspired by deep and abiding doubts. Four widely separated comments from the lectures should suffice in conveying the thrust of his argument:

> What could be better evidence of complete dependence than to subject the validity of the decision of one "Department" as to its authority on a given occasion to review and reversal by another whose own action was conditioned upon the answer to the same issue? Such a doctrine makes supreme the "Department" that has the last word.

> There is nothing in the United States Constitution that gave courts any authority to review the decisions of Congress; and it was a plausible—indeed to my mind an unanswerable—argument that it invaded that "Separation of Powers" which, as many believed, was the condition of all free governments.

> Judges are seldom content merely to annul the particular solution before them; they do not, indeed they may not, say that taking all things into consideration, the legislators' solution is too strong for the judicial stomach. On the contrary, they wrap up their veto in a protective veil of adjectives such as "arbitrary," "artificial," "normal," "reasonable," "inherent," "fundamental," or "essential," whose office usually, though quite innocently, is to disguise what they are doing and impute to it a derivation far more impressive than their personal preferences, which are all that in fact lie behind the decision. If we do need a third chamber it should appear for what it is, and not as the interpreter of inscrutable principles.

[12] Byrnes, "The Supreme Court Must be Curbed," *U.S. News and World Report,* May 18, 1956, p. 50.

It certainly does not accord with the underlying presuppositions of popular government to vest in a chamber, unaccountable to anyone but itself, the power to suppress social experiments which it does not approve.[13]

More interesting still is the context in which Judge Learned Hand maintained that the practice of having judges set aside public policies is just as undesirable as government by an elite of "guardians" advocated by Plato:

Each one of us must in the end choose for himself how far he would like to leave our collective fate to the wayward vagaries of popular assemblies. No one can fail to recognize the perils to which the last forty years have exposed such governments. We are not, indeed, forced to choose between absolutism and the kind of democracy that so often prevailed in Greek cities during the sixth to fourth centuries before our era. The Founding Fathers were acutely, perhaps overacutely, aware of the dangers that had followed that sort of rule, though, as you all know, they differed widely as to what curbs to impose. For myself it would be most irksome to be ruled by a bevy of Platonic Guardians, even if I knew how to choose them, which I assuredly do not.[14]

These variations on a familiar theme in the judicial history of the United States suggest a basic problem in the assessment of the contribution of John Marshall and Alexander Hamilton as architects of the American Constitution. If one accepts Howard Lee McBain's concept of the Constitution as the whole "living" body of principles and practices constituting the American system of government in action—and not merely the parchment of 1787—it becomes necessary to inquire into the forces which have

[13] Hand, *The Bill of Rights* (Cambridge: Harvard University Press, 1958), pp. 4, 10–11, 70, 73.

[14] *Ibid.*, p. 73. Dean Eugene V. Rostow of the Yale Law School is probably our leading exponent of what he has called "the democratic character of judicial review." For a sustained and eloquent defense of this position, see his recently published collection of essays, *The Sovereign Prerogative:* The Supreme Court and the Quest for Law (New Haven: Yale University Press, 1962). A more direct response to Judge Learned Hand's argument was made by the man who delivered the Holmes Lectures a year later. See Herbert Wechsler, "Toward Neutral Principles of Constitutional Law," reprinted in his *Principles, Politics and Fundamental Law* (Cambridge: Harvard University Press, 1961), pp. 3–48.

made that document so flexible and durable a framework of government.[15] Both Hamilton and Marshall are sure to loom large in any such examination.

At least one delegate to the Philadelphia Convention took a modest enough view of the plan of government being drafted to acknowledge that its ultimate worth would depend on the men who were fated to put it into motion. Under the date of August 14, 1787, James Madison reported the following observation by John Francis Mercer of Maryland: "It is a great mistake to suppose that the paper we are to propose will govern the U.States. It is The men whom it will bring into the Governt. and interest in maintaining it that is to govern them. The paper will only mark out the mode & the form—Men are the substance and must do the business. All Govt. must be by force or influence." [16]

Mercer's prophetic insight has a natural relevance when applied to Marshall as well as Hamilton. The reason is, of course, an accident of time. The two men happened to occupy positions of commanding "influence" at a decisive moment in the life of the nation—when the Constitution was launched both as a tool of statecraft and as a touchstone of permissible authority to govern.

Though operating in quite different spheres, Hamilton and Marshall succeeded in leaving the impress of their ideas upon the process of government in the United States. Marshall, working within the cloistered temple of the judiciary, was able to advance the conceptions of national power which are implicit in the programs pioneered by Hamilton within the administrative and legislative arenas. On the other hand, as social conservatives, they believed deeply in the importance of setting limits to the encroachment on private rights, particularly property. Yet each of them, in his own fashion, helped to vindicate theories of governmental authority which were destined to lay the foundation for the virtual collapse of *laissez-faire* notions of public responsibility. From this standpoint, what Paul A. Freund has said

[15] See McBain, *The Living Constitution:* A Consideration of the Realities and Legends of our Fundamental Law (New York: The Macmillan Company, 1927).

[16] *The Records of the Federal Convention of 1787*, Max Farrand, ed. (New Haven: Yale University Press, 1937), II, 289.

about the meaning of John Marshall for the New Deal is suggestive of a leading paradox in American constitutional development. "Although the conception of national economic power had not crystallized by the time of the New Deal, there were decisions . . . which would have sufficed in the hands of a Marshall to validate the major measures taken in the depression." [17]

The same is basically true of Hamilton, as one of our keenest analysts of the intellectual legacy of Thomas Jefferson has conceded. Discussing what he regards as "the crisis of American democracy in the twentieth century"—the attempt to reconcile the liberal response to the problems of industrial capitalism with the tenets of the "Jeffersonian philosophy"—Merrill D. Peterson writes: "The possibility presented itself of a social and political reconstruction under Hamilton's star rather than Jefferson's." It is easy to discern the reason for this "topsy-turvy" situation. "The Jeffersonian philosophy defined liberty largely in terms of the absence of governmental restraint. The conception seemed not only useless but positively harmful in a society where the aggressions against the individual were economic rather than political, begging to be met by more rather than less government." Recalling that the "strongest appeal of Hamilton and Hamiltonian tradition" to the Progressives in the early years of the present century "lay in his bold use of the powers of government for constructive national purposes," Professor Peterson insists that the triumph of Hamilton was vitiated by the "process of revision" to which Jefferson's ideas were subjected during the "era" of Franklin D. Roosevelt.[18]

It must be remembered that the factors which were at the heart of Jefferson's historic conflict with Hamilton account also for his unabated antipathy to Marshall, whom he accused of converting the Constitution into "a mere thing of wax" to be twisted by the judiciary "into any form they please." [19] In a letter to one

[17] Freund, "Umpiring the Federal System," 54 *Columbia Law Review* (1954), 561, 565.

[18] Merrill D. Peterson, *The Jefferson Image and the American Mind* (New York: Oxford University Press, 1960), pp. 330, 333.

[19] Thomas Jefferson to Judge Spencer Roane, Sept. 6, 1819. *The Works of Thomas Jefferson*, Paul L. Ford, ed. (1904), XII, 137.

of Marshall's colleagues, penned toward the end of his life, Jefferson explained once again his approach to the interpretation of the Constitution. "You request me confidentially," Jefferson wrote to Justice William Johnson, "to examine the question whether the Supreme Court has advanced beyond its constitutional limits, and trespassed on those of the State authorities?" After some hesitation, the former President obliged by unburdening himself as follows:

> It may be impracticable to lay down any general formula of words which shall decide at once and with precision in every case, this limit of jurisdiction. But there are two canons which will guide us safely in most of the cases. 1st. The capital and leading object of the constitution was to leave with the States all authorities which respected their own citizens only, and to transfer to the United States those which respected citizens of foreign or other States: to make us several as to ourselves, but one as to all others. . . . 2nd. On every question of construction, carry ourselves back to the time when the constitution was adopted, recollect the spirit manifested in the debates, and instead of trying what meaning may be squeezed out of the text, or invented against it, conform to the probable one in which it was passed.[20]

That constitutional interpretation should have served as the medium through which Marshall manifested his affinity with Hamilton is a fact telling us much about the unique function which the Supreme Court was to assume under his leadership. Was the coincidence due to their common allegiance as Federalists, or was there a deeper cause at work? The key element in a possible answer to this question will be found in a comment made by Charles Evans Hughes in his well-known lectures on the Supreme Court. Speaking with the perspective of one whose study of the Court had been enriched by first-hand acquaintance with its methods and its members, Hughes called attention to the close link between a judge's constitutional viewpoint and his attitudes as a private citizen. We read in the second lecture:

> If conscientious, able and independent men are put on the bench, you cannot predict their course as judges by reference either

[20] Thomas Jefferson to Justice William Johnson, June 12, 1823. *Ibid.*, XII, 257.

to partisan motives or to personal or party loyalties. If you could get further down to the bedrock of conviction as to what are conceived to be fundamental principles of government and social relations, you might be able to get closer to accurate prophecy.[21]

Or, as one of Marshall's eulogists has expressed it, "When Marshall took his seat on the Supreme Bench he brought with him not only his legal genius and training and his wide and various experience in politics and diplomacy, but also certain fixed convictions." [22]

Still another question raised concerning the kinship between Marshall and Hamilton tends to minimize Marshall's creative achievements as Chief Justice. Because so much of his constitutional philosophy reminds one of the Hamiltonian creed, it has been suggested that Marshall was more the imitator than the innovator. This suspicion was voiced by no less profound a student of our legal system than Justice Oliver Wendell Holmes, and under rather unlikely circumstances.

"If American law were to be represented by a single figure, sceptic and worshipper alike would agree without dispute that the figure could be one alone, and that one, John Marshall." This tribute was paid by Justice Holmes in 1901, on the occasion of the one-hundredth anniversary of the day Marshall became Chief Justice of the United States. But it was in the same speech in which Holmes also intimated that Marshall was not quite the original thinker his more avid admirers had depicted him to be. Said Holmes:

> *The Federalist,* when I read it many years ago, seemed to me a truly original and wonderful production for the time. I do not trust even that judgment unrevised when I remember that *The Federalist* and its authors struck a distinguished English friend of mine as finite; for I should feel a greater doubt whether, after

[21] Hughes, *The Supreme Court of the United States* (Garden City: Garden City Publishing Co., 1936), p. 49.
[22] Henry Cabot Lodge, "An Address Upon Chief Justice Marshall," delivered at Chicago, Feb. 4, 1901. Reprinted in *John Marshall, Life, Character and Judicial Services,* As Portrayed in the Centenary and Memorial Addresses and Proceedings Throughout the United States on Marshall Day, 1901. Compiled and edited by John F. Dillon (Chicago: Callaghan and Company, 1903) II, 303, 318

Hamilton and the Constitution itself, Marshall's work proved more
than a strong intellect, a good style, personal ascendancy in his
court, courage, justice and the convictions of his party.[23]

One way in which to pursue the challenging implications of
these words of Justice Holmes is through a comparative study
of the ideas of Marshall and Hamilton. What is meant when it
is asserted that "much of Marshall's career may be viewed as a
process of reading Hamilton's state papers into the Constitution,"
as Max Lerner has phrased it?[24] The extent to which Marshall
may have borrowed from Hamilton is but part of a larger problem in the interpretation of American ideology.

Focusing upon the formative period under the Federal Constitution, the present volume will explore the manner in which
Marshall and Hamilton helped to mold the Constitution into
the dynamic implement of government it has proved itself to
be. There is considerable evidence that Hamilton, in the realm
of social thought and in the field of public policy, and Marshall,
in the emerging domain of constitutional jurisprudence, drew on
a common stream of ideas and values. "The life of Marshall," it
has been remarked, "was itself the constitutional history of the
country, from 1801 to 1835."[25] But both Marshall and Hamilton
were dealing with problems of statecraft in a developing national
community, struggling to adjust itself to the contours of a complicated federal system.

Sometimes there is drama in the simple chronology of history.
When John Marshall, at the age of forty-five, began to preside
over the Supreme Court—on February 4, 1801, to be exact—the

---

[23] Holmes, "John Marshall," reprinted in *The Occasional Speeches of
Justice Oliver Wendell Holmes*, edited by Mark DeWolfe Howe (Cambridge:
Harvard University Press, 1962), pp. 133–134. Speaking on the same day,
James Bradley Thayer took the intellectual measure of Marshall quite dif-
ferently: "In most of Marshall's opinions, one observes the style and the
special touch of a thoughtful and original mind; in some of them the powers
of a great mind in full activity." Thayer, *John Marshall* (Boston: Houghton,
Mifflin and Company, 1901), p. 56.

[24] Lerner, "John Marshall's Long Shadow," reprinted in *Ideas Are Weapons*
(New York: The Viking Press, 1943), p. 31.

[25] Edward J. Phelps, "Chief Justice Marshall and the Constitutional Law
of his Time," an address before the American Bar Association, Aug. 21, 1879,
p. 7. (Library of the Association of the Bar of the City of New York.)

career of Alexander Hamilton, who was only a few months older, was coming to a tragic end. Hamilton died three years later. Marshall thus entered upon the most significant phase of his public life at a moment of bitterness and defeat for Hamilton and for the party which he led—the party that was now routed by the forces of Jeffersonianism. How ironic, then, that Marshall's ensuing thirty-four-year tenure as Chief Justice should have served as an unparalleled opportunity for weaving into the constitutional fabric of American society ideas which were of central concern to Hamilton.

The fact that Hamilton and Marshall played their decisive roles in the early years of the Republic lends special importance to the similarity of their outlook as national leaders. To Hamilton as well as to Marshall there fell what Justice Frankfurter has aptly labeled "the duty of creation." [26] When one thinks of the rare opportunity which was theirs to affect America's future, one need not hesitate to apply to Hamilton also the truism uttered by Holmes with Marshall in mind: "A great man represents . . . a strategic point in the campaign of history, and part of his greatness consists in his being *there*." [27]

The association of Marshall and Hamilton with the art of statecraft raises an old and debatable question about the science of government: What is "statesmanship"? An additional difficulty for Americans is the place of statesmanship in constitutional law. In this connection, the often quoted observations by James Bradley Thayer are particularly pertinent:

> The study of Constitutional Law is allied not merely with history, but with statecraft, and with the political problems of our great and complex national life.
>
> In this wide and novel field of labor our judges have been pioneers. There have been men among them, like Marshall . . . who were sensible of the true nature of their work and of the large method of treatment which it required, who perceived that our constitutions had made them, in a limited and secondary way,

[26] Frankfurter, *The Commerce Clause Under Marshall, Taney and Waite* (Chapel Hill: University of North Carolina Press, 1937), p. 12.

[27] *The Occasional Speeches of Justice Oliver Wendell Holmes* (Howe, ed.), p. 132.

but yet a real one, coadjutors with the other departments in the business of government; but many have fallen short of the requirements of so great a function.[28]

Justice Frankfurter has gone further. In the address with which he opened the 1955 conference on "Government Under Law," marking the two-hundredth anniversary of Marshall's birth, Justice Frankfurter implied that Marshall is the only American judge who legitimately may be considered as a statesman. He said: "The decisive claim to John Marshall's distinction as a great statesman is as a judge. And he is the only judge who has that distinction." [29]

The attempt to deal with the ways in which Hamilton and Marshall contributed to the evolution of the American Constitution leads one to recall Edmund Burke's perceptive inquiry into the problem of maintaining free government. That "greatest of modern conservative thinkers," as Russell Kirk has acclaimed him to be,[30] was enough of a romantic not to overlook the human equation in the art of government. Addressing himself to the question as to what it takes to preserve free institutions, Burke presented a rather arresting hypothesis:

> To make a government requires no great prudence. Settle the seat of power, teach obedience, and the work is done. To give freedom is still more easy. It is not necessary to guide; it only requires to let go the rein. But to form a *free government,* that is, to temper together these opposite elements of liberty and restraint in one consistent work, requires much thought, deep reflection, a sagacious, powerful, and combining mind.[31]

Writing in the same year, Burke's American counterpart hurled a similar challenge, though in much more defiant terms.

[28] Thayer, *Cases on Constitutional Law* (Cambridge: George H. Kent, 1895), pp. V–VI.
[29] Frankfurter, "John Marshall and the Judicial Function," reprinted in *Government Under Law,* Arthur E. Sutherland, ed. (Cambridge: Harvard University Press, 1955), p. 7.
[30] Kirk, *The Conservative Mind* (Chicago: Henry Regnery Company, 1953), p. 3.
[31] Burke, *Reflections on the Revolution in France. The Works of the Right Honorable Edmund Burke* (London: John C. Nimmo, 1899), III, 559–560.

On September 12, 1790, John Adams dispatched a character-istically blunt comment to Samuel Adams:

> What, my old Friend, is this world about to become? Is the
> millennium commencing? Are the kingdoms of it, about to be
> governed by reason? Your Boston town-meetings, and our Harvard
> College, have set the universe in motion. Every thing will be
> pulled down. So much seems certain. But what will be built up?
> Are there any principles of political architecture? What are they?
> Were Voltaire and Rousseau masters of them? Are their disciples
> acquainted with them? Locke taught them principles of liberty.
> But I doubt whether they have not yet to learn the principles of
> government. Will the struggle in Europe, be any thing more than
> a change of impostors and impositions? [32]

But in the special setting of America's experiment with a system of self-government functioning under the weight of numerous limitations on the power to govern, it must be recognized that the right to determine how the balance between "liberty and restraint" shall be struck has been largely pre-empted by one of the organs of government. That organ acts in the name of a written Constitution, proclaiming itself to be "the supreme Law of the Land." Where does our national charter "settle" political power, and what kind of minds have been "required" to make it work? "The Constitution, in making the balance between the different parts of our government a legal rather than a political question," wrote the late Robert H. Jackson, "casts the Court as the most philosophical of our departments. It keeps the most fundamental equilibriums of our society, such as that between centralization and localism, between liberty and authority, and between stability and progress. These issues underlie nearly every movement in an organized society." [33] To the extent that John Marshall and Alexander Hamilton were the initiators of a widely accepted approach toward the task of expounding our Constitution, they were destined to become prototypes of the interpreter-statesman demanded by the American system of constitutional government.

[32] *The Works of John Adams,* Charles Francis Adams, ed. (Boston: Charles C. Little and James Brown, 1851), VI, 411–412.

[33] Jackson, *The Struggle for Judicial Supremacy* (New York: Alfred A. Knopf, 1941), p. 312.

PART I

"The Great Revolution"

1

"An Extreme Jealousy of Power"

It was John Marshall who described the events that culminated in the adoption of the American Constitution as a "great revolution." There is reason to surmise, moreover, that this estimate of a bygone conflict was actually the product of an abiding belief. Marshall gave expression to it near the close of his long tenure as Chief Justice and in a case in which the outcome turned on the interpretation of the intentions of the Founding Fathers. "It is universally understood, it is a part of the history of the day," wrote Marshall in 1833, "that the great revolution which established the constitution of the United States, was not effected without immense opposition." [1]

The aged Chief Justice also reminded his countrymen that the Bill of Rights was added to the Constitution largely because of the widespread apprehension that the greatly strengthened national government might come to threaten the fundamental rights of the people. Said Marshall:

> Serious fears were extensively entertained that those powers which the patriot statesmen, who then watched over the interests of our country, deemed essential to union, and to the attainment of those invaluable objects for which union was sought, might be exercised in a manner dangerous to liberty. In almost every convention by which the constitution was adopted, amendments to guard against the abuse of power were recommended. These amendments demanded security against the apprehended encroachments of the General Government—not against those of the local governments.[2]

[1] *Barron v. Baltimore*, 7 Pet. 243, 250 (1833).
[2] *Ibid.* Marshall's opinion held that the provision in the Fifth Amendment, which prohibits the taking of private property for public use without

Among those who had voiced concern over the failure of the Constitutional Convention to draft a bill of rights was Thomas Jefferson, at the time America's minister to France. Though Jefferson was pleased with many features of the proposed Constitution, he was troubled by several serious reservations. Writing to James Madison from Paris in December of 1787, he confessed that he was "not a friend to a very energetic government" and listed "the omission of a bill of rights" as his first objection to the document which had been framed at Philadelphia the previous summer.[3] That this criticism flowed naturally from his philosophy of self-government is clear from something else Jefferson wrote to Madison: "A bill of rights is what the people are entitled to against every government on earth, general or particular, and what no just government should refuse, or rest on inference." [4]

It is significant that Alexander Hamilton did not share either the anxiety or dissatisfaction of his contemporaries over the absence of a bill of rights in the original Constitution. In Number 84 of *The Federalist*, he strongly argued that the Constitution contained adequate safeguards for personal liberty, including the guarantee of the privilege of the writ of habeas corpus—recalling that Blackstone called the Habeas Corpus Act "the BULWARK of the British Constitution." [5] He even suggested that the inclusion of a more elaborate bill of rights in the American Constitution might have carried dangerous implications: "They [the bills of rights demanded by critics of the Constitution] would contain various exceptions to powers not granted; and, on this very account, would afford a colorable pretext to claim more than

just compensation, applied only to the exercise of the power of eminent domain by the federal government, and did not apply to the states or their local subdivisions.

[3] "I will now add what I do not like. First, the omission of a bill of rights providing clearly and without the aid of sophisms for freedom of religion, freedom of the press, protection against standing armies, restriction against monopolies, the eternal and unremitting force of the habeas corpus laws, and trials by jury in all matters of fact triable by the laws of the land, and not by the law of Nations." Thomas Jefferson to James Madison, Dec. 20, 1787. 12 *The Papers of Thomas Jefferson* 440, Julian P. Boyd, ed. (Princeton: Princeton University Press, 1955).

[4] *Ibid.*

[5] Blackstone, *Commentaries*, IV, 438 (cited by Hamilton).

were granted. For why declare that things shall not be done which there is no power to do?" [6] The essence of Hamilton's rejoinder to the libertarian critics of the Constitution may be gleaned from one terse comment: "The Constitution is itself, in every rational sense, and to every useful purpose, A BILL OF RIGHTS." [7]

Though Hamilton no doubt believed that the fears of those who deplored the absence of a bill of rights were unfounded, he was probably even more perturbed by the fact that they were agitated over a false issue. As he saw it, the need was for more power and energy in government, and not for limitations. This difference in outlook between Hamilton and Jefferson—two men who had played important roles in the American Revolution— is symptomatic of the amorphous nature of the eighteenth-century background of our political institutions.

Whatever contradictory impulses may lurk in the American constitutional tradition, they are directly traceable to the two epochal events which have served to impart to that tradition its paradoxical character. Both the Revolution and the Constitution, to be sure, may be viewed as integral parts of the same ideological ferment which saw Americans give vent to their deepest convictions about government and its place in society. Yet these seminal episodes also reflect quite different notions as to the direction in which the new nation was to move.

I

While in the grip of revolutionary fervor, the patriots of '76 stressed the rights of man. The Declaration of Independence gave expression to their gospel of liberty, and Thomas Jefferson became its symbolic voice. "An extreme jealousy of power is the attendant on all popular revolutions" [8] is the way the man who was destined to become Jefferson's chief political and philosophic antagonist indulgently characterized this mood. Exactly five years

[6] *The Federalist,* No. 84, Benjamin Fletcher Wright, ed. (Cambridge: The Belknap Press of Harvard University Press, 1961), p. 535. All subsequent references to *The Federalist* will be to this edition by Professor Wright.

[7] *Ibid.,* p. 536.

[8] Hamilton, "The Continentalist," July 12, 1781. *The Papers of Alexander Hamilton,* Harold C. Syrett and Jacob E. Cooke, ed. (New York: Columbia University Press, 1961), II, 650.

after America's independence was proclaimed, Alexander Hamilton publicly attributed to the contemporary distrust of power "many of the fatal mistakes which have so deeply endangered the common cause." [9]

Hamilton's disillusionment with the political conditions of the country may be said to have begun even before the Articles of Confederation were officially put into effect. As Washington's secretary and confidential aide during the war, he had become greatly disturbed by the evidence of inefficiency and instability. [10] This experience served to strengthen his conviction about the need for vigor and firmness in affairs of state. His first hand observation of the failures of the Continental Congress led him to say, as early as 1780, that the "fundamental defect" in the existing governmental structure was the "want of power in Congress." [11] Writing from headquarters to Governor George Clinton in March of 1778, he remarked, "I dwell upon the faults of Congress . . . because I think they strike at the vitals of our position and our future prosperity." [12]

The detailed diagnosis is to be found in his letter to James Duane, [13] dated September 3, 1780, a letter which has been justly characterized as one of Hamilton's "first state Papers." [14] That his purpose was of the utmost seriousness, and not merely an academic exercise, is clear from the outset. "I sit down to give you my ideas of the defects of the present system, and the changes necessary to save us from ruin." He ascribed the dangerous situation to three causes: "An excess of the spirit of liberty, which has made the particular states show a jealousy of all power not

---

[9] *Ibid.*

[10] "It is impossible the Contest can be much longer Supported on the present footing. We must have a Government with more Power. We must have a Tax in kind. We must have a Foreign Loan. We must have a Bank on the true Principles of a Bank. We must have an Administration distinct from Congress and in the hands of Single Men under their orders. We must above all things have an Army for the War, and on an Establishment that will Interest the Officers in the Service." Letter to Isaac Sears, October 12, 1780. *The Papers of Alexander Hamilton,* II, 472.

[11] *Ibid.,* II, 650.

[12] *Ibid.,* I, 441.

[13] *Ibid.,* II, 400–418.

[14] Broadus Mitchell, *Alexander Hamilton,* Youth to Maturity, 1755–1788 (New York: The Macmillan Company, 1957), p. 189.

in their own hands; . . . a diffidence in Congress of their own powers, by which they have been timid and indecisive in their resolutions, . . . a want of sufficient means at their disposal to answer the public exigencies." [15]

Hamilton's main object was to demonstrate, as he put it flatly, that "the Confederation itself is defective and requires to be altered." Nevertheless, he also emphasized that many of the difficulties flowed from the failure of Congress to take full advantage of the powers it did possess. The exertion of supreme authority implicit in such "highest acts of sovereignty" as the Declaration of Independence and war and the raising of the military forces should have served as a spur to Congress: "undefined powers are discretionary powers, limited only by the object for which they were given; in the present case the independence and freedom of America."

Turning to the Confederation itself, Hamilton observed that it is "neither fit for war nor peace." Extreme as this indictment appears, the reason for it is even more revealing: "The idea of an uncontrollable sovereignty in each State over its internal police will defeat the other powers given to Congress, and make our union feeble and precarious." He complained that the "power of the purse" had been turned over to the states and argued for authority in Congress to tax imports and to adopt land and poll taxes. "Without certain revenues, a government can have no power." And again, "that power which holds the purse strings absolutely must rule."

It is clear from Hamilton's famous letter to Duane that he was primarily concerned with achieving effective government and not merely with the power relations between Congress and the states. "Another defect in our system is want of method and energy in the administration." This situation resulted from the absence of a "proper executive" and because Congress "meddles" in details of administration. It is not possible for a deliberative body to act "with sufficient decision or with system." Hamilton deplored Congress' growing habit of appointing boards and recommended that departments be headed by one person. Though the war for independence from Great Britain was still going on,

[15] *The Papers of Alexander Hamilton,* II, 401.

Hamilton did not hesitate to admit that he was quite prepared to emulate British institutions. His concluding argument for an "administration by single men" also stands as a rather important clue to the system of government toward which he was groping: "All these reasons conspire to give a preference to the plan of vesting the great executive departments of a state in the hands of individuals. As these men will be, of course, at all times under the direction of Congress, we shall blend the advantages of a monarchy and republic in our constitution." [16]

In calling for a more resolute national government, Hamilton was emphatic in rejecting the idea that it menaced freedom. "Nothing appears more evident to me," he remarked, "than that we run much greater risk of having a weak and disunited federal government, than one which will be able to usurp upon the rights of the people." He criticized the influence of the states in the army and demanded exclusive control by Congress over military appointments, promotions, and supplies. He rejected the idea that greater powers for Congress would be "dangerous to liberty." What the country needed was a "solid and coercive union."

Apparently despairing of the possibility that Congress would venture to exercise the "discretionary powers" he believed it possessed, Hamilton called for a "Convention of all the States" to be composed of delegates who had been made fully aware of the dangers flowing from the want of power in Congress. The new "fundamental law" should give Congress a "complete sovereignty; except as to that part of internal policy which relates to the rights of property and life among individuals, and to raising money by internal taxes." But Hamilton went beyond this generalization. Indeed, his recommendations foreshadowed not only the provisions of the Constitution of 1787 but the measures he was to propose when he became Secretary of the Treasury. His list of powers of Congress was long and specific:

> Congress should have complete sovereignty in all that relates to war, peace, trade, finance, and to the management of foreign affairs; the right of declaring war; of raising armies, officering,

[16] *Ibid.*, II, 405.

paying them, directing their motions in every respect; of equipping fleets, and doing the same with them; of building fortifications, arsenals, magazines, etc.; of making peace on such conditions as they think proper; of regulating trade, determining with what countries it should be carried on; granting indulgences; laying prohibitions on all the articles of export and import; imposing duties, granting bounties and premiums for raising, exporting or importing; and applying to their own use the products of these duties, only giving credit to the States on whom they are raised in the general account of revenues and expenses; instituting admiralty courts, etc.; of coining money, establishing banks on such terms, and with such privileges, as they think proper; appropriating funds, and doing whatever else relates to the operation of finance, transacting everything with foreign nations, making alliances offensive and defensive, treaties of commerce, etc., etc.[17]

As one who had seen "All the workings and progress of the present discontents," Hamilton was determined to build "stable foundations" for the government of the Confederation. In speaking of the importance of a bank erected on the credit "of the public and of individuals," he stressed that what he called an "American bank" would be the instrument for impelling "moneyed men" to uphold the public credit. "The only certain manner to obtain a permanent paper credit," he contended, "is to engage the moneyed interest immediately in it, by making them contribute the whole or part of the stock, and giving them the whole or part of the profits."

Hamilton was twenty-three, or at the most twenty-five,[18] when he wrote this remarkable letter to Duane. "At a time when the centrifugal tendencies of the respective states were most in evidence," writes a recent biographer, "he called boldly for a centralized, unified national government. At a time when Congress had shown itself weak, incompetent and corrupt, he demanded more power for it." [19] Hamilton apparently was aware that the changes

[17] *Ibid.*, II, 408.
[18] Until recently it was assumed that Hamilton was born in 1757. There is now reason to believe that he was born two years earlier. See Broadus Mitchell, *op. cit.*, pp. 11–13.
[19] Nathan Schachner, *Alexander Hamilton* (New York: D. Appleton-Century Company, 1946), pp. 112–113.

he was urging were well-nigh revolutionary in their import. "There are epochs in human affairs," he declared, "when even novelty is useful." A reinvigorated Confederation, a permanent military force, and a national bank would restore the people's confidence in the energy of government. "In future, my dear sir," Hamilton admonished, "two things let me recommend as fundamental rules of conduct to Congress: to attach the army to them by every motive; to maintain an air of authority (not domineering) in all their measures with the States." [20]

II

This simultaneous preoccupation with questions of governmental organization as well as with issues of economic policy continued to pervade Hamilton's private correspondence and public expressions. Whether writing to friends, or speaking as a member of the Confederation Congress, or as a member of the New York legislature,[21] he drove home the urgent need for a revision of the existing political order which would create the will and the means for dealing with the problems common to all the States. His most significant utterance during the years preceding the meeting of the Constitutional Convention of 1787 was the series of six essays which came to be known as "The Continentalist." They appeared in the *New York Packet* in the period from July 12, 1781 through July 4, 1782.

In the first of these essays,[22] Hamilton noted that those who launched the Revolution had but "very vague notions" as to the "practical business of government." [23] Whatever ideas they had might have been suited to the colonial "sphere" and not to the government of an independent nation. It was time to acknowledge that there had been "many false steps, many chimerical projects and utopian speculations, in the management of our civil as well as military affairs." Should the country persist in these errors, it would prove that "we are incapable of those enlightened and liberal views necessary to make us a great and a

[20] *The Papers of Alexander Hamilton*, II, 417.

[21] Hamilton served as a member of Congress for a year, 1782–83, and again in 1788. In January of 1787 he became a member of the New York State Assembly.

[22] *The Papers of Alexander Hamilton*, II, 649–652.

[23] *Ibid.*, II, 649.

flourishing people." In terms of fundamental principles and political sagacity, the gravest mistake was the failure to strike a proper balance between freedom and authority, between liberty and power. Hamilton's statement of this dilemma deserves to be recalled:

> History is full of examples, where in contests for liberty, a jealousy of power has either defeated the attempts to recover or preserve it in the first instance, or has afterward subverted it by clogging government with too great precautions for its felicity, or by leaving too wide a door for sedition and popular licentiousness. In a government framed for durable liberty, not less regard must be paid to giving the magistrate a proper degree of authority, to make and execute the laws with rigour, than to guard against encroachments upon the rights of the community. As too much power leads to despotism, too little leads to anarchy, and both eventually to the ruin of the people.[24]

It was "jealousy of power" which had kept America from "reaping all the advantages" from the experience of other nations and which led her to make the constitutions "feeble and imperfect." The state constitutions were likely to be improved in this respect, but the same should not be expected of the federal government: "If it is too weak at first, it will continually grow weaker." This was so because local ambitions and interests tended to undermine and to encroach upon the prerogatives of the central government. A weak federation always faces the specter of disintegration, brought on by the desire on the part of some of the more powerful members to place themselves at the head of new confederacies. "Political societies in close neighborhood must either be strongly united under one government, or there will infallibly exist emulations and quarrels; this is human nature, and we have no reason to think ourselves wiser or better than other men." [25]

The "symptoms" of the impending dissolution of the union were already to be seen, Hamilton announced. Congress was not alone responsible for the situation. Its "greatest" error was its failure to take advantage of the "powers implied in its original

[24] *Ibid.,* II, 651.
[25] *Ibid.,* II, 660.

trust" and its acquiescence in the desire of states to retain "all power" in their own hands.

But Hamilton's chief criticism of the Confederation may be gathered from his assertion that "Congress has been responsible for the administration of affairs, without the means of fulfilling that responsibility." It lacked the vital power of regulating trade, and yet such a power was as "necessary for the purposes of commerce as of revenue." It is Hamilton's argument for endowing the national Congress with authority over trade and finance which has been seized upon as proof that he was an apostle of mercantilism. "There are some, who maintain, that trade will regulate itself, and is not to be benefitted by the encouragements, or restraints of government. Such persons will imagine, that there is no need of a common directing power. This is one of those wild speculative paradoxes, which have grown into credit among us, contrary to the uniform practice and sense of the most enlightened nations." [26]

Moreover, since all the states "have a common interest in trade," there ought to be "a common direction." Only through uniform commercial regulation could the states be kept from pursuing narrow local interests to the detriment of the common good. "Unless we . . . learn to estimate measures by their general tendencies, we shall never be a great or a happy people, if we remain a people at all." Without a power "to advance the general prosperity of trade," both the landed interest and "the laboring poor" will be sacrificed to the trading interest of the particular state. Every state will hesitate to impose duties on commerce lest the state without such taxes derive a competitive advantage. Thus did the man who came to be viewed as a cham-

[26] *Ibid.*, III, 76. It has been suggested that much of Hamilton's thinking in the field of economics and statesmanship was influenced by his reading, during the early years of the Revolution, of Malachy Postlethwayt's *Universal Dictionary of Trade and Commerce.* "Postlethwayt's Dictionary constitutes the most important document yet discovered showing the background and immediate sources of Hamilton's principal writings. . . . Had they [scholars] consulted the Dictionary, they could have found that in most of Hamilton's reports there are traces of Postlethwayt's economic theories and, indeed, whole paragraphs quoted from the Dictionary." See E. P. Panagopoulos, "Hamilton's Notes in His Pay Book of the New York State Artillery Company," *American Historical Review,* vol. LXII, no. 2, 310, 312 (Jan., 1957).

pion of the commercial interest speak as a friend of a balanced national economy:

> Nothing can be more mistaken, than the collision and rival-ship, which almost always subsist between the landed and trading interests, for the truth is they are so inseparably interwoven, that one cannot be injured, without injury, nor benefitted, without benefit to the other. Oppress trade, lands sink in value, make it flourish, their value rises, incumber husbandry, trade declines, en-courage agriculture, commerce revives.[27]

III

"No one," says Richard B. Morris, "saw the perils earlier than Hamilton, and no one kept pounding away at the theme during the Confederation period more insistently." [28] Indeed, if the years Hamilton was writing from Washington's headquarters are included, it would be correct to say that his relentless cam-paign in behalf of a stronger union persisted a whole decade. The reason Hamilton gave to Governor Clinton for dwelling on the "faults of Congress" [29] well epitomize the motivating force behind his polemical and legislative efforts during the ten years preceding the meeting of the Convention which drafted the Constitution of the United States. Throughout this period of letter writing, pamphleteering, and speech making, he was care-ful to maintain that his plans in no way threatened the con-tinued existence of the states as sovereign members of the Union. In the second of his "Continentalist" essays,[30] he had written:

> The security therefore of the public liberty must consist in such a distribution of the sovereign power, as will make it morally impossible for one part to gain an ascendancy over the others, or for the whole to unite in a scheme of usurpation. . . . In federal governments, each member has a distinct sovereignty, makes and executes laws, imposes taxes, distributes justice, and exercises every other function of government. It has always within itself the means of revenue, and on an emergency can levy forces.[31]

[27] *The Papers of Alexander Hamilton*, III, 102.
[28] Morris, *Alexander Hamilton and the Founding of the Nation* (New York: The Dial Press, 1957), p. 91.
[29] *The Papers of Alexander Hamilton*, I, 441.
[30] *Ibid.*, II, 654–657.
[31] *Ibid.*, II, 654–655.

He voiced the reassuring belief that the states would always be
closer to the people than the national government.[32] Perhaps no
other single statement conveys Hamilton's majestic vision of
America's future than the lines with which he closed the sixth
and final "Continentalist" essay:

> There is something noble and magnificent in the perspective of
> a great Foederal Republic, closely linked in the pursuit of a com-
> mon interest, tranquil and prosperous at home, respectable
> abroad; but there is something proportionably diminutive and
> contemptible in the prospect of a number of petty states, with the
> appearance only of union, jarring, jealous and perverse, without
> any determined direction, fluctuating and unhappy at home, weak
> and insignificant by their dissensions, in the eyes of other nations.
> Happy America! if those, to whom thou hast intrusted the guard-
> ianship of thy infancy, know how to provide for thy future repose;
> but miserable and undone, if their negligence or ignorance permits
> the spirit of discord to erect her banners on the ruins of thy
> tranquility! [33]

IV

It has been remarked that the American Constitution was
"a product of human experience; not of abstract reason." [34]
More concretely, it may be said that the document framed in the
city of Philadelphia in the summer of 1787 was largely shaped by
the attitude of the delegates toward the economic and political
condition of the country after the Revolution. Of none was this
more true than of the young delegate from New York. It was
Hamilton who viewed that situation as amounting to a crisis
imperiling the very survival of the new nation.

"Among the many historic assemblies which have wrought
revolution in the affairs of mankind," Charles and Mary Beard

[32] "The particular governments will have more empire over the minds of
their subjects, than the general one, because their agency will be more direct,
more uniform, and more apparent. The people will be habituated to look up
to them as the arbiters and guardians of their personal concerns, by which the
passions of the vulgar, if not of all men, are most strongly affected; and in every
difference with the confederated body will side with them against the common
sovereign." *Ibid.*, II, 656.

[33] *Ibid.*, III, 106.

[34] Robert L. Schuyler, *The Constitution of the United States* (New York:
The Macmillan Company, 1923), p. 5.

have written, "it seems safe to say that there never has been one
that commanded more political talent, practical experience, and
sound substance than the Philadelphia Convention of 1787." [35]
Though deeply versed in the political philosophy of their own
and earlier times, the delegates were obviously influenced more
by their recent experiences.

Hamilton spearheaded the struggle for the ratification of the
Constitution in the New York Convention, which met at Poughkeepsie from June 17 to July 26, 1788. In a speech on June 21,
he expressed the hope that "We have now found a cure for the
evils under which we have so long labored." The proposed Constitution, he added, "affords a genuine specimen of representative
and republican government." [36] Yet on the day the Philadelphia
Convention completed its historic labors—September 17, 1787—
James Madison reports Hamilton as acknowledging that "No
man's ideas were more remote from the plan than his [Hamil-
ton's] were known to be." He nevertheless expressed the "anxiety that every member should sign" the newly written Constitution.[37]

The fact is that Hamilton's own "cure" for the defects of the
Confederation was too extreme for the delegates at Philadelphia.
One suspects, however, that his sense of political realism kept
him from taking his "propositions" for a constitution too seri-
ously. He was aware that it would "shock public opinion." Dr.
William Samuel Johnson is recorded as saying, on Thursday,
June 21, 1787, "A gentleman from New York, with boldness and
decision, proposed a system totally different from both [the
Virginia and New Jersey Plans]; and though he has been praised
by every body he has been supported by none." [38]

Hamilton ventured to inject his views only after Edmund
Randolph of Virginia and William Paterson of New Jersey had
offered their plans for revision of the Articles of Confederation.
Randolph, who outlined his State's proposals as early as the

[35] Charles A. and Mary R. Beard, *The Rise of American Civilization* (New
York: The Macmillan Company, 1930), p. 310.
[36] *The Papers of Alexander Hamilton*, V, 45.
[37] *The Records of the Federal Convention of 1787*, Farrand, ed., II, 645–
646.
[38] The notes of Robert Yates, *Ibid.*, I, 363.

third day of the Convention, began with an accolade to the
framers of the Articles which was also in the nature of a resumé
of current dissatisfactions:

> In speaking of the defects of the confederation, he [Randolph]
> professed a high respect for its authors, and considered, them as
> having done all that patriots could do, in the then infancy of the
> science, of constitutions, and of confederacies—when the ineffi-
> ciency of requisitions are unknown—no commercial discord had
> arisen among any states—no rebellion had appeared as in Massts.
> —foreign debts had not become urgent—the havoc of paper
> money had not been foreseen—treaties had not been violated—
> and perhaps nothing better could be obtained from the jealousy
> of the states with regard to their sovereignty.[39]

The most important of the resolutions Randolph introduced, the
sixth, stated that the "National Legislature ought to be impow-
ered to enjoy the Legislative Rights vested in Congress by the
Confederation and moreover to legislate in all cases to which
the separate States are incompetent, or in which the harmony
of the United States may be interrupted by the exercise of individual Legislation; to negative all laws passed by the several
States, contravening in the opinion of the National Legislature
the articles of Union." [40]

The series of proposals which Paterson submitted on June 15
resolved that, in addition to the powers which the Congress
possessed under the existing Articles, it be "authorized to pass
acts for raising a revenue, by levying a duty or duties on all goods
or merchandizes of foreign growth or manufacture, imported into
any part of the U. States, . . . to pass acts for the regulation of
trade and commerce as well with foreign nations as with each
other." [41] On the following day, Paterson hastened to explain
that the Convention had no authority to go beyond his state's
plan, which "accorded with the powers of the Convention" and
"the sentiments of the people." The Convention was not empowered to make radical changes in the Confederation: "Our

[39] *The Records of the Federal Convention of 1787*, I, 18–19.
[40] *Ibid.*, I, 21.
[41] *Ibid.*, I, 243.

object is not such a government as may be best in itself, but such a one as our Constituents have authorized us to prepare, and as they will approve." [42] The union rested on the "equal sovereignty" of all the states, and all the states would have to approve of all alterations.

Implicit in Paterson's position was, of course, the assumption that the union under the Articles of Confederation was the result of a compact or association among sovereigns. When James Wilson of Pennsylvania spoke on June 19, he denied "the doctrine that when the Colonies became independent of G. Britain, they became independent also of each other. He read the declaration of Independence, observing thereon that the *United Colonies* were declared to be free & independent States; and inferring that they were independent, not *Individually* but *Unitedly* and that they were confederated as they were independent, States." [43] Madison's notes tell us that "Col. Hamilton assented to the doctrine of Mr. Wilson." Earlier in the debate on the same day, Wilson indicated that "He thought, contrary to the opinion of (Col. Hamilton) that they [the States] might (not) only subsist but subsist on friendly terms with the former [the national government]. They were absolutely necessary for certain purposes which the former could not reach." But "Mr. Wilson observed that by a Natl. Govt. he did not mean one that would swallow up the State Govts. as seemed to be wished by some gentlemen. He was tenacious of the idea of preserving the latter." [44] Hamilton apparently rose to complain that he had been misunderstood.

[42] *Ibid.*, I, 250. "He [Paterson] reads the 5th Art. of Confederation giving each State a vote—and the 13th. declaring that no alteration shall be made without unanimous consent. This is the nature of all treaties. What is unanimously done, must be unanimously undone." *Ibid.*

On February 21, 1787, the Congress under the Articles of Confederation —responding to the recommendation of the delegates from the five states who had attended the unsuccessful Annapolis meeting of the previous September—adopted a resolution providing that the proposed convention should be held "for the sole and express purpose of revising the Articles of Confederation and reporting to Congress and the several legislatures such alterations and provisions therein as shall when agreed to in Congress and confirmed by the states render the federal constitution adequate to the exigencies of Government & the preservation of the Union." *Ibid.*, III, 14.

[43] *Ibid.*, I, 324.

[44] *Ibid.*, I, 322.

V

What was it, then, that Hamilton had proposed on June 18 which had moved Wilson and others to suspect that he desired a federal system of government which would "swallow up" the States? He was "unfriendly" to both the Randolph and Paterson plans, but especially to that from New Jersey, "being fully convinced, that no amendment of the Confederation, leaving the States in possession of their sovereignty could possibly answer the purpose." Hamilton reminded the delegates that the world had known federated systems in which the power to govern had been distributed differently. He obviously favored the implication in the Virginia plan that the federal power was "to operate on individuals." Expressing impatience over the doubts as to how far the Convention could go, he declared: "The States sent us here to provide for the exigencies of the Union. To rely on and propose any plan not adequate to these exigencies, merely because it was not clearly within our powers, would be to sacrifice the means to the end." He next summarized the principles of effective government and found them resting on the "side" of the states in the existing American Confederation:

> The great & essential principles necessary for the support of Government are (1) an active & constant interest in supporting it. . . . (2) the love of power, Men love power. . . . (3) an habitual attachment of the people. . . . The whole force of this tie is on the side of the State Govt. . . . (4) Force by which may be understood a *coercion of laws or a coercion of arms*. . . . (5) *influence*. he did not (mean) corruption, but a dispensation of those regular honors & emoluments, which produce an attachment to the Govt. almost all the weight of these is on the side of the States; and must continue so as long as the States continue to exist. All the passions then we see, of avarice, ambition, interest, which govern most individuals, and all public bodies, fall into the current of the States, and do not flow in the stream of the Genl. Govt. the former therefore will generally be an overmatch for the Genl. Govt. and render any confederacy, in its very nature precarious.[45]

[45] *Ibid.*, I, 284–285.

His examination of these principles led Hamilton to conclude that all the normal inducements of "avarice, ambition and interest which govern most individual and all public bodies" prevailed in the government of the states, but not in the general government under the Articles. For this reason, he believed that the states would remain an "overmatch" for the general government and "render any confederacy, in its very nature, precarious." Hamilton then asked and answered a question which pretty much revealed the fundamental object of his plan: "How then are all these evils to be avoided? Only by such a compleat sovereignty in the general Governmt. as will turn all the strong principles & passions above mentioned on its side." [46] Though the "extent" of the territory to be governed "embarrassed him," Hamilton nevertheless urged that "two sovereignties can not co-exist within the same limits." If the states were "extinguished" and a general government erected, great economies would result. The states, he argued, "are not necessary for any of the great purposes of commerce, revenue, or agriculture." Subordinate authorities, he was aware, would be necessary, but, he wanted to know, "cui bono, the vast & expensive apparatus now appertaining to the States." [47]

But if Hamilton felt himself to have been misunderstood as regards the position he would have assigned to the states, his remarks on the British government planted the suspicion that he was at heart a monarchist, a suspicion with which his political enemies were to taunt him till the end of his life. In introducing his plan to the Convention, he voiced admiration for British traditions and characterized the House of Lords as a "noble institution." On this subject, Hamilton ought to be allowed to speak for himself, as reported by Madison:

> In his private opinion he [Hamilton] had no scruple in declaring, . . . that the British Govt. was the best in the world: and that he doubted much whether any thing short of it would do in America. . . . The members most tenacious of republicanism, he observed, were as loud as any in declaiming agst the vices of de-

[46] *Ibid.,* I, 286.
[47] *Ibid.,* I, 287.

mocracy. This progress of the public mind led him to anticipate
the time, when others as well as himself would join in the praise
bestowed . . . on the British Constitution, namely, that it is the
only Govt. in the world "which unites public strength with individual security."—In every community where industry is encouraged, there will be a division of it into a few & the many. Hence
separate interests will arise. There will be debtors & creditors &c.
Give all power to the many, they will oppress the few. Give all
power to the few, they will oppress the many. Both therefore
ought to have power, that each may defend itself agst. the other.
To the want of this check we owe our paper money—instalment
laws &c. To the proper adjustment of it the British owe the excellence of their Constitution. Their house of Lords is a most noble
institution. Having nothing to hope for by a change, and a sufficient interest by means of their property in being faithful to the
National Interest, they form a permanent barrier agst every
pernicious innovation, whether attempted on the part of the
Crown or of the Commons.[48]

[48] *Ibid.*, I, 288–289. Hamilton was here giving expression to a view of
social conflict which both James Madison and John Adams had discussed
much more elaborately on the eve of the Philadelphia Convention. In April
1787, Madison published a pamphlet—"Vices of the Political System in the
United States"—in which he wrote: "All civilized societies are divided into
different interests and factions, as they happen to be creditors or debtors—
rich or poor—husbandmen, merchants or manufacturers—members of different religious sects—followers of different political leaders—inhabitants of
different districts—owners of different kinds of property etc. etc. In republican government the majority, however composed, ultimately give the law.
Whenever therefore an apparent interest or common passion unites a
majority what is to restrain them from unjust violations of the rights and
interests of the minority, or of individuals? . . . . The great desideratum
in Government is such a modification of the sovereignty as will render it
sufficiently neutral between the different interests and factions, to controul
one part of the society from invading the rights of another, and at the same
time sufficiently controuled itself, from setting up an interest adverse to that
of the whole Society." *The Writings of James Madison,* Gaillard Hunt, ed.
(New York: G. P. Putnam's Sons, 1901), II, 366–368.

The same year there appeared John Adams' now famous treatise on government. For the members of the Convention, it may be assumed, the
most important and interesting section of the work was the sixth letter, entitled "The Right Constitution of a Commonwealth Examined." In it we
read: "In every society where property exists, there will be a struggle between
rich and poor. Mixed in one assembly, equal laws can never be expected.
They will either be made by numbers, to plunder the few who are rich, or
by influence, to fleece the many who are poor. Both rich and poor, then,
must be made independent, that equal justice may be done, and equal liberty

After these comments on the virtues of the British system, Hamilton told the delegates that the "inference" to be drawn is that "We ought to go as far in order to attain stability and permanency as Republican principles will admit." And how were such "stability and permanency" to be achieved in America? One branch of the proposed national legislature, the Senate, should consist of persons who "hold their places for life or at least during good behavior," and the national executive, the "governour," should "also be for life." With its members serving for life, the Senate would embody "a permanent will, a weighty interest." But would life tenure give us republican government? Yes, said Hamilton, "if all the Magistrates are appointed, and vacancies filled, by the people, or a process of election originating with the people."

Aware though he was that it "went beyond the ideas of most members," Hamilton proceeded to submit for consideration by the delegates "a sketch of a plan" embodying the political precepts he had been discussing. The essential import of his plan may be gleaned from the following provisos:

I. The Supreme Legislative power of the United States of America to be vested in two different bodies of men; the one to be called the Assembly, the other the Senate who together shall form the Legislature of the United States with power to pass all laws whatsoever subject to the Negative hereafter mentioned.

II. The Assembly to consist of persons elected by the people to serve for three years.

III. The Senate to consist of persons elected to serve during good behavior; their election to be made by electors chosen for that purpose by the people; . . .

IV. The supreme Executive authority of the United States to be vested in a Governour to be elected to serve during good behavior—the election to be made by Electors chosen by the people in the Election Districts aforesaid—the authorities & func-

enjoyed by all. To expect that in a single sovereign assembly no load shall be laid upon any but what is common to all, nor gratify the passions of any, but only to supply the necessities of their country, is altogether chimerical." Adams, *A Defence of the Constitutions of Government of the United States of America,* reprinted in *The Works of John Adams,* Charles Francis Adams, ed., VI, 68–69.

tions of the Executive to be as follows: to have a negative on all laws about to be passed, and the execution of all laws passed, . . .

VII. The Supreme Judicial authority to be vested in Judges to hold their office during good behavior with adequate and permanent salaries. . . .

VIII. The Legislature of the United States to have power to institute Courts in each State for the determination of all matters of general concern. . . .

X. All laws of the particular States contrary to the Constitution or laws of the United States to be utterly void; and the better to prevent such laws being passed, the Governour or president of each state shall be appointed by the General Government and shall have a negative upon the laws about to be passed in the State of which he is Governour or President.[49]

Madison's summary of the speech in which Hamilton presented his plan makes it clear that the New Yorker was not altogether without hope that his scheme would ultimately prevail. So convinced was he of the impending breakdown of the governmental system that he apparently permitted himself to believe that the country would reject the other less drastic proposals for revamping the Articles of Confederation and would adopt his recommendations for meeting so grave an emergency.

He [Hamilton] sees the Union dissolving or already dissolved —he sees evils operating in the States which must soon cure the people of their fondness for democracies—he sees that a great progress has already been made and is still going on in the public mind. He thinks therefore that the people will in time be unshackled from their prejudices; and whenever that happens, they will themselves not be satisfied at stopping where the plan of Mr. R. [Randolph] would place them, but be ready to go as far at least as he proposes.[50]

Hamilton's political ideas were too extreme for his fellow delegates. His desire to reduce the states to mere administrative arms of the general government was completely frustrated. Neither did his proposal for giving life tenure to the Senate and the national executive receive serious attention. As the debates con-

[49] *The Records of the Federal Convention of 1787*, Farrand, ed., I, 291–293.
[50] *Ibid.*, I, 291.

tinued, the astute delegate from New York no doubt became convinced that however grave the crisis, the way out did not lie along the revolutionary path he was quite prepared to traverse. He would have to settle for a less radical reconstitution of the governmental system.

Like Benjamin Franklin, Hamilton might well have said that he "expected no better." [51] Having come to this conclusion, he had no hesitation in calling on the delegates to sign the plan of government the Convention formulated. He threw himself into the battle for its ratification with all the fervor and talents of which he was capable. But he made his own motive entirely clear: "Is it possible to deliberate between anarchy and Convulsion on one side, and the chance of good to be expected from the plan on the other." [52]

[51] "Thus I consent, Sir, to this Constitution because I expect no better, and because I am not sure, that it is not the best." Benjamin Franklin, speaking on the closing day of the Convention, September 17, 1787. *Ibid.*, II, 643.

[52] *Ibid.*, II, 646.

2

"The Excellences of Republican Government"

In recent years, historians have sought to show that the period of the Articles of Confederation was not at all the "critical" era portrayed by John Fiske.[1] Yet even if it were true that those seeking approval of the Constitution exaggerated the crisis of the times, their view of the situation would still be important. "Our Convention," Thomas Jefferson complained soon after receiving a copy of the Constitution, "has been too much impressed with the insurrection in Massachusetts." [2] The same no doubt could have been said with respect to many another of the episodes and problems aired by the proponents of ratification. Overdrawn though their picture may have been, it helps us see the extent of the alarm and to understand the remedy proposed.

I

It is in the numbers of *The Federalist* papers attributed to Hamilton in which one will find the most pessimistic account of contemporary conditions.[3] Considering his sustained effort to scrap the Articles of Confederation, the bias was as logical as it was politically necessary. The tone is set in the opening sentences of the very first number of *The Federalist*:

[1] Fiske, *The Critical Period of American History* (Boston and New York: Houghton, Mifflin and Company, 1897). For a quite different picture of the period, see Merrill Jensen, *The New Nation* (New York: Alfred A. Knopf, 1950).

[2] Thomas Jefferson to William S. Smith, November 13, 1787. 12 *The Papers of Thomas Jefferson* 356–357 (Boyd, ed.).

[3] The question as to who—John Jay, James Madison, or Alexander Ham-

After an unequivocal experience of the inefficiency of the sub-
sisting federal government, you are called upon to deliberate on
a new Constitution for the United States of America. The subject
speaks its own importance comprehending in its consequences
nothing less than the existence of the UNION, the safety and
welfare of the parts of which it is composed, the fate of an empire
in many respects the most interesting in the world. It has been
frequently remarked that it seems to have been reserved to the
people of this country, by their conduct and example, to decide
the important question, whether societies of men are really capable
or not of establishing good government from reflection and
choice, or whether they are forever destined to depend for their
political constitutions on accident and force. If there be any
truth in the remark, the crisis at which we are arrived may with
propriety be regarded as the era in which that decision is to be
made; and a wrong election of the part we shall act may, in this
view, deserve to be considered as the general misfortune of mankind.[4]

Though *The Federalist* is primarily a brief for enlarging the
scope of national power, it is inspired and informed by a much
deeper purpose. That purpose was to expound and vindicate a
philosophy of good government. The collection of essays is a
remarkable fusion of polemical analysis and historical illustration. Its immediate aim was, of course, to convince those locked
in the struggle over the ratification of the Constitution that the
only way to rescue America's experiment with political freedom
was to give greater power and prestige to the general government
—to create "a more perfect Union." The union under the
Articles of Confederation, said Hamilton, presented the "awful

ilton—wrote which of the eighty-five essays has been in dispute from the
beginning. One of the most careful discussions of the problem will be found
in Douglass Adair's "The Authorship of the Disputed Federalist Papers,"
William and Mary Quarterly, 3rd. Series, I, April and July 1944. Professor
Adair concludes that Jay is the author of only five of the essays—Numbers
2, 3, 4, 5, and 64. Hamilton is the author of Numbers 1, 6–9, 11–13, 15–17,
21–36, 59–61, and 66–85, inclusive. Numbers 18–30 were written jointly by
Madison and Hamilton; the remaining essays were penned by Madison. But
the controversy with regard to the authorship of certain of the numbers
continues.
[4] *The Federalist,* No. 1, p. 89 (Wright, ed.).

spectacle" of "a nation, without a national government." [5] It
was in the nature of the "political monster of an *imperium in
imperio.*" [6]

Hamilton undertook to demonstrate that what he characterized as "the present shadow of a federal government" [7] stemmed
from a fundamental "imperfection" in the system erected by the
Articles of Confederation. Indeed, the "bane" of that system was
a principle "incompatible with the idea of government" itself—
the dependence of the national government upon the voluntary
cooperation of the states. "The great and radical vice in the
construction of the existing Confederation," wrote Hamilton,
"is in the principle of LEGISLATION for STATES or GOV-
ERNMENTS, in their CORPORATE or COLLECTIVE CA-
PACITIES, and as contradistinguished from the INDIVIDUALS
of which they consist." [8] In exercising the powers delegated to it
by the Articles, the central government was unable to enforce
its will on the individual citizen. As a result, national measures
were mere "recommendations" or "advice," which the "States
observe or disregard at their option."

For all practical purposes, the union under the Articles was
a mere league or alliance among independent communities. "We
must extend the authority of the Union," insisted Hamilton, "to
the persons of the citizens—the only proper objects of government." The very idea of government "implies the power of making laws" and laws must have sanctions or penalties for disobedi-
ence. Only by arming the general government of the union with
direct coercive authority over individuals will a system of judicially administered law be possible. "This penalty . . . can only
be inflicted in two ways: by the agency of the courts and ministers
of justice, or by military force; by the coercion of the magistracy,
or by the coercion of arms. The first kind can evidently apply to
men; the last kind must of necessity, be employed against bodies
politic, or communities, or States." [9]

[5] *Ibid.*, No. 85, p. 547.
[6] *Ibid.*, No. 15, p. 157.
[7] *Ibid.*, No. 15, p. 162.
[8] *Ibid.*, No. 15, p. 158.
[9] *Ibid.*, No. 15, p. 159.

II

Yet it is not by dwelling on the now familiar story of the feebleness of the government under the Articles that one will perceive Hamilton's deepest convictions about the nature of government. More revealing is his discussion of the social unrest in the states and the way in which he used that situation as an argument for adoption of the Constitution. The rampant struggle between debtors and creditors and the consequent attacks on the rights of property loom large in his diagnosis of the "disease" and of the remedy. When the time came to summarize, in the concluding number of *The Federalist*, the benefits that would be derived from the Constitution, Hamilton listed first "the restraints which the preservation of the Union will impose on local factions and insurrections, and on the ambition of powerful individuals in single States, who may acquire credit and influence enough, from leaders and favorites, to become the despots of the people." [10] In the same statement, he applauded those "precautions" in the new Constitution which were directed "against the repetition of those practices on the part of the State governments, which have undermined the foundations of property and credit, have planted mutual distrust in the breasts of all classes of citizens, and have occasioned an almost universal prostration of morals." [11]

In essay after essay, Hamilton continued to argue that both liberty and property were threatened by the "pestilential" spread of factional strife. He looked to an energetic national government to quell incipient threats to social peace. "A firm Union will be of the utmost moment to the peace and liberty of the States, as a barrier against domestic faction and insurrection." [12] Against disturbances threatening "the peace of society and the stability of government," he remarked, "too many checks cannot be provided." [13] To Hamilton, Shays' Rebellion—which he describes as "an actual insurrection" and a "civil war"—bespoke its own fearful object lesson for all the states:

[10] *Ibid.*, No. 85, p. 542.
[11] *Ibid.*
[12] *Ibid.*, No. 9, p. 124.
[13] *Ibid.*, No. 21, p. 188.

Without a guaranty [to the States of protection against domestic violence] the assistance to be derived from the Union in repelling those domestic dangers which may sometimes threaten the existence of the State constitutions, must be renounced. Usurpation may rear its crest in each State, and trample upon the liberties of the people, while the national government could legally do nothing more than behold its encroachments with indignation and regret. A successful faction may erect a tyranny on the ruins of order and law, while no succor could constitutionally be afforded by the Union to the friends and supporters of the government. The tempestuous situation from which Massachusetts has scarcely emerged, evinces that dangers of this kind are not merely speculative. Who can determine what might have been the issue of her late convulsions, if malcontents had been headed by a Caesar or by a Cromwell? Who can predict what effect a despotism, established in Massachusetts, would have upon the liberties of New Hampshire or Rhode Island, of Connecticut or New York? [14]

For Hamilton the peril to the American states arising from "domestic factions and convulsions" was even "more alarming" than dangers stemming from foreign intrigues and hostility. His obsessive fear of factions was closely linked with his conception of human nature itself. In order to understand the potential sources of friction among the states as well as within their borders, he stressed, it was important to remember that "men are ambitious, vindictive, and rapacious." In popular government as well as in monarchies, the community may be convulsed as the result of policies occasioned by the indulgence on the part of "leading individuals" of their purely private interests and ambitions. "If Shays had not been a *desperate debtor*," Hamilton illustrated, "it is much to be doubted whether Massachusetts would

[14] *Ibid.*, No. 21, p. 187. It is instructive to compare Hamilton's stricture on the use of violence with the lesson drawn by Jefferson. Said Hamilton: "The natural cure for an ill-administration, in a popular or representative constitution, is a change of men." *Ibid.*, No. 21, p. 188. By way of discounting the exaggerated importance some men were attaching to Shays' Rebellion and in order to set it in its proper perspective, Jefferson wrote: "And what country can preserve its liberties if their rulers are not warned from time to time, that their people preserve the spirit of resistance? Let them take arms. . . . What signify a few lives lost in a century or two? The tree of liberty must be refreshed from time to time with the blood of patriots and tyrants. It is its natural manure." 12 *The Papers of Thomas Jefferson* 256.

have been plunged into a civil war." [15] Experience, "that best oracle of wisdom," [16] shows that "human selfishness" shapes the conduct of political bodies as it does that of individuals. Only by keeping in mind "the true springs by which human conduct is actuated" is it possible to arrive at a realistic view of political behavior.[17] Men have organized government out of an awareness that, without compulsion, individuals will ignore the common interest in the pursuit of purely private desires: "Why has government been instituted at all? Because the passions of men will not conform to the dictates of reason and justice, without constraint." [18]

In collective bodies, such as state legislatures, the danger that the general good will be ignored is even greater. "A spirit of faction, which is apt to mingle its poison in the deliberations of all bodies of men, will often hurry the persons of whom they are composed into improprieties and excesses, for which they blush in a private capacity." [19] All of this was said by Hamilton by way of emphasizing that without a firm central government to guard the national interest, the states could be expected to continue to consult their own immediate interests and convenience in disregard of the effect on the nation as a whole. The neglect of the national interest by local lawmakers was due to their lack of that "knowledge of national circumstances and reasons of state which is essential to a right judgment." [20] Hamilton's comments on the universal tendency of institutions and persons to resist the imposition of limits on their authority add up to a rather interesting theory about the nature of political power:

> . . . there is, in the nature of sovereign power, an impatience of control, that disposes those who are invested with the exercise of it to look with an evil eye upon all external attempts to restrain or direct its operations. From this spirit it happens, that in every political association which is formed upon the principle of uniting in a common interest a number of lesser sovereignties, there will

[15] *The Federalist,* No. 6, p. 110.
[16] *Ibid.,* No. 15, p. 160.
[17] *Ibid.*
[18] *Ibid.*
[19] *Ibid.*
[20] *Ibid.,* p. 161.

be found a kind of eccentric tendency in the subordinate or inferior orbs, by the operation of which there will be a perpetual
effort in each to fly off from the common centre. This tendency
is not difficult to be accounted for. It has its origin in the love of
power. Power controlled or abridged is almost always the rival
and enemy of that power by which it is controlled or abridged.
This simple proposition will teach us, how little reason there is to
expect, that the persons intrusted with the administration of the
affairs of the particular members of a confederacy will at all times
be ready with perfect good-humor, and an unbiased regard to the
public weal, to execute the resolutions or decrees of the general
authority. The reverse of this results from the constitution of
human nature.[21]

As one follows Hamilton's "dark catalog of public misfortune," with its dramatic recital of the events and measures which
had brought America to "the last stage of national humilia-
tion," [22] it becomes quite apparent that he ascribed the calamity

[21] *Ibid.*, pp. 160–161.
[22] *Ibid.*, p. 156. Probably the best contemporaneous refutation of Hamilton's version of the crisis is to be found in Richard Henry Lee's "Letters from
the Federal Farmer to the Republican." In the first letter, appearing on
October 8, 1787, he wrote: "The first principal question that occurs is,
Whether, considering our situation, we ought to precipitate the adoption of
the proposed constitution? If we remain cool and temperate, we are in no
immediate danger of any commotions; we are in a state of perfect peace, and
in no danger of invasions; the state governments are in the full exercise of
their powers; and our governments answer all present exigencies, except the
regulation of trade, securing credit, in some cases, and providing for the interest, in some instances, of the public debts; and whether we adopt a change
three or nine months hence, can make but little odds with the private circumstances of individuals; their happiness and prosperity, after all, depend prin-
cipally upon their own exertions. We are hardly recovered from a long and
distressing war: The farmers, fishmen, etc. have not fully repaired the waste
made by it. Industry and frugality are again assuming their proper station.
Private debts are lessened, and public debts incurred by the war have been,
by various ways, diminished; and the public lands have now become a pro-
ductive source for diminishing them much more. I know uneasy men, who
with very much to precipitate, do not admit all these facts; but they are
facts well known to all men who are thoroughly informed in the affairs of
this country. It must, however, be admitted, that our federal system is defective, and that some of the state governments are not well administered;
but, then, we impute to the defects in our governments many evils and embarrassments which are most clearly the result of the late war." *Pamphlets
on the Constitution of the United States,* P. L. Ford, ed. (Brooklyn, 1888), pp.
280–281. For a systematic and objective analysis of the position of those who
opposed ratification, see Jackson Turner Main, *The Antifederalists—Critics*

to two basic causes. Within most of the states, both liberty and property—and, indeed, republican government itself—were rendered insecure by the power of unbridled legislative majorities to act in disregard of considerations of public justice. Under the influence of factional interests, such as the clamor of debtors for paper money and relief from their obligations, the state governments were in the throes of group conflict which had erupted into actual armed insurrection. The other factor which had brought the country to the "very brink of the precipice" was the lack of authority in the central government to curb the parochial and disruptive actions of the states and to compel them to accept measures required for the good of the nation as a whole. "Each State, yielding to the persuasive voice of immediate interest or convenience," Hamilton stated grimly, "has successively withdrawn its support, till the frail and tottering edifice seems ready to fall upon our heads, and to crush us beneath its ruins." [23]

III

In the final number of *The Federalist*, Hamilton confessed that he did not have "entire confidence" in the arguments which had been presented in the previous eighty-four essays for the adoption of the Constitution. "I am persuaded," he nevertheless added, "that it is the best which our political situation, habits, and opinions will admit, and superior to any the Revolution has produced." [24] At the Convention, he had contended that the "turbulent and changing" masses "seldom judge or determine right" and urged the need of a permanent governmental body to "check the imprudence of democracy." [25]

The inevitable question must be asked: What was there about the proposed system of government which made Hamilton feel that it was the best hope for achieving the purposes and changes he sought? In dealing with this difficult problem, it must be acknowledged that the seeming paradox of Hamilton's position is traceable to two contradictions implicit in his analysis of conditions under the Articles of Confederation. In the first place,

of the Constitution (Chapel Hill: The University of North Carolina Press, 1961).
[23] *The Federalist*, No. 15, p. 162.
[24] *Ibid.*, No. 85, p. 543.
[25] *Records of the Federal Convention of 1787*, Farrand, ed., I, 299.

there was the view of human nature which he shared with such of his contemporaries as John Adams and James Madison, the view that man was inherently selfish, contentious, and short-sighted. "Is it not time," he queried rhetorically in the second of his essays, "to awake from the deceitful dream of a golden age, and to adopt as a practical maxim for the direction of our political conduct that we, as well as the other inhabitants of the globe, are yet remote from the happy empire of perfect wisdom and perfect virtue?" [26]

If the American Constitution is a product of "an age of realism," as Richard Hofstadter has suggested, Hamilton was certainly its leading representative.[27] But of course, the "realism" of Alexander Hamilton was more than a matter of philosophic conviction. Its more significant aspect is conveyed by his forbidding image of life in America in the decade preceding the Philadelphia Convention. His portrayal of the degeneration of popular government into virtual anarchy involved Hamilton in the additional necessity of demonstrating how the proposed Constitution would avoid these evils and yet retain republican institutions. In a sense, the dilemma was comparable to the mixed emotions stirred by the turbulent history of the republics of the ancient world: "It is impossible to read the history of the petty republics of Greece and Italy without feeling sensations of horror and disgust at the distractions with which they were continually agitated, and at the rapid succession of revolutions by which they were kept in a state of perpetual vibration between the extremes of tyranny and anarchy." [28] Yet Hamilton repudiated the infer-

[26] *The Federalist*, No. 6, p. 113.

[27] Hofstadter, *The American Political Tradition* (New York: Alfred A. Knopf, 1948), p. 1.

[28] *The Federalist*, No. 9, p. 124. Professor Douglass Adair has advanced the interesting view that the use of history by the Founding Fathers was a product of their belief that it was possible to study political institutions with "scientific" accuracy. He writes: "The three hundred pages of comparative-historical research in John Adams' *Defense of the Constitutions of the United States* (1787), and the five-hour closely argued historical analysis in Alexander Hamilton's Convention speech of June 18, 1787, were both 'scientific' efforts to relate the current difficulties of the thirteen American republics to the universal tendencies of republicanism in all nations and in all ages. History, scientifically considered, thus helped *define* both the nature of the crisis of 1787 for these leaders and their audience, and also determine in large part the 'reforms' that, it could be predicted, would end the crisis." See Adair,

ence drawn by the "advocates of despotism" that the experience of those republics proves that "free" or "republican" government was "inconsistent with the order of society." He expressed the hope, moreover, that America would become a "permanent monument" to the error of any such theory.

How, then, did Hamilton reconcile his support of the Constitution with his assessment of conditions in post-Revolutionary America, an assessment which was not too unlike that of the critics of the ancient republics? "If it had been found impracticable to have devised models of a more perfect structure," he observed, "the enlightened friends to liberty would have been obliged to abandon the cause of that species of government as indefensible." [29] Hamilton attempted to resolve the apparent contradiction by citing the advances that had been made in the art of government:

> The science of politics, . . . like most other sciences, has received great improvement. The efficacy of various principles is now well understood, which were either not known at all, or imperfectly known to the ancients. The regular distribution of power into distinct departments; the introduction of legislative balances and checks; the institution of courts composed of judges holding their offices during good behavior; the representation of people in the legislature by deputies of their own election: these are wholly new discoveries or have made their principal progress toward perfection in modern times. They are means, and powerful means, by which the excellences of republican government may be retained and its imperfections lessened or avoided.[30]

To this list of institutional arrangements for making popular government both workable and durable, Hamilton added the principle of the enlarged geographic "orbit" within which republicanism could be made to function. Some of the opponents of ratification had invoked Montesquieu to argue that a coercive national administration was unsuited to a vast expanse of territory like the United States. What Elbridge Gerry, a member of the Philadelphia Convention who had refused to sign the Con-

" 'That Politics May be Reduced to a Science': David Hume, James Madison, and the Tenth Federalist," *The Huntington Library Quarterly* (Early American History Number) vol. XX, no. 4, August 1957, 343–360, at p. 347.

[29] *The Federalist*, No. 9, p. 125.

[30] *Ibid.*

stitution, said on this point is typical: "The difficulty, if not impracticability, of exercising the equal and equitable powers of government by a single legislature over an extent of territory that reaches from the Mississippi to the Western lakes, and from them to the Atlantic Ocean, is an insuperable objection to the adoption of the new system." [31]

Conceding that Montesquieu had maintained that the republican principle was better suited to a small territory,[32] Hamilton insisted that "that great man"—as he speaks of the Frenchman—had also recognized that a confederate republic was a proper "expedient for extending the sphere of popular government and reconciling the advantages of monarchy with those of republicanism." [33] He went further. Turning the tables on the critics, he accused them of failing to see that if Montesquieu were taken literally, even the existing states in the American union were too large for the republican principle. "If we therefore take his

[31] *Pamphlets on the Constitution of the United States*, P. L. Ford, ed., p. 13. In the statement of their reasons for not signing the Constitution, which they had submitted to Governor George Clinton of New York, Robert Yates and John Lansing gave as one of two principal objections their "conviction of the impracticability of establishing a general government, pervading every part of the United States, and extending essential benefits to all." Patrick Henry told the Virginia Ratifying Convention, June 9, 1788, "One government cannot reign over so extensive a country as this is, without absolute despotism." *The Debates in the Several State Conventions*, on the adoption of the Federal Constitution, edited by Jonathan Elliot (Philadelphia: J. B. Lippincott Co., 1836–1845; 1888 edition), III, 150, subsequently to be cited as Elliot's *Debates*.

[32] Montesquieu had written: "In an extensive republic, the public good is sacrificed to a thousand private views; it is subordinate to exceptions, and depends on accidents. In a small one, the interest of the public is more obvious, better understood, and more within the reach of every citizen; abuses have less extent, and, of course are less protected." *The Spirit of the Laws*, Book VIII, ch. 16. (New York: The Colonial Press, 1899), I, 120.

[33] Hamilton quotes the following from Montesquieu: "It is very probable that mankind would have been obliged at length to live constantly under the Government of a single person, had they not contrived a kind of Constitution that has all the internal advantages of a republican, together with the external force of a monarchical, government. I mean a CONFEDERATE REPUBLIC.

"This form of Government is a Convention by which several smaller *States* agree to become members of a larger *one*, which they intend to form. It is a kind of assemblage of societies that constitute a new one, capable of increasing, by means of new associations, till they arrive to such a degree of power as to be able to provide for the security of the united body." *The Federalist*, No. 9, p. 127.

[Montesquieu's] ideas on this point as the criterion of truth," Hamilton argued, "we shall be driven to the alternative either of taking refuge at once in the arms of monarchy, or of splitting ourselves into an infinity of little, jealous, clashing, tumultuous commonwealths, the wretched nurseries of unceasing discord, and the miserable objects of universal pity or contempt." [34]

[34] *Ibid.*, No. 9, p. 126. It is in Number 10 of *The Federalist*, universally attributed to the pen of James Madison, in which one will find the best statement of the case for federal union as the most effective safeguard for popular government against the insidious effects of factional strife. It has been suggested that Madison's "most amazing political prophesy" was his view that "the size of the United States and its variety of interests could be made a guarantee of stability and justice under the new Constitution." Douglass Adair, " 'That Politics May be Reduced to a Science': David Hume, James Madison, and the Tenth Federalist," *loc. cit.*, 348. Professor Adair contends that at the time Madison was greatly influenced by the philosophy of David Hume, particularly the Scotsman's theories as set forth in his *The Idea of a Perfect Commonwealth*, 1752.

3

"The Majesty of
National Authority"

"All theories of politics," Benjamin F. Wright has written, "are based upon a set of presuppositions concerning the nature of man." [1] There can be no question but that this generalization applies with particular force to the political ideas of the men who penned our classic defense of the Constitution. So much stress has been placed on James Madison's appreciation of the economic basis of politics that it is sometimes forgotten that he also recognized a deeper source of social conflict. Thus, the very passage in the tenth number of *The Federalist* in which he speaks of "the most common and durable source of factions" begins with the following observation:

> The latent causes of faction are thus sown in the nature of man; and we see them everywhere brought into different degrees of activity, according to the different circumstances of civil society. A zeal for different opinions concerning religion, concerning government, and many other points, as well of speculation as of practice; an attachment to different leaders ambitiously contending for pre-eminence and power; or to persons of other descriptions whose fortunes have been interesting to the human passions, have, in turn, divided mankind into parties, inflamed them with mutual animosity, and rendered them much more disposed to vex

[1] Wright, "The Federalist on the Nature of Political Man," *Ethics*, vol. LIX, No. 2, Part II (Jan. 1949), p. 2. For a more elaborate discussion of the political philosophy of the authors of the *Federalist Papers*, see Gottfried Dietze, *The Federalist: A Classic on Federalism and Free Government* (Baltimore: The Johns Hopkins Press, 1960).

and oppress each other than to co-operate for their common good. So strong is this propensity of mankind to fall to mutual animosities, that where no substantial occasion presents itself, the most frivolous and fanciful distinctions have been sufficient to kindle their unfriendly passions and excite their most violent conflict. But the most common and durable source of factions has been the various and unequal distribution of property.[2]

The view of man taken by the framers of the Constitution was pessimistic indeed. Hamilton's belief as to the "depravity of human nature" and the "folly and wickedness of mankind" [3] were shared not only by his literary collaborators, but probably by most of the Founding Fathers. Nor did they, unlike more utopian builders of political systems, suffer from the illusion that the basic pattern of human behavior would change once the political revolution they contemplated were wrought. In this respect, the Founding Fathers were true disciples of David Hume. Hume had dismissed Thomas More's *Utopia* and Plato's *Republic* as worthless speculations, and expressed the belief that "All plans of government, which suppose great reformation in the manners of mankind, are plainly imaginary." [4]

It was precisely because they were so deeply convinced that men were inclined to be governed by "momentary passions" and "immediate interests" [5] that the Founding Fathers turned to institutional devices for protecting society by curbing those impulses. A comment made by John Adams on the eve of the Philadelphia Convention is a good reflection of this attitude: "The best republics will be virtuous, and have been so; but we may hazard a conjecture, that the virtues have been the effect of the well ordered constitution, rather than the cause." [6]

I

Hamilton depicted the proposed Constitution as embodying a double-barreled defense against social, economic, and political

[2] *The Federalist*, No. 10, p. 131 (Wright, ed.).

[3] *Ibid.*, No. 78, p. 496.

[4] Hume, *Essays, Moral, Political and Literary* (London: Longmans, Green, and Co., 1882), I, 481.

[5] *The Federalist*, No. 6, p. 111.

[6] Adams, *A Defence of the Constitutions of Government of the United States of America*, reprinted in *The Works of John Adams*, Charles Francis Adams, ed., VI, 219.

instability. Its provisions, he argued, erected powerful barriers against efforts—at both the state and national levels—to shape public policies in behalf of selfish and unprincipled factions. How was this dual objective to be achieved?

It is clear that Hamilton placed chief reliance upon a strong and energetic national government. That this was going to be the dominating theme of his particular contribution can be discerned from the very opening number of *The Federalist*. He chided the opponents of the Constitution who preached that "vigor in government" endangers liberty. "An enlightened zeal for the energy and efficiency of government will be stigmatized as the offspring of a temper fond of despotic power and hostile to the principles of liberty," [7] was the way he sardonically summarized their attitude. For him the correct principle was simple enough: "The vigor of government is essential to the security of liberty." [8]

Little phrases suggestive of this conviction recur with such frequency that they only serve to confirm one's impression of the tenacity with which it was held: "A vigorous national government"; [9] "unity of government"; [10] "one government pervading all the States"; [11] "One national government"; [12] "the majesty of national authority." [13] Hamilton's unmistakable premise was that the fear to entrust government with ample powers is unjustified in a free society, and is actually dangerous: "A government, the constitution of which renders it unfit to be trusted with all the powers which a free people *ought to delegate to any government* would be an unsafe and improper depository of the national interests." [14]

Hamilton's belief that liberty depended on governmental strength was one idea which James Madison accepted fully. In Number 37, concerned with some of the dilemmas which had

[7] *The Federalist*, No. 1, p. 91.
[8] *Ibid.*
[9] *Ibid.*, No. 11, p. 139.
[10] *Ibid.*, p. 141.
[11] *Ibid.*, No. 12, p. 145.
[12] *Ibid.*, p. 146.
[13] *Ibid.*, No. 16, p. 165.
[14] *Ibid.*, No. 23, p. 202.

faced the Convention, Madison singled out for extended comment the difficult problem of fusing freedom with vigorous government. "Among the difficulties encountered by the Convention," he reports, a very important one "must have lain in combining the requisite stability and energy in government, with the inviolable attention due to liberty and to the republican form." [15] When he turned to the practical problem of maintaining such a regime of liberty, however, he was emphatic in arguing that the fate of republican institutions hinges on vigor in government:

> Energy in government is essential to that security against external and internal danger, and to prompt and salutary execution of the laws, which enter into the definition of good government. Stability in government is essential to national character, and to the advantages annexed to it, as well as to that repose and confidence in the minds of the people, which are among the chief blessings of civil society.[16]

Like Madison, Hamilton spoke as a believer in the principle of popular sovereignty. "The fabric of American empire," he wrote in Number 22, "ought to rest on the solid basis of THE CONSENT OF THE PEOPLE. The streams of national power ought to flow immediately from that pure, original foundation of all legitimate authority." [17]

In discussing the need for the powers which the Constitution conferred on the newly created national government, Hamilton takes the attitude that the framers had done no more than was essential to effective rule. Without such an arsenal of powers the United States would have continued to be a mere league. "There is an inherent and intrinsic weakness in all federal constitutions," he remarks, adding, "too much pains cannot be taken in their organization, to give them all the force which is compatible with the principles of liberty." [18]

Hamilton stressed that if the country wanted an actual government, and not merely an association of autonomous common-

[15] *Ibid.*, No. 37, p. 267.
[16] *Ibid.*
[17] *Ibid.*, No. 22, p. 199.
[18] *Ibid.*, No. 17, p. 168.

wealths, it would have to accept the supremacy of the national power:

> If a number of political societies enter into a larger political society, the laws which the latter may enact, pursuant to the powers intrusted to it by its constitution, must necessarily be supreme over those societies, and the individuals of whom they are composed. It would otherwise be a mere treaty, dependent on the good faith of the parties, and not a government, which is only another word for political power and supremacy.[19]

II

Whether considering the need for uniform commercial regulation, the common defense of the country, or financial independence, Hamilton saw each of these interests as essential to national cohesion. He seemed to be guided by a few simple imperatives. Hamilton described the voluntary contributions (under the so-called quota and requisition process) which the states were expected to make available for the support of the central government as a "system of imbecility" and blamed them for being "chiefly" responsible for the perilous situation in which the country found itself. He urged that the national government be permitted to raise its own revenues by methods "authorized in every well-ordered constitution of civil government." The maxim on which he was basing these criticisms of the Articles of Confederation he had already made clear: "There must be interwoven, in the frame of the government, a general power of taxation, in one shape or another." [20]

---

[19] *Ibid.*, No. 33, p. 247. Madison, too, perceived strong government to be the best assurance of social peace and stable conditions in the community: "A sovereignty over sovereigns, a government over governments, a legislation for communities, as contradistinguished from individuals, as it is a solecism in theory, so in practice it is subversive of the order and ends of civil polity, by substituting violence in place of *law*, or the destructive *coercion* of the *sword* in place of the mild and salutary *coercion* of the *magistracy*." *Ibid.*, No. 20, pp. 185–186.

In his edition of *The Federalist*, Professor Jacob E. Cooke cites Number 20 as having been written "With the Assistance" of Hamilton. *The Federalist*, with Introduction and Notes by Jacob E. Cooke, ed. (Middletown, Conn.: Wesleyan University Press, 1961), p. 124.

[20] *The Federalist*, No. 30, pp. 233, 232. Not only did Hamilton insist that the regulation of commerce absolutely demanded "federal superintendence,"

In his conception of what he called "the economy of national affairs," Hamilton saw money as an essential weapon of national strength. "Money is, with propriety, considered as the vital principle of the body politic; as that which sustains its life and motion and enables it to perform its most essential function. A complete power, therefore, to procure a regular and adequate supply of it, as far as the resources of the community will permit, may be regarded as an indispensable ingredient in every constitution." [21]

The phrase—"liberal or enlarged plans of public good" [22]— is a revealing clue to Hamilton's dynamic conception of the potential uses of the powers of the nation. The way to provide for the future is to leave the government free to make broad use of its powers to cope with contingencies which could not be anticipated at the time the powers were delegated.

> Constitutions of civil government are not framed upon a calculation of existing exigencies, but upon a combination of these with the probable exigencies of ages, according to the natural and tried course of human affairs. Nothing, therefore, can be more fallacious than to infer the extent of any power, proper to be lodged in the national government, from an estimate of its immediate necessity. There ought to be a capacity to provide for future contingencies as they may happen: and as these are illimitable in their nature, it is impossible safely to limit that capacity.[23]

Though this was said by Hamilton with special reference to the need for an independent power of the purse, it is fair to say that the sentiment was essentially an argument against restricting Congress' capacity for action within narrow limits. "It is both unwise and dangerous," he declared, "to deny the federal government an unconfined authority, as to all those objects which are intrusted to its management." [24]

To Hamilton government inevitably meant power—and power

but he also envisaged the building up of a navy as essential to the commercial progress of America. "If we Mean to be a commercial people, or even to be secure on our Atlantic side, we must endeavor, as soon as possible, to have a navy." *Ibid.,* No. 24, p. 208.
[21] *Ibid.,* No. 30, p. 232.
[22] *Ibid.,* p. 235.
[23] *Ibid.,* No. 34, p. 249.
[24] *Ibid.,* No. 23, p. 202.

ought to be exercised in ways and to the extent dictated by need. So thoroughly convinced was he of this simple truism that he allowed himself to argue that the sweep of the national power would be the same even without the clause authorizing Congress "to make all laws which shall be necessary and proper for carrying into execution the foregoing powers, and all other powers vested by this Constitution in the Government of the United States, or in any Department or Officer thereof." [25] Thus, after acknowledging that the "necessary and proper" clause and the "supremacy" clause [26] "have been held up to the people . . . as the pernicious engines by which their local governments were to be destroyed and their liberties exterminated," Hamilton went on to say:

> The constitutional operation of the intended government would be precisely the same, if these clauses were entirely obliterated, as if they were repeated in every article. They are only declaratory of a truth which would have resulted by necessary and unavoidable implication from the very act of constituting a federal government, and vesting it with certain specified powers.[27]

And of the "necessary and proper" clause—"the sweeping clause, as it has been affectedly called"—he says, "The declaration itself, though it may be chargeable with tautology or redundancy, is at least perfectly harmless." [28]

It is interesting to contrast these observations of Hamilton with the view of Madison, from whom we learn that "few parts of the constitution have been assailed with more intemperance" than the "necessary and proper" clause. In Number 44 of *The Federalist,* Madison wrote, "Without the *substance* of this power, the whole Constitution would be a dead letter." [29] This theory

[25] *Constitution,* Art. I, sec. 8, par. 18.

[26] "This Constitution, and the Laws of the United States which shall be made in Pursuance thereof; and all Treaties made, or which shall be made, under the Authority of the United States, shall be the supreme Law of the Land; and the Judges in every State shall be bound thereby, anything in the Constitution or Laws of any State to the Contrary notwithstanding." *Ibid.,* Article VI, par. 2.

[27] *The Federalist,* No. 33, p. 245.

[28] *Ibid.,* pp. 245–246.

[29] *Ibid.,* No. 44, p. 320.

was entirely in accord with Madison's belief that the "change" wrought by the Constitution consisted "much less in the addition of New Powers to the Union, than in the invigoration of its original powers." [30]

III

The second institutional device on which Hamilton depended for keeping republican or popular government from degenerating into anarchy was the series of provisions which separated and diffused powers among the coordinate branches of the government. It was James Madison rather than Hamilton, however, who assumed the major part of the burden of defending the Constitution against the charge that in the organization of the new federal government, insufficient attention had been given to "this essential precaution in favor of liberty." [31]

In terms of fundamental theory, the best discussion in *The Federalist* of the separation of powers principle will be found in Numbers 47 and 51, both presumably written by Madison. "No political truth is certainly of greater intrinsic value, or is stamped with the authority of more enlightened patrons of liberty," writes Madison in Number 47, "than the political maxim that the legislative, executive, and judiciary departments ought to be separate and distinct." [32] Even Montesquieu—"The oracle who is always consulted and cited on this subject" [33]—would have approved Madison's terse statement of the celebrated precept: "The accumulation of all powers, legislative, executive, and judiciary, in the same hands, whether of one, a few, or many, and whether hereditary, self-appointed, or elective, may justly be pronounced the very definition of tyranny." [34]

Madison argues that since Montesquieu regarded the constitution of England as the "mirror of political liberty," the only correct way to judge whether the American Constitution conformed to the separation of powers principle was to recognize that under the British constitution "the legislative, executive, and judiciary

[30] *Ibid.*, No. 45, p. 329.
[31] *Ibid.*, No. 47, p. 336.
[32] *Ibid.*
[33] *Ibid.*, p. 337.
[34] *Ibid.*, p. 336.

departments are by no means totally separate and distinct from each other." Madison added:

> In saying "There can be no liberty where the legislative and executive powers are united in the same person, or body of magistrates," or "if the power of judging be not separated from the legislative and executive powers," he [Montesquieu] did not mean that these departments ought to have no *partial agency* in, or no *control* over, the acts of each other. His meaning, as his own words import, and still more conclusively as illustrated by the example in his eye, can amount to no more than this, that where the *whole* power of one department is exercised by the same hands which possess the *whole* power of another department, the fundamental principles of a free constitution are subverted.[35]

But perhaps the best philosophic defense of what he terms "the sacred maxim of free government" is to be found in the fifty-first essay of *The Federalist*, credited to himself by Hamilton [36] but now generally assigned to Madison:

> To what expedient . . . shall we finally resort, for maintaining in practice the necessary partition of power among the several departments, as laid down in the Constitution? The only answer that can be given is, that as all these exterior provisions are found to be inadequate, the defect must be supplied, by so contriving the interior structure of the government as that its several constituent parts may, by their mutual relations, be the means of keeping each other in their proper places. . . .
> But the great security against a gradual concentration of the several powers in the same department, consists in giving to those who administer each department the necessary constitutional means and personal motives to resist encroachments of the others. The provision for defence must in this, as in all other cases, be made commensurate to the danger of attack. Ambition must be made to counteract ambition. The interest of the man must be connected with the constitutional rights of the place. It may be a reflection on human nature, that such devices should be necessary to control the abuses of government. But what is government itself, but the greatest of all reflections on human nature? If men

[35] *Ibid.*, pp. 337–338.
[36] Douglass Adair, "The Authorship of the Disputed Federalist Papers," *William and Mary Quarterly*, 3rd Series, I (1944), particularly pp. 254–264.

were angels, no government would be necessary. If angels were to govern men, neither external nor internal controls on government would be necessary.[37]

Hamilton shared Madison's view that the separation of powers principle did not demand a complete isolation of the departments from each other. Thus, in discussing the objections to the provisions conferring on Congress the impeachment power, he wrote:

> The first of these objections is, that the provision in question confounds legislative and judiciary authorities in the same body, in violation of that important and well-established maxim which requires a separation between the different departments of power. The true meaning of this maxim has been discussed and ascertained in another place, and has been shown to be entirely compatible with a partial intermixture of those departments for special purposes, preserving them, in the main, distinct and unconnected. This partial intermixture is even, in some cases, not only proper but necessary to the mutual defence of the several members of the government against each other. An absolute or qualified negative in the executive upon the acts of the legislative body, is admitted, by the ablest adepts in political science, to be an indispensable barrier against the encroachments of the latter upon the former. And it may, perhaps, with no less reason be contended, that the powers relating to impeachments are, . . . an essential check in the hands of that body upon the encroachments of the executive.[38]

IV

This elaborate system of checks and balances was once described by Charles A. Beard as "the essential element of the Constitution." It sprang from the conviction, he suggested, that "the popular branch of the government cannot be allowed full sway, and least of all in the enactment of laws touching the rights of property." [39] Indeed, even before the Constitutional Convention of 1787 met at Philadelphia, there were indications that a good many Americans of substance and influence were beginning to

---

[37] *The Federalist*, No. 51, pp. 355–356.
[38] *Ibid.*, No. 66, p. 431.
[39] Beard, *The Supreme Court and the Constitution* (New York: The Macmillan Company, 1912, 1938 ed.), p. 95.

doubt the capacity of legislative assemblies to enact just or impartial laws. The early state constitutions, while professing faith in the separation of governmental powers, apportioned these powers in such a way as to make the legislature dominant.

It was probably inevitable that the lawmakers should have come to be blamed for the social unrest which marked the years following the American Revolution. As the antagonism between debt-ridden farmers, who controlled the legislatures in most of the states, and the men of finance and commerce grew more intense, a discontented but powerful minority turned to courts for protection against measures hostile to their interests. Thus did the search for greater economic and political stability lead gradually to the emergence of the judiciary as the guardian of private rights, particularly property.

The philosophy and expectations behind this reaction are well mirrored in the debate at the Philadelphia Convention over the proposal, embodied in the Virginia or Randolph plan, calling for the creation of a Council of Revision. Composed of members of the national legislature and a certain number of judges, the Council was to be vested with the power to review laws before they went into effect.

Madison reports Gouverneur Morris as having "dwelt on the importance of public Credit, and the difficulty of supporting it without some strong barrier against the instability of legislative Assemblies." [40] One of the principal supporters of legislative revision was James Wilson of Pennsylvania, who told the Convention, "The Judiciary ought to have an opportunity of remonstrating against projected encroachments on the people as well as on themselves." Reminding the delegates that "it had been said that the Judges, as expositors of the Laws would have an opportunity of defending their constitutional rights," Wilson argued that this did not go far enough: "Laws may be unjust, may be unwise, may be dangerous, may be destructive; and yet not be so unconstitutional as to justify the Judges in refusing to give them effect." [41]

Objecting to the proposed use of the judges of the Supreme

---

[40] *Records of the Federal Convention of 1787,* Farrand, ed., II, 299.
[41] *Ibid.,* II, 73.

Court to protect the people against unwise or dangerous legislation, Nathaniel Ghorum of Massachusetts insisted that "As Judges they (were) not to be presumed to possess any peculiar knowledge of the mere policy of public measures." [42] And while speaking against adoption of the Wilson-Madison proposal for giving the judges a share in the veto of national legislation, Elbridge Gerry declared: "It [the Council of Revision] was making statesmen of the Judges; and setting them up as guardians of the Rights of the people. He [Gerry] relied for his part on the Representatives of the people as the guardians of their Rights and interests." [43]

But, of course, the power of courts to nullify legislation was destined to become, in time, a vital part of the grand constitutional design for curbing the excesses of popular majorities. During the bitter debate over the ratification of the Constitution, no one was more forthright than Alexander Hamilton in stating the purpose ultimately to be served by checks and balances. Strongly of the belief, as he had phrased it at the Philadelphia Convention, that government must be capable of "resisting the popular current," [44] he quite naturally seized upon the system of mutual restraints embodied in the Constitution as a major instrument for assuring social stability. It is in Hamilton's "examination of the judiciary department" [45] where one will find an especially candid and forceful statement of this position. The essay delineates in particular the role he was hoping judges would come to play in the American system of government. Hamilton championed judicial review long before John Marshall succeeded in making it synonymous with the Constitution.

In an earlier essay, Hamilton had remarked that "the want of a judiciary power" was the condition which "crowned" the defects of the government under the Articles of Confederation. He went on to say that "laws are a dead letter without courts to expound and define their true meaning and operation." [46] Yet

[42] *Ibid.*
[43] *Ibid.*, II, 75.
[44] *Ibid.*, I, 309.
[45] *The Federalist*, No. 78, p. 489.
[46] *Ibid.*, No. 23, p. 197.

when one turns to his fuller discussion of the system of courts established by the Constitution, it is apparent that the New Yorker was looking to the federal judges to perform a function infinitely more significant than the mere interpretation of the meaning of laws.

Hamilton's now classic defense of judicial power is, in essence, an argument for the existence of an institution able to restrain the more popularly constituted branches of the government. Courts, he explains, "were designed to be an intermediate body between the people and the legislature." They were to be the "bulwarks" of the Constitution "against legislative encroachments." It was necessary to protect society against "legislative invasions" of the Constitution "instigated by the major voice of the Community." Defending lifetime tenure for federal judges, Hamilton contended that the independence of judges was an "essential safeguard" against those "ill-humors in society" which may jeopardize "the private rights of particular classes of citizens, by unjust and partial laws." He expected the judiciary to be a force "in mitigating the severity and confining the operation of such laws." [47]

Hamilton did not confine his belief in the importance of restraining the popular impulse in government to the pages of *The Federalist* papers. One of his strongest statements on the subject is to be found in a speech at the New York Ratifying Convention. Arguing on June 24, 1788, against a proposal to make Senators ineligible for re-election, he said:

> There are few positions more demonstrable than that there should be in every republic some permanent body, to correct the prejudices, check the intemperate passions, and regulate the fluctuations of a popular assembly. . . . A body instituted for these purposes must be so formed as to exclude as much as possible from its own character those infirmities and that mutability which it is designed to remedy. It is, therefore, necessary that it should be small, that it should hold its authority during a considerable period, and that it should have such an independence

[47] *Ibid.*, No. 78, pp. 494–495.

in the exercise of its powers, as will divest it, as much as possible, of local prejudices.[48]

And on the following day, he pressed this view even more bluntly by citing contemporary experience:

> Is not the State of Rhode Island at this moment struggling under difficulties and distresses, for having been led blindly by the spirit of the multitude? What is her legislature but the picture of a mob? In this state, we have a senate, possessed of the proper qualities of a permanent body. Virginia, Maryland, and a few other States are in the same situation. The rest are either governed by a single democratic assembly, or have a senate constituted entirely upon democratic principles. These have been more or less embroiled in factions, and have generally been the image and echo of the multitude.[49]

One cannot be sure that at the time he contributed the essay on the judiciary Hamilton actually envisaged, in all of its ramifications, the type of governmental practice hammered out by Marshall many years later. What is clear is that Hamilton appreciated, perhaps intuitively, that what he euphemistically calls "the interpretation of the laws" embraced "the right of the courts to pronounce legislative acts void." Most striking of all is his prophetic observation that the power of courts to safeguard society against "unjust and partial laws" would have "more influence upon the character of governments, than but few may be aware of." [50]

[48] *The Papers of Alexander Hamilton*, V, 68.
[49] *Ibid.*, p. 82.
[50] *The Federalist*, No. 78, p. 495.

4

"The Powers . . . Ought to Be Construed Liberally"

◆◇◆◇◆◇◆◇◆◇◆◇◆◇◆◇◆◇◆◇◆◇◆

As a member of the New York Ratifying Convention and an active and vigorous participant in its deliberations, Alexander Hamilton said much in support of the proposed federal Constitution which clearly presaged both the attitudes and policies he was to espouse as America's first Secretary of the Treasury. "Sir, when you have divided and nicely balanced the departments of government;" he told the convention at Poughkeepsie, "When you have strongly connected the virtue of your rulers with their interest; when, in short, you have rendered your system as perfect as human forms can be; you must place confidence; you must give power." [1] One theme dominated his utterances. He neatly summarized it in his long speech on the powers of the Senate when he argued that no less important than the "zeal for liberty" generated by the Revolution was the "principle of strength and stability in the organization of our government, and of vigor in its operations." The whole context in which Hamilton makes this comment is worth recalling:

> In the commencement of a revolution, which received its birth from usurpations of tyranny, nothing was more natural than that the public mind should be influenced by an extreme spirit of jealousy. To resist these encroachments, and to nourish this spirit, was the great object of all our public and private institutions. Zeal for liberty became predominant and excessive. In forming our confederation, this passion alone seemed to actuate us,

[1] June 27, 1788. *The Papers of Alexander Hamilton,* V, 95.

and we appear to have had no other view than to secure ourselves from despotism. The object certainly was a valuable one, and deserved our utmost attention. But, Sir, there is another object, equally important, and which our enthusiasm rendered us little capable of regarding. I mean a principle of strength and stability in the organization of our government, and of vigor in its operations.[2]

In retrospect, it can be seen that all of Hamilton's prior experience and polemical activity were an ideal preparation for his service in Washington's Cabinet. Seldom has there been so complete an intellectual apologia for a program of statecraft. Perhaps only the policies of governments established by successful revolutions follow such a pattern.

I

But Hamilton did not cease being the advocate when he became Washington's chief planner of national policy. His success in winning the support both of the President and Congress was due, in no small degree, to the fact that he was quite prepared to defend the constitutionality as well as the necessity of the measures he was proposing. An outstanding instance is his plan calling for the incorporation of a national bank.

In the House of Representatives the opposition to the measure was led by James Madison, who questioned its constitutionality. Both Attorney General Edmund Randolph and Secretary of State Jefferson shared Madison's misgivings. Before signing the bill, Washington requested the Secretary of the Treasury to submit a formal opinion on the constitutional objections to the proposed bank.

Among the powers delegated to Congress by the Constitution, Jefferson insisted, there was none to create a national bank. Nor was he willing to rely on Congress' power "to make all laws necessary and proper" for carrying into effect its enumerated powers. "To take a single step beyond the boundaries thus specially drawn around the powers of Congress," warned Jefferson, "is to take possession of a boundless field of power, no longer susceptible of any definition." [3] He was equally unimpressed by the argu-

---

[2] June 24, 1788. *Ibid.*, V, 68.
[3] Thomas Jefferson, "Opinion on the Constitutionality of a National Bank

ment that the government would find the national bank convenient. "Convenience is not necessity" was his simple rejoinder.[4]

Hamilton's opinion on the constitutionality of the national
bank is much more than a carefully reasoned refutation of the
legal arguments against the bill awaiting Washington's signa-
ture. It is a powerful restatement of his own philosophy of government. He found one feature of the position taken by Randolph and Jefferson particularly vulnerable. "In entering upon
the argument," he observes at the outset, "it ought to be premised
that the objections of the Secretary of State and the Attorney
General are founded on a general denial of the authority of the
United States to erect corporations." [5] This contention struck
him as contrary to the principle that every government must be
free to establish institutions it deems essential to its needs and
functions. "Now it appears to the Secretary of the Treasury,"
Hamilton advised the President, "that this *general principle* is
inherent in the very *definition* of government, and *essential* to
every step of the progress to be made by that of the United
States." [6]

That the government launched by the Constitution was also
to avail itself of such instrumentalities Hamilton deduced from
an even more basic political maxim. "Every power vested in a
government is in its nature *sovereign,* and includes, by *force* of
the *term,* a right to employ all the *means* requisite and fairly
applicable to the attainment of the *ends* of such power, and
which are not precluded by restrictions and exceptions specified
in the Constitution, or not immoral, or not contrary to the *essential ends* of political society." [7] The "supremacy" clause is
"decisive" in showing that the national government was meant
to be sovereign "in relation to the objects intrusted to the management of the government."

of the United States," Feb. 15, 1791, *Works of Thomas Jefferson,* Ford, ed.,
VI, 198.
    [4] *Ibid.*
    [5] "Opinion as to the Constitutionality of the Bank of the United States,"
February 23, 1791, *The Works of Alexander Hamilton,* Henry Cabot Lodge, ed.
(New York: G. P. Putnam's Sons, 1904), III, 446.
    [6] *Ibid.*
    [7] *Ibid.*

In the light of this fundamental principle of effective government, it made no difference that the government of the United States was confined by the Constitution to certain specified objects. "It is not denied that there are implied, as well as express powers, and that the former are as effectually delegated as the latter." Once it is admitted that the Constitution conferred implied as well as express powers, it must follow that the national government was free to make use of corporations chartered by it. This is so because such corporations are the instruments for effectuating the ends or purposes of government as represented by the powers actually delegated.

What, then, was the constitutional problem? "The only question must be in this, as in every other case," said Hamilton, "whether the mean to be employed, or, in this instance, the corporation to be erected, has a natural relation to any of the acknowledged objects or lawful ends of the government." Referring to Jefferson's answer to this question, he accused the Secretary of State of maintaining that the government could make use only of such "means" without which it would be incapable of carrying out its express powers. "It is essential to the being of the national government, that so erroneous a conception of the meaning of the word *necessary* should be exploded," [8] emphatically declared Hamilton. As Marshall was to do three decades later when the issues over the bank were joined before the Supreme Court, Hamilton called on the dictionary and on human experience in expounding the meaning of an important constitutional phrase:

> It is certain, that neither the grammatical nor popular sense of the term requires that construction. According to both, *necessary* often means no more than *needful, requisite, incidental, useful,* or *conducive to.* It is a common mode of expression to say, that it is *necessary* for a government or a person to do this or that thing, when nothing more is intended or understood, than that the interests of the government or person require, or will be prompted by, the doing of this or that thing. . . . The whole turn of the clause containing it [the word "necessary" in the necessary and proper clause of the Constitution] indicates, that it was

[8] *Ibid.,* III, 452.

the intent of the Convention, by that clause, to give a liberal latitude to the exercise of the specified powers. . . .

To understand the word as the Secretary of State does, would
be to depart from its obvious and popular sense, and to give it a
restrictive operation, an idea never before entertained. It would
be to give it the same force as if the word *absolutely* or *indispensably* had been prefixed to it. . . .

The *degree* in which a measure is necessary can never be a *test*
of the legal right to adopt it; that must be a matter of opinion,
and can only be a *test* of expediency. The *relation* between the
measure and the *end;* between the *nature* of the *means* employed
towards the execution of a power, and the object of that power,
must be the criterion of constitutionality, not the more or less
of *necessity* or *utility*. . . .

This restrictive interpretation of the word *necessary* is also
contrary to this sound maxim of construction; namely, that the
powers contained in a constitution of government, especially
those which concern the general administration of the affairs of a
country, its finances, trade, defence, etc., ought to be construed
liberally in advancement of the public good. . . . The means
by which national exigencies are to be provided for, national in-
conveniences obviated, national prosperity promoted, are of such
infinite variety, extent, and complexity, that there must of necessity be great latitude of discretion in the selection and application
of those means. Hence, consequently, the necessity and propriety
of exercising the authorities intrusted to a government on principles of liberal construction.[9]

After setting forth these principles of liberal constitutional
interpretation, Hamilton proceeded to argue that the right to
create banks had a clear connection with several of the specific
powers which the Constitution delegates to Congress. There was,
he insisted, a more or less "direct relation" between the proposed
national bank and Congress' power of collecting taxes, borrowing
money, regulating commerce among the states, and the power
to raise and maintain armed forces.[10] In other words, the incor-

[9] *Ibid.*, III, 452–455.
[10] "The Congress shall have Power To lay and collect Taxes, Duties, Imposts and Excises, to pay the Debts and provide for the common Defence
and general Welfare of the United States; . . .
"To borrow Money on the credit of the United States;

poration of the bank was a "constitutional measure" for putting into practical operation certain of the general responsibilities which the Constitution had committed to the national government. The test of constitutionality is simple: "This criterion is the *end,* to which the measure relates as a *mean.* If the end be clearly comprehended within any of the specified powers, and if the measure have an obvious relation to that *end,* and is not forbidden by any particular provision of the Constitution, it may safely be deemed to come within the compass of the national authority." [11]

II

Judged by the importance of the role which the federal government has come to play in the promotion of social welfare, none of Hamilton's prophetic ideas is more strikingly significant than his conception of the "general welfare" clause. It is unfolded in the "Report on Manufactures" which he submitted to the House of Representatives on December 5, 1791.[12] Hamilton was dealing with the question whether the federal government had a "constitutional right" to encourage the development of manufacturing in the United States by favoring it with protective tariffs and other bounties. He had no doubts. Such legislation could be enacted by virtue of the provision authorizing Congress "To lay and collect Taxes, Duties, Imposts, and Excises, to pay the debts, and provide for the common Defence and general Welfare of the United States." [13]

Except for the three restrictions which the Constitution itself imposes on Congress' taxing power, Hamilton urged that its power to raise revenue be viewed as "plenary and indefinite." [14]

"To regulate Commerce with foreign Nations, and among the several States, and with the Indian Tribes; . . . . .

"To raise and support Armies, ..." *Constitution,* Art. I, sec. 8, par. 1, 2, 3, and 12.

[11] Hamilton, *Works,* Lodge, ed., III, 458. Marshall's language on the relation between means and ends is as follows: "Let the end be legitimate, let it be within the scope of the Constitution, and all means, which are appropriate, which are plainly adapted to that end, which are not prohibited, but consist with the letter and spirit of the Constitution, are constitutional." *McCulloch v. Maryland,* 4 Wheat. 316, 437 (1819).

[12] Hamilton, *Works,* Lodge, ed., IV, 70.

[13] *Constitution,* Art. I, sec. 8, par. 1.

[14] These three restrictions are: (1) "all Duties, Imposts and Excises shall

Even more useful to future architects of federal spending would be his assertion that the "objects" to which money raised by Congress might be devoted "are no less comprehensive than the payment of the public debts, and the providing for the common defence and the general welfare." Unless the words "general welfare" were given a broad construction "numerous exigencies incident to the affairs of a nation would have been left without a provision." The framers inserted so comprehensive a phrase as is the "general Welfare" clause because they believed that "it was not fit that the constitutional authority of the Union to appropriate its revenue should have been restricted within narrower limits than the 'general welfare,' and because this necessarily embraces a vast variety of particulars, which are susceptible neither of specification nor of definition." [15]

But Hamilton was doing more than expounding constitutional theory. His practical object was to supply a rationale which would free Congress to adopt measures he deemed essential to the nation's growth and power. Constitutional exegesis was thus to serve as an implement with which both to inspire and to defend necessary public policies:

> It is, therefore, of necessity, left to the discretion of the National Legislature to pronounce upon the objects which concern the general welfare, and for which, under that description, an appropriation of money is requisite and proper. And there seems to be no room for a doubt that whatever concerns the general interests of learning, of agriculture, of manufactures, and of commerce, are within the sphere of the national councils, as far as regards an application of money.
>
> The only qualification of the generality of the phrase in question, which seems to be admissible, is this: That the object to which an appropriation of money is to be made be general, and not local; its operation extending in fact or by possibility throughout the Union, and not being confined to a particular spot.[16]

be uniform throughout the United States;" Art. I, sec. 8, par. 1; (2) "No Capitation, or other direct, Tax shall be laid, unless in Proportion to the Census or Enumeration;" Art. I, sec. 9, par. 4; (3) "No Tax or Duty shall be laid on Articles exported from any State;" Art. I, sec. 9, par. 5.

[15] Hamilton, *Works,* IV, 151.

[16] *Ibid.,* IV, 151–152.

III

No wonder the men who a century and a half later struggled
to vindicate the New Deal's resort to federal spending (as an en-
gine for economic recovery and social betterment) found Hamilton's views so congenial and useful. All one need do is examine
his definition of general welfare—with its reference to learning,
agriculture, manufacture, and commerce as permissible objects
of federal expenditure—and he will perceive at least one reason
for a major paradox of our time. The ideological successors of
Thomas Jefferson have turned to the constitutional philosophy
of his implacable antagonist. A terse and dramatic comment of
Justice Cardozo in 1937 connected the two epochs: "It is too late
today for the argument to be heard with tolerance that in a
crisis so extreme the use of the moneys of the nation to relieve
the unemployed and their dependents is a use for any purpose
narrower than the promotion of the general welfare." [17] And in
his opinion sustaining the right of Congress to adopt the old-age
provisions of the Social Security Act, Cardozo actually invoked
Hamilton: "The conception of the spending power advocated
by Hamilton and strongly reinforced by Story has prevailed over
that of Madison, which has not been lacking in adherents." [18]

Besides Hamilton's, two other views of the meaning and effect
of the "general welfare" clause have been entertained in our history. The most extreme theory is the contention that this clause
permits Congress to advance the general welfare, independently
of (or by means other than) the taxing-spending power. The
notion that the federal government possesses a separate substantive power to promote the general welfare of the nation has never
been accepted by the courts. If this conception of the general
welfare clause were ever adopted, Justice Joseph Story pointed
out, all that need happen is that "under color of the generality
of the words to 'provide for the common defence and the general
welfare' the government of the United States [would], in reality,

---

[17] This comment will be found in Justice Cardozo's opinion for a majority
of the Supreme Court which upheld the constitutionality of the unemploy-
ment compensation provisions of the Social Security Act of 1935. *Steward Ma-
chine Co. v. Davis,* 301 U.S. 548, 586–587 (1937).

[18] *Helvering v. Davis,* 301 U.S. 619, 640 (1937).

be a government of general and unlimited powers, notwithstanding the subsequent enumeration of specific powers." [19]

According to the doctrine advocated by James Madison, the expenditure of funds raised by federal taxation must be devoted to purposes embraced by the powers which the Constitution delegated to Congress. In other words, the power to tax and spend for the general welfare cannot be used as a basis for federal control of matters to which the regulatory powers of the national government do not extend.[20]

Hamilton's interpretation of the range of the "general welfare" clause is essentially a compromise between these two positions. He believed that the sole limitation to which Congress' power to tax and spend was subject was that it be exercised to provide for the general or national welfare, rather than to confer purely local or isolated benefits.

When John Marshall came to discuss—in his biography of Washington—the controversy generated by Hamilton's plan for a national bank, he chronicled what he obviously regarded as an unfortunate consequence of the conflict. "This measure [the bank bill] made a deep impression on many members of the legislature, and contributed, not inconsiderably, to the complete organization of those distinct and visible parties which, in their long and dubious conflict for power, have since shaken the United States to their centre." [21] Even Thomas Jefferson, who dismissed the

[19] Story, *Commentaries on the Constitution of the United States* (Boston: Hilliard, Gray, and Company, 1833), II, 367. Marshall shared Story's view of the "general welfare" clause: "I have never believed that the words 'to pay the debts and provide for the common defence and general welfare of the United States' were to be considered as a substantive grant of power but as a declaration of objects for which taxes might be levied." John Marshall to Timothy Pickering, March 28, 1828. *Proceedings of the Massachusetts Historical Society* (Second Series, 1901), XIV, 323.

[20] See Madison's letter to Andrew Stevenson, Nov. 27, 1830, reprinted in *The Writings of James Madison,* Gaillard Hunt, ed., IX, 1819–1836.

[21] Marshall, *The Life of George Washington* (Philadelphia: Caleb P. Wayne, 1807), V, 299. Marshall appended a long note to the fifth volume in which he summarizes, quite objectively, the views of both Hamilton and Jefferson. But his concluding comment would seem to indicate where his own sympathies lay. Speaking of Hamilton's argument, he writes: "The Secretary of the Treasury next proceeded, by a great variety of arguments and illustra-

Chief Justice's *Life* of the first President as a "party diatribe," [22] may have found Marshall's assessment of the political effects of the legislation not altogether unacceptable.

But if Jefferson was disturbed by the constitutional implications of Hamilton's theory of implied powers, Hamilton's reading of the "general welfare" clause of the Constitution apparently impressed him with its danger to the Republic even more. Nor did time lessen his fears, as a letter he penned a quarter of a century later clearly shows. Writing from Monticello to Spencer Roane in 1815, Jefferson summed up his philosophy in uncompromising terms:

> I hope our courts will never countenance the sweeping pretensions which have been set up under the words "general defence and public welfare." These words only express motives which induced the Convention to give to the ordinary legislature certain specified powers which they enumerate, and which they thought might be trusted to the ordinary legislature, and not to give them the unspecified also; or why any specification? They could not be so awkward in language as to mean, as we say, "all and some." And should this construction prevail, all limits to the federal government are done away. This opinion, formed on the first rise of the question, I have never seen reason to change, whether in or out of power; but, on the contrary, find it strengthened and confirmed by five and twenty years of additional reflection and experience: and any countenance given to it by any regular organ of the government, I should consider more ominous than anything which has yet occurred.[23]

Jefferson went on to apologize for these comments by saying that they were motivated by "my zeal for the administration of our

---

tions, to prove the position that the measure in question was a proper mean for the execution of the several powers which were enumerated, and also contended that the right to employ it resulted from the whole of them taken together. To detail those arguments would occupy too much space, and is the less necessary, because their correctness obviously depends on the correctness of the principles which have been already stated." *Ibid.*, note No. III, pp. 3–11 at p. 11.

[22] Thomas Jefferson to John Adams, August 10, 1815. *The Works of Thomas Jefferson*, Ford, ed., XI, 485.

[23] Thomas Jefferson to Spencer Roane, Oct. 15, 1815. *Ibid.*, XI, 489–490.

government according to its true spirit, federal as well as republican." [24]

That contemporary America should be more in tune with Hamilton's conception of the constitutional possibilities for promoting the public welfare through federal action may be too obvious a phenomenon to require further proof. What does need to be said, perhaps, is that this inversion of the logic of ideology is probably as good a testimonial to the resourcefulness of the American Constitution as the history of the document has furnished. To the extent, therefore, that Alexander Hamilton helped to bring about its adoption and to infuse it with principles of liberal interpretation, to that extent he made the Constitution an instrument of lasting utility to Americans—all Americans, regardless of political persuasion. As one of his most informed biographers once expressed it: "It was in this last decisive struggle, in securing the acceptance of the work of the Convention, that Hamilton rendered his greatest services to the cause of the Constitution— services more important and more effective than those of any other one man at this last stage of what was in truth a great political revolution." [25]

[24] *Ibid.*, XI, 490.
[25] Henry Cabot Lodge, *Alexander Hamilton* (Boston: Houghton Mifflin Co., 1882; Standard edition, 1910), p. 62. Lodge called attention to a paradoxical turn of events which occurred while both Hamilton and Jefferson were still opposing each other on the stage of political combat. "By one of the strange but not uncommon contradictions which we meet with in human history, there fell to the lot of Hamilton's keenest foe to carry out the most imperial part of the great Federalist's national policy. It was reserved to Jefferson to acquire by purchase [the Louisiana Purchase], and in what was then thought to be defiance of the Constitution, the vast territory which Hamilton planned only a few years before to win by arms." *Ibid.*, p. 260.

PART II

"By This Tribunal Alone"

5

"The Very Essence of Judicial Duty"

In September of 1831 John Marshall went to Philadelphia on a desperate mission. He came to consult an eminent surgeon, seeking relief from a terribly painful condition.

By way of asking him to address them at a formal dinner, the Bar of the City adopted resolutions expressing admiration and affection for the old and ailing Chief Justice. In his letter declining the invitation, Marshall observed that the thing which had given him the greatest satisfaction was that he and his associates on the Supreme Court had "never sought to enlarge the judicial power beyond its proper bounds, nor feared to carry it to the fullest extent that duty required." [1]

Made in the twilight years of his tenure on the court and at a moment of deep discouragement, this comment would seem to be a defensive one. But there is another way of looking at it. Marshall's statement to the lawyers of Philadelphia, coming as it did less than four years before the end of his life, may be viewed as both a challenge to his critics and a veritable epitome of his fundamental contribution to the emergence of judicial power in the United States.

Characteristically, Marshall was expressing a complex and subtle issue in terms of unavoidable choice. He was proclaiming for all to hear that he had adhered to the simple necessity of the dictates of judicial duty. But this assurance would hardly have

[1] Albert J. Beveridge, *The Life of John Marshall* (Boston: Houghton Mifflin Co., 1916–1919), IV, 522.

satisfied Thomas Jefferson, who had allowed himself to write to a colleague of Marshall's only eight years earlier: "There is no danger I apprehend so much as the consolidation of our government by the noiseless and therefore unalarming, instrumentality of the Supreme Court." [2] And three years before that, Jefferson had taken to task the author of a widely publicized book for expounding a heretical view of the judicial function. "You seem . . . to consider the judges," he objected, "as the ultimate arbiters of all constitutional questions; a very dangerous doctrine indeed, and one which would place us under the despotism of an oligarchy." Jefferson's letter continued:

> Our judges are as honest as other men, and not more so. They have, with others, the same passions for party, for power, and the privilege of their corps. . . . Their power [is] the more dangerous as they are in office for life, and not responsible, as the other functionaries are, to the elective control. The Constitution has erected no such single tribunal, knowing that to whatever hands confided, with the corruption of time and party, its members would become despots. It has more wisely all the departments co-equal and co-sovereign within themselves.[3]

It was Justice Joseph Story who brought this letter by Jefferson to Marshall's attention. In his reply, Marshall, who remarked that the letter "rather grieves than surprises me," used the opportunity to suggest an explanation for Jefferson's attitude toward the judiciary:

> For Jefferson's opinion as respects this department [the judiciary] it is not difficult to assign the cause. He is among the most ambitious, and I suspect among the most unforgiving of men. His great power is over the mass of the people, and this power is chiefly acquired by professions of democracy. Every check on the wild impulse of the moment is a check on his own power, and he is unfriendly to the source from which it flows. He looks of course with ill will at an independent judiciary.[4]

[2] Thomas Jefferson to Justice William Johnson, March 4, 1823. *The Works of Thomas Jefferson*, Ford, ed. (1904), XII, 280.

[3] Thomas Jefferson to William Charles Jarvis, Sept. 28, 1820. *Ibid.*, XII, 162.

[4] John Marshall to Joseph Story, July 13, 1821. Proceedings of the Massachusetts Historical Society (2nd Series, 1901), XIV, 328.

Placed in juxtaposition, these observations by Marshall and by Jefferson throw into bold relief what is perhaps the really basic, and even still unresolved, question concerning the nature and scope of the Supreme Court's power as the "ultimate" interpreter of the American Constitution. In Marshall's own phrase, that question is: What are the "proper bounds" and what is the abuse of judicial power?

I

In a fundamental sense, Marshall's boast to the bar of Philadelphia in 1831 is but an echo of his notable apologia for judicial power in *Marbury v. Madison*,[5] rendered just two years after he assumed the office of Chief Justice. And his opinion in this case was but an elaboration of a view he had voiced at the Virginia Ratifying Convention of 1788. In the course of urging approval of the proposed Constitution, the young Virginian undertook to allay the fears of those who had charged that Congress was being given unlimited powers. Marshall's comments on this occasion deserve to be recalled as foreshadowing the whole tenor of his central conviction as expounder of the Constitution:

> If they [Congress] were to make a law not warranted by any of the powers enumerated, it would be considered by the judges as an infringement of the Constitution which they are to guard. They would not consider such a law as coming under their jurisdiction. They would declare it void. . . .
>
> To what quarter will you look for protection from an infringement of the Constitution, if you will not give the power to the judiciary? There is no other body that can afford such a protection.[6]

Marbury v. Madison is the case in which Marshall avoided a direct collision with Jefferson by declining to issue the writ which would have forced Secretary of State Madison to surrender the commission in which John Adams had named Marbury as a justice of the peace for the District of Columbia. Relying on section 13 of the Judiciary Act of 1789—which had authorized the Supreme Court to issue writs of *mandamus*—Marbury requested the Court

[5] 1 Cranch 137 (1803).
[6] Elliot's *Debates*, III, 554.

to issue such a writ. In adopting Section 13, said Marshall, Congress had enlarged the "original jurisdiction" of the Court beyond the two fields specified in the Constitution itself. "In all Cases affecting Ambassadors, other public Ministers and Consuls, and those in which a State shall be a Party, the Supreme Court shall have original jurisdiction." Logically, this provision in Article III might have been treated as signifying an intention to assure immediate and direct access to the Supreme Court in the two types of litigation it mentions. Instead, Marshall read it to mean that no other parties could be permitted to come before the High Court without first being heard in lower courts.

As early as 1803, then, Marshall made the extraordinary pronouncement that a law, duly enacted by a coordinate branch of the government, was nevertheless unconstitutional or no law at all.[7] But as if this assertion were not bold enough, he went on to raise a seemingly gratuitous question—whether the Supreme Court had the right to make such a pronouncement. As Justice Samuel F. Miller once pointed out, "Since the court declared in the end that they had no jurisdiction in the case," the decision in *Marbury v. Madison* was in many respects *obiter*.[8]

For Marshall, the inquiry as to whether the Court was meant to have the right to set aside an act of Congress apparently presented no special difficulty. "The question," he begins, "whether an act repugnant to the Constitution can become the law of the land is a question deeply interesting to the United States; but, happily, not of an intricacy proportioned to its interest." And why was the question so easy of solution? "It seems only necessary," Marshall continues, "to recognize certain principles supposed to have been long and well established, to decide it." [9]

[7] What James Bradley Thayer said on the occasion of the centenary of Marshall's accession to the Chief Justiceship is still an accurate statement: "It has been said in high quarters that there were earlier decisions of the Supreme Court holding an act of Congress unconstitutional; but nothing yet in print justifies the statement. This was the first case. And it was more than half a century before such a decision was again rendered by this Court." (Manuscript in Harvard Law Library.)

[8] Miller, *Lectures on the Constitution of the United States* (New York and Albany: Banks and Brothers, Law Publishers, 1891), p. 386.

[9] 1 Cranch 137, 175.

His exposition of fundamental political precepts makes it plain that for Marshall, as for Hamilton, judicial review of legislation flowed logically—indeed inevitably—from the very nature of the institutions created by the Constitution. In this discussion Marshall revealed his own basic conception of the American system of government. It almost seems, moreover, as if he were determined to answer, from the outset, the objection to judicial review traditionally made by those who adhered to an opposite political philosophy. That argument is, of course, that judicial review is inconsistent with the principle of popular rule—government by what Jefferson calls in the Declaration of Independence "the consent of the governed."

How, then, does Marshall equate the Supreme Court's right to hold acts of Congress to be invalid with the notion that in approving the Constitution, Americans intended their government to reflect the will of the people? He does this by portraying the act of adopting a written Constitution—and he characterizes written constitutions as "the greatest improvement on political institutions"—as embodying the ultimate will of the people. As he says:

> That the people have an original right to establish, for their future government, such principles as, in their opinion, shall most conduce to their own happiness is the basis on which the whole American fabric has been erected. The exercise of this original right is a very great exertion; nor can it, nor ought it, to be frequently repeated. The principles, therefore, so established, are deemed fundamental. And as the authority from which they proceed is supreme, and can seldom act, they are designed to be permanent.
>
> This original and supreme will organizes the government, and assigns to different departments their respective powers. It may either stop here, or establish certain limits not to be transcended by those departments.
>
> The government of the United States is of the latter description. The powers of the legislature are defined and limited; and that those limits may not be mistaken, or forgotten, the constitution is written.[10]

[10] *Ibid.*, pp. 175–176.

The American Constitution was thus seen by Marshall as depending on two essential ingredients. Its provisions embody the "supreme will" of the people, and the chief import of these provisions was to restrict the exercise of power by the different departments. A certain rhetorical question raised by Marshall suggests the vital connection between the limits imposed by the Constitution and the power he was claiming for the Court. "To what purpose are powers limited and to what purpose is that limitation committed to writing, if these limits may at any time be passed by those intended to be restrained?" But of course Marshall does not leave this question unanswered. "The distinction between a government with limited and unlimited powers is abolished," he declared, "if those limits do not confine the persons on whom they are imposed and if acts prohibited and acts allowed are of equal obligation." He could see "no middle ground" between the view that the Constitution "controls any legislative act repugnant to it" and the view that would permit a legislative assembly to change the Constitution by ordinary legislation.

> The Constitution is either a superior paramount law, unchangeable by ordinary means, or it is on a level with ordinary legislative acts, and, like other acts, is alterable when the Legislature shall please to alter it.
> If the former part of the alternative be true, then a legislative act contrary to the Constitution is not law: if the latter part be true, then written constitutions are absurd attempts, on the part of the people, to limit a power in its own nature illimitable.[11]

Marshall's many variations on this theme were no mere exercise in syllogistic reasoning. They were meant to clarify and to prepare the way for a most important conclusion: "Certainly all those who have framed written constitutions contemplate them as forming the fundamental and paramount law of the nation, and consequently the theory of every such government must be that an act of the Legislature repugnant to the Constitution is void." More emphatic still is the Chief Justice's comment that "this theory is essentially attached to a written constitution, and,

[11] *Ibid.*, p. 176.

is consequently, to be considered, by this court, as one of the fundamental principles of our society." [12]

In the light of these "fundamental principles," what are courts to do when they find that the legislative branch of the government has attempted to do something which the Constitution forbids? For the courts to regard such enactments as a "law" would be "an absurdity too gross" to be tolerated.

> It is emphatically the province and duty of the judicial department to say what the law is. Those who apply the rule to particular cases, must of necessity expound and interpret that rule. . . .
>
> So, if a law be in opposition to the constitution; if both the law and the constitution apply to a particular case, so that the court must either decide that case conformably to the law, disregarding the constitution; or conformably to the constitution, disregarding the law; the court must determine which of these conflicting rules governs the case. This is of the very essence of judicial duty.[13]

At the heart of Marshall's conception of judicial power is his view of the American constitutional system as a sort of legal hierarchy. Not all of the law's commands are of equal obligation. Standing at the apex of the legal order is the Constitution, and obedience to the mandate of the Constitution is the primary or fundamental loyalty.

Nor does Marshall treat the dilemma faced by judges—when confronted with a conflict between legislative will and constitutional prescription—as a mere theoretical or philosophic abstraction. He goes on to cite several clauses of the Constitution which restrict legislative authority; and by the time he is through analyzing their import, it is clear that in his mind there was no such dilemma at all. The Constitution, he points out, bans taxes on exports, forbids the enactment of bills of attainder and *ex post facto* laws, and requires the testimony of two witnesses in proving the charge of treason. Suppose Congress were to adopt laws which are contrary to these provisions, and judges were called upon to reconcile the legislative enactments with the prohibitions of the Constitution? Certainly the judges of the Supreme Court,

[12] *Ibid.,* pp. 176–177.
[13] *Ibid.,* p. 177.

who have sworn to uphold the Constitution, have no choice but
to "say" that Congress had violated the Constitution. Not to do
so would make "a solemn mockery" out of the oath imposed on
judges.

Marshall's purpose in giving these illustrations is clear. To
him they prove that "the framers of the Constitution contemplated that instrument as a rule for the government of courts,
as well as of the Legislature." His emphasis on the importance
of the oath has an almost emotional ring to it:

> Why otherwise does it [the Constitution] direct the judges to
> take an oath to support it? This oath certainly applies in an es-
> pecial manner, to their conduct in their official character. How
> immoral to impose it on them, if they were to be used as the in-
> struments, and the knowing instruments, for violating what they
> swear to support.[14]

The superior claim of the Constitution upon the allegiance
of judges is also further justified by Marshall with the argument
that the "supremacy" clause [15] assigns primacy to the document
itself. "It is also not entirely unworthy of observation," the Chief
Justice notes, "that, in declaring what shall be the supreme law
of the land, the Constitution itself is mentioned first, and not the
laws of the United States generally, but those only which shall
be made in *pursuance* of the Constitution, have that rank."

II

It is not necessary to share James Kent's flattering estimate
that Marshall's argument for judicial review approached "the
precision and certainty of a mathematical demonstration" [16] in
order to recognize that Marshall presented a powerful and persuasive defense of the Supreme Court's right to set aside governmental policies it deems to be unconstitutional. There were

---

[14] *Ibid.*, p. 179.

[15] "This Constitution, and the Laws of the United States which shall be
made in Pursuance thereof; and all Treaties made, or which shall be made,
under the Authority of the United States, shall be the supreme Law of the
Land; and the Judges in every State shall be bound thereby, any Thing in
the Constitution or Laws of any State to the Contrary notwithstanding." *Constitution*, Art. VI, clause 2.

[16] Kent, *Commentaries on American Law*, 12th edition by O. W. Holmes,
Jr. (Boston: Little, Brown and Company, 1873), p. 453.

flaws in his reasoning, but the logical inadequacies of Marshall's opinion in *Marbury v. Madison* have in no way diminished his stature as the "great Chief Justice." On the contrary, much of the mythology surrounding the Supreme Court's prerogative to have the last say as to the meaning of the Constitution continues to draw upon Marshall's historic statement of 1803. It remains true, as Max Lerner wrote in 1937, that the justification for the doctrine of judicial supremacy "is a body of inferences, a system of 'givens' and 'therefors,' an intellectual construction." [17]

The Constitution does not, in so many plain words, authorize the Supreme Court to exercise the power of annulling actions of the other branches of the government. Neither did Marshall invent judicial review. What can be said with confidence is that in *Marbury v. Madison*, Marshall seems to have been motivated by one compelling purpose. His aim was to furnish the Court and the country with a rationale for subjecting the whole domain of governmental activity to overall control by the judiciary. The resulting "intellectual construction" is a reflection of that purpose.

Of special interest is Marshall's use of what might be called a process of attribution. Without referring to the actual proceedings of the Constitutional Convention of 1787 and without offering any other documentation, he ascribes to the framers of the Constitution a philosophy of government which makes out of judicial review the indispensable instrument for preserving the Constitution. The most significant of these attributions is, obviously, the alleged intention of confining the legislative power within limits enforceable by the Supreme Court as binding law. From a practical point of view, this postulate necessarily implies the "supremacy" of the Constitution above all other forms of law.[18]

---

[17] Lerner, "Minority Rule and the Constitutional Tradition," reprinted in *The Constitution Reconsidered,* Conyers Read, ed. (New York: Columbia University Press, 1938), p. 191.

[18] "A concept . . . which is absolutely basic to the American doctrine of judicial review," Charles L. Black, Jr. has recently written, is *"the concept that the Constitution is a kind of law."* Professor Black criticizes Marshall for "understressing" the concept: "He [Marshall] emphasized the obvious fact that the Constitution is superior to ordinary law—but that fact

Building on this generalized view of the grand constitutional design of the Founding Fathers, Marshall invoked the specific language of the Constitution itself in support of his basic conclusion. As he says, at the very end of his opinion, "Thus, the particular phraseology of the Constitution of the United States confirms and strengthens the principle, supposed to be essential to all written Constitutions, that a law repugnant to the Constitution is void; and that *courts,* as well as other departments, are bound by that instrument." [19] He found three provisions particularly pertinent: the clause empowering federal courts to decide cases arising under the Constitution,[20] the clause prescribing the oath to be taken by judges, and the "supremacy" clause.

Yet no less eminent and scholarly a jurist than the late Learned Hand was impelled to refute the suggestion that the language of the Constitution warranted the Court in assuming the power of judicial review. "When the Constitution emerged from the Convention in September 1787," he has said, "the structure of the proposed government, if one looked to the text, gave no ground for inferring that the decisions of the Supreme Court, and *a fortiori* of the lower courts, were to be authoritative upon the Executive and the Legislature." Judge Hand nevertheless concluded that "it was probable, if indeed it was not certain, that without some arbiter whose decisions should be final the whole system would have collapsed." [21]

Hand seems to have derived his theory of the ultimate justi-

alone implies little as to the location of the final responsibility for construing it. And he curiously understressed the really pivotal point in the argument for locating this responsibility in the courts—the point that *our* Constitution . . . is, on the overwhelming probabilities arising from its own language and structure and from the evidence of the intent of those who made it, to be taken as *law.*" Black, *The People and the Court* (New York: The Macmillan Company, 1960), pp. 6, 26–27.

[19] 1 Cranch 137, 179.

[20] "The judicial power shall extend to all cases, in Law and Equity, arising under this Constitution, the Laws of the United States, and Treaties made, or which shall be made, under their Authority." *Constitution,* Art. III, sec. 2.

[21] Hand, *The Bill of Rights,* pp. 27, 29. For a fine recent discussion of the recurring question as to the intention of the framers on judicial review, see Alan F. Westin's Introduction to Charles A. Beard's *The Supreme Court and the Constitution* (Englewood Cliffs: Prentice-Hall, 1962).

fication for the power of judicial review from the traditional
behavior of courts and judges in dealing with the meaning of
documents. His somewhat grudging acknowledgment of the "legitimacy" of the Supreme Court's authority presents an interesting hypothesis: "For centuries it has been an accepted canon
in interpretation of documents to interpolate into the text such
provisions, though not expressed, as are essential to prevent the
defeat of the venture at hand." For this reason, it was "altogether
in keeping with established practice for the Supreme Court to
assume an authority to keep the states, Congress, and the President within their prescribed powers." Judge Hand finally concedes that "it was not a lawless act to import into the Constitution such a grant of power." [22]

Some students of the Supreme Court have been intrigued by
the adroitness with which Marshall outmaneuvered Jefferson in
the power struggle implicit in *Marbury v. Madison*. A particularly outstanding example of this approach is the statement by
Edward S. Corwin:

> Marshall's opinion in *Marbury v. Madison* was a political *coup*
> of the first magnitude, and by it he achieved half a dozen objects,
> some of the greatest importance. In the first place, while avoiding
> a direct collision with the executive power, he stigmatized his
> enemy Jefferson as a violator of the laws which as President he
> was sworn to support. . . . Yet again Marshall scored in exhibit-
> ing the Court in the edifying and reassuring light of declining,
> even from the hands of Congress, jurisdiction to which it was not
> entitled by the Constitution, an attitude of self-restraint which em-
> phasized tremendously the Court's claim to the function of judicial
> review, now first definitely registered in deliberate judicial de-
> cision.[23]

Still another reason for caution in assessing the significance of the
case is that it was not until the decision in *Dred Scott v. Sand-*

---

[22] Hand, *The Bill of Rights*, pp. 14, 15, 29. For a most persuasive defense
of his belief, as he phrased it, that "the power of the courts is grounded in the
language of the Constitution and is not a mere interpolation," see Herbert
Wechsler, "Toward Neutral Principles of Constitutional Law," 73 *Harvard
Law Review* 1 (Nov. 1959); reprinted in Wechsler, *Principles, Politics and
Fundamental Law*, pp. 3–11.

[23] Corwin, *John Marshall and the Constitution*, p. 65.

ford,[24] more than half a century later, that the Court ventured
again to strike down an Act of Congress. Indeed, Marshall's
biographer has made the interesting suggestion that the eventual
acceptance of the doctrine of judicial review was quite fortuitous.
"As it turned out, but for *Marbury v. Madison*," writes Beveridge,
"the power of the Supreme Court to annul acts of Congress probably would not have been insisted upon thereafter." His reason
for thinking so is that time would have worked against the success of the principle:

> For, during the thirty-two years that Marshall remained on the
> Supreme Bench after the decision of that case [*Marbury v. Madi-
> son*], and for twenty years after his death, no case came before the
> court where an act of Congress was overthrown; and none had
> been invalidated from the adoption of the Constitution to the
> day when Marshall delivered his epochal opinion. So that, as a
> matter of historical significance, had he not then taken this stand,
> nearly seventy years would have passed without any question aris-
> ing as to the omnipotence of Congress. After so long a period of
> judicial acquiescence in Congressional supremacy it seems likely
> that opposition to it would have been futile.[25]

III

It is no doubt true that not even Marshall himself appreciated,
at the time of *Marbury v. Madison*, the potential impact of the
principle he was enunciating. The ebb and flow of the history
of that doctrine certainly demonstrates that in actual practice,
the function of judicial review has depended for its vitality upon
the role the Supreme Court has chosen to play in the governmental process. Yet the striking fact remains that it is to Marshall
that the Court has turned for authoritative exposition whenever
the scope of its power has been brought into question. This has
been as true of occasions concerned with the Court's oversight of
the other departments of the Federal Government as of conflicts
over its function in maintaining the federal balance.

Thus, in the recent so-called *Little Rock* case,[26] the Court

----

[24] 19 Howard 393 (1857).

[25] Beveridge, *The Life of John Marshall*, III, 131–132.

[26] *Cooper v. Aaron*, 358 U.S. 1 (1958). The Court took the unusual and
dramatic step of mentioning by name all of the members of the Court as

cited two of Marshall's delineations of judicial power. After recalling his assertion in *Marbury v. Madison* that "it is emphatically the province and duty of the judicial department to say what the law is," the opinion goes on to state: "This decision declared the basic principle that the Federal judiciary is supreme in the exposition of the law of the Constitution, and that principle has ever since been respected by this Court and the Country as a permanent and indispensable feature of our constitutional system." [27] And by way of defending its insistence upon the duty resting on all state officials to obey federal court orders, the Supreme Court quoted the following language from another of Marshall's opinions: "If the legislatures of the several states may, at will, annul the judgments of the courts of the United States, and destroy the rights acquired under those judgments, the Constitution itself becomes a solemn mockery." [28]

The second of the Court's allusions to Marshall is to the rather complicated 1809 case of *United States v. Peters,*[29] a case in which the Supreme Court of that day was confronted by the refusal on the part of a federal district judge to enforce his own decree. Judge Peters had taken this strange stand because, as he explained, he "was unwilling to embroil the United States with Pennsylvania." After Judge Peters had rendered his original decision, the legislature of Pennsylvania passed a law undertaking to immunize the parties who had lost in Judge Peters' court from

joining in the opinion. The statement in the *United States Reports* reads as follows: "Opinion of the Court by The Chief Justice, Mr. Justice Black, Mr. Justice Frankfurter, Mr. Justice Douglas, Mr. Justice Burton, Mr. Justice Clark, Mr. Justice Harlan, Mr. Justice Brennan, and Mr. Justice Whittaker." At p. 4.

[27] *Ibid.*, p. 18.

[28] *Ibid.*

[29] *United States v. Peters,* 5 Cranch 115 (1809). The paragraph in the Peters decision from which the Court quoted in the *Little Rock* case is as follows: "If the legislatures of the several States may, at will, annul the judgments of the courts of the United States, and destroy the rights acquired under those judgments, the Constitution itself becomes a solemn mockery; and the nation is deprived of the means of enforcing its laws by the instrumentality of its tribunals. So fatal a result must be deprecated by all; and the people of Pennsylvania, not less than the citizens of every other state, must feel a deep interest in resisting principles so destructive of the union, and in averting consequences so fatal to themselves." *Ibid.*, p. 136.

any judgment against them which might emanate from a federal court. When the issues were joined, Pennsylvania, which claimed that the property the defendants were being asked to surrender really belonged to the state, relied on the Eleventh Amendment of the Constitution,[30] arguing that since the suit was in essence against the state itself, the federal judiciary had no jurisdiction over the litigation.

Strictly speaking, it may be said that Marshall disposed of the controversy by holding that the action in the District Court had been brought against private individuals. The mere fact that Pennsylvania had an interest in the outcome did not convert the dispute into a suit against the state.[31] However, Marshall used the occasion to proclaim a constitutional principle of far-reaching importance for the integrity of the power of federal courts. That principle is that the states have no authority to determine for themselves the extent of the jurisdiction of federal courts. They may not, that is to say, defy judgments of the courts of the United States under the guise of questioning their right to decide a particular case.

Something we read almost at the start of his opinion in the *Peters* case indicates that to Marshall Pennsylvania's attitude smacked of "interposition" or nullification. As he writes, "The act in question does not, in terms, assert the universal right of the state to interpose in every case whatever; but assigns, as a motive for its interposition in this particular case, that the sentence, the execution of which it prohibits, was rendered in a

[30] Amendment XI reads as follows: "The judicial power of the United States shall not be construed to extend to any suit in law or equity, commenced or prosecuted against one of the United States by Citizens of another State, or by Citizens or Subjects of any Foreign State." Adopted in 1798, this Amendment overruled, in effect, a Supreme Court decision which permitted Georgia to be sued by a citizen of another state. *Chisholm v. Georgia*, 2 Dallas 419 (1793).

[31] "Since, then, the State of Pennsylvania had neither possession of, nor right to, the property on which the sentence of the District Court was pronounced, and since the suit was neither commenced nor prosecuted against that state, there remains no pretext for the allegation that the case is within that amendment of the constitution which had been cited; and, consequently, the State of Pennsylvania can possess no constitutional right to resist the legal process which may be directed in this cause." 5 Cranch 115, 141.

cause over which the Federal courts have no jurisdiction." [32] Whatever the pretext, Marshall was implying, Pennsylvania was in effect setting itself up as the judge of whether the judicial power of the United States was being used properly or constitutionally. This a state cannot do. The Chief Justice was firm in announcing the Court's conclusion that the "ultimate right to determine the jurisdiction of the courts of the union" is conferred by the Constitution, not upon the states, but upon what he calls "the supreme judicial tribunal of the nation." [33] Again, as in *Marbury v. Madison*, what began as an inquiry into the *power* of courts ended with a call to *duty*, as Marshall's closing words show: "It will be readily conceived that the order which this court is enjoined to make by the high obligations of duty and of law, is not made without extreme regret at the necessity which has induced the application. But it is a solemn duty, and therefore must be performed." [34]

Perhaps an even more significant Marshall utterance, which the 1958 Court might well have cited, is his opinion in *Cohens v. Virginia*.[35] It is in that case, decided in 1821, where one will find Marshall's most elaborate and convincing discussion of judicial power as it relates to what the Supreme Court called in the *Little Rock* case "the maintenance of our federal system of government." [36] It stands as an integral part of the philosophy of *Marbury v. Madison*.

The crucial problem in *Cohens v. Virginia* was whether judgments of state courts were subject to review by the Supreme Court of the United States. Though Marshall's opinion reaffirmed a principle embodied in a decision written by Justice Joseph Story some five years earlier,[37] it precipitated widespread and bitter criticism which persisted for years. In *Martin v. Hunter's Lessee*,

---

[32] *Ibid.*, p. 136.
[33] *Ibid.*
[34] *Ibid.*, p. 141.
[35] 6 Wheat. 264 (1821).
[36] 358 U.S. 1, 4.
[37] *Martin v. Hunter's Lessee*, 1 Wheat. 304 (1816). In 1810, the Virginia Court of Appeals had upheld the legality of a grant of land made by the state in 1789 and rejected a claim to the land under Lord Fairfax and the peace treaty with England.

Story's opinion held that the Supreme Court had the power to review decisions of state courts which deny rights claimed under the Constitution, laws, and treaties of the United States. This ruling was in keeping with Section 25 of the Judiciary Act of 1789.[38]

Story and his colleagues had been asked to enforce a decision which they had rendered three years earlier, a decision which the Court of Appeals of Virginia refused to obey. Virginia's highest tribunal had taken the position that neither the Constitution nor Section 25 of the Judiciary Act of 1789 gave the Supreme Court jurisdiction over the litigation and that it would therefore decline "obedience" to the Court's mandate. Justice Story relied on two principal arguments in meeting this attack on the right of the Supreme Court to review state court decisions. He pointed out, in the first place, that the appellate jurisdiction vested in the Supreme Court by the third article of the Constitution is not limited to any particular courts. "It is the *case,* then, not *the Court,* that gives the jurisdiction." [39] And if a particular case in the state courts makes it necessary to apply the Constitution, laws, or treaties of the United States, the "supremacy" clause binds the state judges to decide the questions in accordance with "the supreme Law of the Land; . . . anything in the Constitution or laws of any State to the contrary notwithstanding." Story stressed that "the framers of the constitution did contemplate that cases within the judicial cognizance of the United

[38] Section 25 of the Judiciary Act of 1789 reads as follows: "And be it further enacted, that a final judgment or decree in any suit, in the highest court of law or equity of a State in which a decision in the suit could be had, where is drawn in question the validity of a treaty or statute of, or an authority exercised under the United States, and the decision is against their validity; or where is drawn in question the validity of a statute of, or an authority exercised under any State, on the ground of their being repugnant to the Constitution, treaties or the laws of the United States, and the decision is in favor of their validity, or where is drawn in question the construction of any clause of the Constitution, of a treaty, or a statute of, or commission held under the United States, and the decision is against the title, privilege or exemption specially set up or claimed by either party, under such clause of the said Constitution, treaty, statute or commission, may be reexamined and reversed or affirmed in the Supreme Court of the Unifed States upon a writ of error."
[39] 1 Wheat. 304, 338.

States not only might but would arise in the State Courts, in the exercise of their ordinary jurisdiction." [40]

IV

It was to be expected that Marshall's vigorous restatement in *Cohens v. Virginia* of the Court's views in *Martin v. Hunter' Lessee* would reawaken old resentments. Voices of protest were raised particularly high in Virginia and Ohio, among them that of Thomas Jefferson. Writing to John Taylor while the case was still being argued, Jefferson condemned the "sophistries" of the lawyers who had appeared in the case and said that "this last act of venality (for it cannot be of judgment) makes me ashamed that I was ever a lawyer." [41] Jefferson's friend on the Virginia Court of Appeals, Judge Spencer Roane, using the pseudonym of Algernon Sidney in the *Richmond Enquirer*, subjected the Court's decision to a series of attacks lasting two weeks.[42] When Marshall wrote to Justice Story a week later, he offered to send him the *Enquirer* and remarked that Algernon Sidney "will be supposed to be the champion of states rights, instead of what he really is, the champion of dismemberment." [43]

From beginning to end, Marshall's opinion in *Cohens v. Vir-*

---

[40] *Ibid.*, p. 339.

[41] Thomas Jefferson to John Taylor, February 14, 1821. *The Writings of Thomas Jefferson*, A. E. Bergh, ed. (Washington, D.C.: The Thomas Jefferson Memorial Association, 1905), XVII, 312.

[42] The articles appeared in the *Richmond Enquirer* between May 25 and June 8, 1821.

[43] John Marshall to Joseph Story, June 15, 1821. Proceedings of the Mass. Historical Society (Second Series, 1901), XIV, 328. Marshall's letter to Story reveals how deeply disturbed he was by the attacks on the decision in *Cohens v. Virginia*. He wrote: "The opinion of the Supreme Court in the Lottery case has been assaulted with a degree of virulence transcending what has appeared on any former occasion. Algernon Sidney is written by the gentleman who is so much distinguished for his feelings towards the Supreme Court, and if you have not had the opportunity of seeing the Enquirer I will send it to you. There are other minor gentry who seek to curry favor and get into office by adding their mite of abuse, but I think for coarseness and malignity of invention, Algernon Sidney surpasses all party writers who have ever made pretensions to any decency of character. There is on this subject no such thing as a free press in Virginia, and of consequence the calumnies and misrepresentations of this gentleman will remain uncontradicted and will by many be believed to be true." *Ibid.*, pp. 327–328.

ginia, as was true of Story's opinion in *Martin v. Hunter's Lessee,* shows that the two Justices equated the challenge to the Court's authority with a mortal threat to the whole system of government established by the Constitution. When Story replied to Marshall's letter of June 15, 1821, he assured the Chief Justice that Massachusetts had not as yet been "inoculated" with the "disease" raging in Virginia and reported to him that the "best lawyers" in his state "consider your opinion in Cohens v. Virginia as a most masterly and convincing argument, and as the greatest of your judgments." He added, "If you were known here only by this last opinion, you could not wish for more unequivocal fame." [44]

How can one account for Story's lavish praise of the Chief Justice's performance in *Cohens v. Virginia?* Was it induced by the ardor of intimate friendship, or was there a deeper cause at work? The basic reason, it may be assumed, was Story's wholehearted acceptance of Marshall's conception of the Constitution and of the Court's function in applying it. "The truth is," he told Marshall in the same letter, "that the whole doctrine of Virginia on the subject of the Constitution appears to me so fundamentally erroneous, not to say absurd, that I have a good deal of difficulty in reading with patience the elaborate attempts of her political leaders to mislead and deceive us." [45]

Some years after both Story and Marshall were dead, Story's son was frank to acknowledge that the result of his father's long association with the Chief Justice was "a cordial adherence to the views of Marshall, whom he considered then and ever afterwards as the expounder of the true principles of the Constitu-

[44] Joseph Story to John Marshall, June 27, 1821. Charles Warren, "The Story-Marshall Correspondence," *William and Mary College Quarterly,* Second Series, Vol. 21, p. 7 (January 1941).

[45] *Ibid.* In comparing the "doctrine of Virginia on the subject of the Constitution" with the outlook in Massachusetts, Story disclosed the spacious view of the Constitution which he shared with Marshall: "Massachusetts is attached to the Union and has no jealousy of its powers; and no political object to answer in crying up 'State Rights'—We should dread to see the government reduced as Virginia wished it, to a confederacy; and we are disposed to construe the Constitution of the United States as a frame of government and not as a petty charter granted to a paltry corporation for the purpose of regulating a fishery or collecting a toll." *Ibid.*

tion." This was said by William W. Story after he had recalled that his father, who had been named to the Supreme Court by James Madison, was a member of the party headed by Jefferson and that "the views of the party to which he belonged were widely different from those of the illustrious Chief Justice Marshall." Another comment by the younger Story suggests the extent to which constitutional interpretation affected party warfare: "As the doctrines in Martin v. Hunter's Lessee were at all points opposite to those of Mr. Jefferson and the Republicans, my father was exposed to the accusation of being a renegade of party. This neither troubled nor influenced him." [46]

Justice Story had launched his rejoinder to Virginia—in *Martin v. Hunter's Lessee*—somewhat dramatically, with the observation that on the "right decision" of the questions raised by its defiance of the Court's jurisdiction "rest some of the most solid principles which have hitherto been supposed to sustain and protect the constitution itself." [47] Chief Justice Marshall began his analysis of the issues in *Cohens v. Virginia* by saying that they were "of great magnitude, and may be truly said vitally to affect the Union." [48]

The case was in the nature of an appeal to the Supreme Court from a court in Norfolk, in which P. J. and M. J. Cohens had been convicted for violating a state law prohibiting the sale of lottery tickets. Virginia's Court of Appeals had refused to hear their case on the ground that only the Norfolk court had jurisdiction over the particular subject. The Cohens were claiming that the activity in which they engaged was perfectly lawful under the act of Congress permitting a lottery in the District of Columbia. It was this defense which served as the basis for their effort to get the Supreme Court to reverse their conviction.

Once again Virginia questioned both the right and propriety of having the Supreme Court entertain attacks upon the decisions of state courts. Her lawyers made a fundamental assault on the Court's jurisdiction. But the very way in which Marshall sum-

[46] William W. Story, *Life and Letters of Joseph Story* (Boston: Little, Brown & Co., 1851), I, 276.

[47] I *Wheat.* 304, 323.

[48] 6 *Wheat.* 264, 377.

marized their arguments made it clear that to him much more
was at stake than the respective powers of the national and state
judiciaries; the fate of the "more perfect Union" itself seemed to
hang in the balance. Marshall wrote:

> They maintain that the nation does not possess a department
> capable of restraining peaceably, and by authority of law, any
> attempt which may be made, by a part, against the legitimate
> powers of the whole; and that the government is reduced to the
> alternative of submitting to such attempts, or of resisting them by
> force. They maintain that the constitution of the United States
> has provided no tribunal for the final construction of itself, or of
> the laws or treaties of the nation; but that this power may be
> exercised in the last resort by the Courts of every State in the
> Union. That the constitution, laws, and treaties, may receive as
> many constructions as there are States; and that this is not a
> mischief, or, if a mischief, is irremediable.[49]

And turning to the Court's responsibilities in the light of these
"abstract propositions," he immediately added: "If such be the
constitution, it is the duty of the Court to bow with respectful
submission to its provisions. If such be not the constitution, it is
equally the duty of this Court to say so; and to perform that task
which the American people have assigned to the judicial department."[50]

As Story had done in *Martin v. Hunter's Lessee*, Marshall first
examined the scope of the Court's appellate power as outlined
in the second section of Article III of the Constitution. Basically,
whether or not a case falls within the Supreme Court's province
depends on the subject matter of the controversy or who the
parties are. "The judicial power shall extend to all cases, in Law
and Equity, arising under this Constitution, the Laws of the
United States, and Treaties made, or which shall be made, under
their Authority." After making this general grant of power to
the judicial branch of the national government, the third article
of the Constitution goes on to confer jurisdiction on federal
courts in two classes of cases. In the first category, whether or
not a case comes within their jurisdiction depends on the subject

[49] *Ibid.*
[50] *Ibid.*

matter of the litigation, regardless of who the litigants or the parties happen to be. Thus, if the outcome in a case hinges on the interpretation of a provision of the Constitution, laws of the United States, or a treaty, it raises a "federal question" and therefore may potentially reach the Supreme Court. In the second class of cases, the jurisdiction of federal courts may be invoked because of the identity of the parties. Cases between two or more states, suits in which the United States itself is a party, and cases between citizens of different states—all illustrate the latter basis for access to the federal courts.

Marshall took fifty-five pages in which to say that his Court had jurisdiction to review the decision of the Virginia court. When he turned to the merits of the controversy, he held that the act of Congress enabling the District of Columbia to have a lottery law was not a proper defense, since it did not have any effect in Virginia. This finding is presented in an opinion of only seven pages.[51] Obviously, the really important aspect of the case is not what lawyers would call the precise "holding"—the conclusion that when the decisions of state courts turn on the interpretation of the Constitution, laws or treaties of the United States, the Supreme Court may review those decisions. It is the reasons advanced by Marshall for saying that the Court must have this power which make his opinion significant as well as interesting.

Counsel for Virginia could not deny, of course, that the Constitution, in express terms, authorizes the federal courts to decide cases "arising" under it or under the laws or treaties of the United States. But what they did undertake to argue was that the constitutional position of the states in the American Union presupposes an imporant exception to the judicial power; more specifically, that a "sovereign" and "independent" state could not be sued unless it gave its consent.

v

Marshall drew a quite opposite inference from the authority the Constitution assigns to the states. Without rejecting the

[51] Marshall wrote two opinions in *Cohens v. Virginia*. The opinion concerned with the Court's jurisdiction, delivered March 3, 1821, begins on page 375 and ends on 430. His opinion on the merits, read two days later, will be found on pp. 440–447.

proposition that a state was not to be sued except with its permission, he began his refutation of Virginia's argument by observing that a state's consent was not "requisite" in every instance.
It is not too much to say that the bulk of Marshall's opinion in
Cohens v. Virginia is an attempt to demonstrate that the surrender
of sovereignty implicit in the existence of the states as members
of the federal union carries with it a corresponding loss of immunity from suit. By adhering to a Union governed by a Constitution which is the "supreme law of the land," the states have lost
the right to be the final judges of their powers. As Marshall put it,
"if upon a just construction of that instrument [the Constitution],
it shall appear that the State has submitted to be sued, then it has
parted with this sovereign right of judging in every case on the
justice of its own pretensions, and has entrusted that power to a
tribunal in whose impartiality it confides." [52]

The sentence just quoted contains the key to the whole tenor
of Marshall's elaborate refutation of Virginia's attitude toward
federal judicial power. Abstract though it may appear to be, it
prepares us for the logic with which the Chief Justice was about
to forge the vital link between the dual character of the American
system of government and the need for a national Supreme Court
with power to preserve the Constitution as the law for all. First
comes the reminder that the federal Union is "essential" to the
future freedom and happiness of the American people:

> The American States, as well as the American people, have
> believed a close and firm Union to be essential to their liberty
> and to their happiness. They have been taught by experience,
> that this Union cannot exist without a government for the whole;
> and they have been taught by the same experience that this gov-
> ernment would be a mere shadow, that must disappoint all their

---

[52] 6 Wheat. 264, 380. The rather stilted language with which Marshall first
suggests that such would be his line of reasoning is a good example of his
habit of using abstract propositions to build a practical result. He wrote: "The
jurisdiction of the Court, then, being extended by the letter of the constitution to all cases arising under it, or under the laws of the United States, it
follows that those who would withdraw any case of this description from that
jurisdiction must sustain the exemption they claim on the spirit and true
meaning of the constitution, which spirit and true meaning must be so apparent as to overrule the words which its framers have employed." *Ibid.*, pp.
379–380.

hopes, unless invested with large portions of that sovereignty which belongs to independent States. Under the influence of this opinion, and thus instructed by experience, the American people, in the conventions of their respective States, adopted the present constitution.[53]

There then follow several comments designed to show that the "supremacy" clause removes all doubts as regards the superior status of the federal government and that the Supreme Court has the responsibility for "maintaining" the distribution of power between nation and states in the American commonwealth:

This [the "supremacy" clause] is the authoritative language of the American people; and, if gentlemen please, of the American States. It marks, with lines too strong to be mistaken, the characteristic distinction between the government of the Union, and those of the States. The general government, though limited as to its objects, is supreme with respect to those objects. This principle is a part of the constitution; and if there be any who deny its necessity, none can deny its authority.

To this supreme government ample powers are confided; and if it were possible to doubt the great purposes for which they were so confided, the people of the United States have declared, that they are given "in order to form a more perfect union, establish justice, ensure domestic tranquility, provide for the common defence, promote the general welfare, and secure the blessings of liberty to themselves and their posterity."

With the ample powers confided to this supreme government, for these interesting purposes, are connected many express and important limitations on the sovereignty of the States, which are made for the same purposes. The powers of the Union, on the great subjects of war, peace, and commerce, and on many others, are in themselves limitations of the sovereignty of the States; but in addition to these, the sovereignty of the States is surrendered in many instances where the surrender can only operate to the benefit of the people, and where, perhaps, no other power is conferred on Congress than a conservative power to maintain the principles established in the constitution. The maintenance of these principles in their purity, is certainly among the great duties of the government. One of the instruments by which this duty may

[53] *Ibid.*, pp. 380–381.

be peaceably performed, is the judicial department. It is authorized
to decide all cases of every description, arising under the Constitution or laws of the United States.[54]

For the Court to accept Virginia's objection to its jurisdiction,
Marshall insists, it would be necessary to hold that the federal
courts may not exercise their power to decide cases arising under
the Constitution and laws of the United States when a state
happens to be a party in the case. He says repeatedly that there
is no basis—either in logic or in history—for any such exception
to the federal judicial power. On the contrary, he interprets the
second section of Article III as clearly precluding the exception
contended for by Virginia. He calls attention to the fact that in
the enumeration of the cases in which the federal courts are
given jurisdiction because of the character of the parties, "we
find controversies between two or more States, between a state
and citizens of another state, between a state and foreign states,
citizens or subjects."

Marshall's forthright answer to Virginia will be found in one
simple sentence: "One of the express objects, then, for which the
judicial department was established, is the decision of controversies between States and between a State and individuals." [55]
Pressing his attack, he argues that the exception which Virginia
was seeking would reduce the judicial article of the Constitution
to a logical contradiction. If the view for which Virginia was
pleading were to prevail, it would mean that the Constitution
vested in the Supreme Court original jurisdiction over cases in
which a state would be a party but denied it appellate jurisdiction over controversies wherein a state was involved. The much
more serious consequence would be that the "American people"
would be denied impartial adjudication of their claims should
their rights be threatened by state action:

> The mere circumstance, that a State is a party, gives jurisdic-
> tion to the Court. How, then, can it be contended, that the very
> same instrument, in the very same section, should be so construed,
> as that this same circumstance should withdraw a case from the

[54] *Ibid.,* pp. 381–382.
[55] *Ibid.,* p. 383.

jurisdiction of the Court, where the constitution or laws of the United States are supposed to have been violated? The constitution gave to every person having a claim upon a State, a right to submit his case to the Court of the nation. However unimportant his claim might be, however little the community might be interested in its decision, the framers of our constitution thought it necessary for the purposes of justice, to provide a tribunal as superior to influence as possible, in which that claim might be decided. Can it be imagined, that the same person considered a case involving the constitution of our country and the majesty of the laws, questions in which every American citizen must be deeply interested, as withdrawn from this tribunal, because a State is a party? [56]

But it was not the illogicality of Virginia's reading of the judicial article of the Constitution which interested Marshall the most. It was the practical effects of that construction to which he addressed himself with particular force. The gravest of the "mischievous consequences" of Virginia's theory was that "it would prostrate the government and its laws at the feet of every State in the union." To deny to the Supreme Court the ultimate authority to control the judgments of state courts would have the effect of depriving the federal government of an essential instrument for enforcing its will in the States. The result would be, Marshall warns, that each state would then "possess a *veto* on the will of the whole." [57]

Conceding that the federal courts alone would be incapable of stemming the tide were the states bent on destroying the Union, Marshall maintained that the critical danger was that the display of the national government's inability to "protect itself" would serve to enhance the incidence of defiance of federal authority. History demonstrated that laws having the support of

[56] *Ibid.*, pp. 383–384.

[57] *Ibid.*, p. 385. "What power of the government could be executed by its own means, in any State disposed to resist its execution by a course of legislation? The laws must be executed by individuals acting within the several States. If these individuals may be exposed to penalties, and if the Courts of the Union cannot correct the judgments by which these penalties may be enforced, the course of the government may be, at any time, arrested by the will of one of its members. Each member will possess a *veto* on the will of the whole." *Ibid.*

the "great majority of the American people" have at times been treated as "unconstitutional" by one or more states.[58] "We have no assurance that we shall be less divided than we have been," Marshall observes prophetically. Neither was there good ground for believing that the state courts would be less influenced by local "prejudices" than were state legislatures. It is quite apparent that Marshall had little faith in the impartiality of state judges.[59] Writing at a time when the nation and the states were still looked upon as mutually hostile and competitive centers of political power, the Chief Justice was determined to consolidate the position of the Supreme Court as an instrument for resolving these inevitable conflicts. His eloquent words on this point are still timely:

> These collisions may take place in times of no extraordinary commotion. But a constitution is framed for ages to come, and is designed to approach immortality as nearly as human institutions can approach it. Its course cannot always be tranquil. It is exposed to storms and tempests, and its framers must be unwise statesmen indeed, if they have not provided it, as far as its nature will permit, with the means of self-preservation from the perils it may be destined to encounter. No government ought to be so defective in its organizaton, as not to contain within itself the means of securing the execution of its own laws against other dangers than those which occur every day. Courts of justice are the means most usually employed; and it is reasonable to expect that a government should repose on its own Courts, rather than on others. There is certainly nothing in the circumstances under which our constitution was formed; nothing in the history of the times, which would justify the opinion that the confidence reposed in the States

[58] The two specific examples cited by Marshall are the resistance to the assumption of the debts contracted during the American Revolution and the opposition to certain federal taxes. Perhaps he was thinking of the Whiskey Rebellion.

[59] "In many States the judges are dependent for office and for salary on the will of the legislature. . . . When we observe the importance which that constitution attaches to the independence of judges, we are the less inclined to suppose that it can have intended to leave these constitutional questions to tribunals where this independence may not exist, in all cases where a State shall prosecute an individual who claims the protection of an act of Congress." 6 Wheat. 264, 386–387.

was so implicit as to leave in them and their tribunals the power of
resisting or defeating, in the form of law, the legitimate measures
of the Union.[60]

Donning the mantle of historian and teacher, Marshall
sought to show that counsel for Virginia simply did not understand the fundamental purposes of the framers of the Constitution in creating a separate and independent national judiciary. Two considerations in particular had to be kept in mind.
If the Supreme Court were to refuse to entertain complaints
alleging state violations of federal rights, that part of Article
III which gives the Court jurisdiction over cases "arising"
under the Constitution and laws of the United States "would
be mere surplusage." But the more serious flaw in the grounds
urged by Virginia's attorneys was their failure to recognize that
the really "important" and "interesting" object—perhaps the
"greatest object"—the framers had in view when they provided
for a federal judiciary was "the preservation of the Constitution
and laws of the United States, so far as they can be preserved by
judicial authority." [61] By a neat bit of judicial sleight of hand, the
Chief Justice takes Virginia's objection to having the Court hear
the Cohens and turns it into an argument for the power to do
so. He wrote:

> If a suit, brought in one Court, and carried by legal process
> to a supervising Court, be a continuation of the same suit, then
> this suit is not commenced nor prosecuted against a State. It is
> clearly in its commencement the suit of a State against an indi-
> vidual, which suit is transferred to this Court, not for the purpose
> of asserting any claim against the State, but for the purpose of

---

[60] *Ibid.*, pp. 387–388. Marshall referred to the experience under the Articles
of Confederation—when some of the states refused to honor the requisitions
on them made by Congress—as showing that the framers of the Constitution
were concerned with the problem of securing compliance with national
measures. "With the knowledge of this fact, and under its full pressure," he
explained, "a convention was assembled to change the system." It was to be
expected that the framers would confer on the federal judiciary "the power
of construing the constitution and laws of the Union in every case, in the
last resort, and of preserving them from all violation from every quarter, so
far as judicial decisions can preserve them." *Ibid.*, p. 388.
[61] *Ibid.*, p. 391.

asserting a constitutional defence against a claim made by a
State.[62]

Implicit in this extended rejoinder to Virginia was, of course,
the assumption that state tribunals are part of a single judicial
system headed by the Supreme Court of the United States.
Though both national and state courts enjoyed concurrent jurisdiction in cases concerned with rights claimed under the federal
Constitution, "the necessity of uniformity, as well as correctness
in expounding the constitution and laws of the United States,
would itself suggest the propriety of vesting in some single
tribunal the power of deciding, in the last resort, all cases in
which they are involved." [63] This subordination of the state
judiciaries to ultimate "supervision" by the Supreme Court was
altogether compatible with the character of the states as "constituent parts" of the union; for the states "are members of one great
empire—for some purposes sovereign, for some purposes subordinate." [64] The rationale behind this restraining power of the
Court, Marshall stated emphatically, is the controlling principle
that "the constitution and laws of a state, so far as they are

[62] *Ibid.*, p. 409. In rejecting Virginia's objection that the appeal of the
Cohens to the Supreme Court was barred by the Eleventh Amendment,
Marshall pointed out that the amendment was adopted in order to allay the
fear that the federal courts would entertain suits seeking to collect from the
states the debts they owed at the time the Constitution was written. The
"motive" of the amendment "was not to maintain the sovereignty of a State
from the degradation supposed to attend a compulsory appearance before
the tribunal of the nation" but to protect the state governments against
creditors. Marshall insisted that the case of the Cohens was not "governed"
by the Eleventh Amendment, but by "the constitution as originally framed,"
going on to explain: "In its origin, the judicial power was extended to all
cases arising under the constitution or laws of the United States, without
respect to parties." *Ibid.*, p. 412.

[63] *Ibid.*, p. 416. Marshall was here echoing a view expressed even more
emphatically by Hamilton. "If there are such things as political axioms, the
propriety of the judicial power of a government being coextensive with its
legislative, may be ranked among the number. The mere necessity of uniformity in the interpretation of the national laws, decides the question. Thirteen independent courts of final jurisdiction over the same causes, arising
upon the same laws, is a hydra in government from which nothing but
contradiction and confusion can proceed." *The Federalist*, No. 80, p. 500
(Wright, ed.).

[64] 6 *Wheat.* 264, 414.

repugnant to the constitution and laws of the United States, are absolutely void." [65] He invoked the great "authority" of *The Federalist* papers—which he characterized as "a complete commentary on our constitution"—in support of the commanding position he was claiming for the Supreme Court. Said Marshall:

> The opinion of the Federalist has always been considered as of great authority. It is a complete commentary on our constitution, and is appealed to by all parties in the questions to which that instrument has given birth. Its intrinsic merit entitles it to this high rank, and the part two of its authors performed in framing the constitution put it very much in their power to explain the views with which it was framed. These essays having been published while the constitution was before the nation for adoption or rejection, and having been written in answer to objections founded entirely on the extent of its powers, and on its diminution of state sovereignty, are entitled to the more consideration where they frankly avow that the power objected to is given, and defend it." [66]

[65] *Ibid.*

[66] *Ibid.*, p. 418. Marshall quoted Hamilton's question and answer respecting the concurrent jurisdiction of federal and state courts:

"What relation would subsist between the national and State courts in these instances of concurrent jurisdiction? I answer, that an appeal would certainly lie from the latter, to the Supreme Court of the United States. The Constitution in direct terms gives an appellate jurisdiction to the Supreme Court in all the enumerated cases of federal cognizance in which it is not to have an original one, without a single expression to confine its operation to the inferior federal courts. The objects of appeal, not the tribunals from which it is to be made, are alone contemplated. From this circumstance, and from the reason of the thing, it ought to be construed to extend to the State tribunals. Either this must be the case, or the local courts must be excluded from a concurrent jurisdiction in matters of national concern, else the judiciary authority of the Union may be eluded at the pleasure of every plaintiff or prosecutor. Neither of these consequences ought, without evident necessity, to be involved; the latter would be entirely inadmissible, as it would defeat some of the most important and avowed purposes of the proposed government, and would essentially embarrass its measures. Nor do I perceive any foundation for such a supposition. Agreeably to the remark already made, the national and State systems are to be regarded as *one whole*. The courts of the latter will of course be natural auxiliaries to the execution of the laws of the Union, and an appeal from them will as naturally lie to the tribunal which is destined to unite and assimilate the principles of national justice and the rules of national decisions. The evident aim of the plan of the convention is, that all the causes of the specified classes shall, for

VI

Those who worked to mobilize public opinion against Marshall's conception of judicial power were deeply disturbed by its implications for the future of federal-state relations. As soon as the Supreme Court agreed to hear the appeal of the Cohens, Virginia's chief executive alerted the legislature to the dangers posed by the Court's action. The committee to which the matter was referred responded to the Governor's message by submitting a formal report and by proposing resolutions on the subject. It strongly condemned the theory that one government in the American Union has the right to "abrogate" the laws of the other government. The exercise of any such power by the national government, it admonished, "would directly affect the existence of the state governments, the balance of the Constitution, and the integrity of the Union." The Constitution was pictured as making the national and state legislatures "independent of each other" in their respective spheres, and it was insisted that "if the federal legislature cannot abrogate state laws, the federal judiciary cannot abrogate state judgments." As for the Supreme Court's claim to be the court of last resort, the committee advanced the view that "the word supreme as descriptive of the federal tribunal . . . implies that the supremacy bestowed upon the Supreme Court is over the inferior courts, to be ordained and established by Congress, and not over the state courts." [67]

And when the time came for Spencer Roane to deal with the opinion in *Cohens v. Virginia,* he penned an attack for the *Richmond Enquirer* which seemed to Jefferson "to pulverize every word which had been delivered by Judge Marshall." [68] Roane

weighty public reasons, receive their original or final determination in the courts of the Union. To confine, therefore, the general expressions giving appellate jurisdiction to the Supreme Court, to appeals from the subordinate federal courts, instead of allowing their extension to the State courts, would be to abridge the latitude of the terms, in subversion of the intent, contrary to every sound rule of interpretation." *The Federalist,* No. 82, pp. 516–517.

[67] Quoted by Charles Grove Haines in his *The Role of the Supreme Court in American Government and Politics* (New York: Russell and Russell, 1960), p. 429.

[68] Thomas Jefferson to Justice William Johnson, June 12, 1823. *The Works of Thomas Jefferson,* XII, 254. In the same letter, Jefferson described "all" of the decision in the *Cohens* case as "extrajudicial," except for the holding that Washington's lottery law was inoperative in the states. *Ibid.*

charged that the decision threatened the very existence of the states and therefore of the federal system itself. He warned that if either government were ever conceded the right to pass on the powers of the other, the "equilibrium established by the Constitution" would be destroyed.[69] Roane saw the Union as the creature of a "compact" or "treaty" between equals; the national government as but one party to the federal compact was not competent to be the final judge of the powers of the other party. "I boldly deny, therefore," Roane protested, "that the Judiciary of the general government has any greater interest in the system of the federal government than have those of the States, or any greater inducement to preserve it. Nor are they the exclusive judges of a matter." [70]

Marshall, on the other hand, continued to regard all criticisms of the Supreme Court as veiled threats to subvert the Union itself. As he wrote at the time of Roane's polemic against the ruling in the *Cohens* case, "A deep design to convert our government into a mere league of states has taken strong hold of a powerful and violent party in Virginia. The attack upon the judiciary is in fact an attack upon the Union." [71] Marshall was apparently convinced that Roane's journalistic crusade against the federal judiciary was inspired by Jefferson. "There is some reason to believe," he told Story, "that the essays written against the Supreme Court were, in a degree at least, stimulated by this gentleman, and that although the coarseness of the language belongs exclusively to the author, its acerbity has been increased by his communications with the great Lama of the mountains." [72]

Thus did a seemingly trivial case induce examination of fundamental issues. Indeed, Marshall's highly repetitious opinion in *Cohens v. Virginia* is strikingly reflective of nearly all of the basic attitudes and techniques with which his contribution as Chief Justice has come to be identified. From a strictly technical standpoint, to be sure, the case was concerned with the range

[69] Haines, *op. cit.*, p. 438.
[70] *Ibid.*, p. 440.
[71] John Marshall to Joseph Story, Sept. 18, 1821. *Proceedings of the Massachusetts Historical Society* (2nd Series, 1901), XIV, 330.
[72] *Ibid.*

or scope of the jurisdiction the Constitution extended to the federal courts. Yet in the course of analyzing the problem in the light of a vast and varied number of considerations, Marshall managed to frame an opinion which seldom deviated for long from the two central ideas which dominated his approach to the Constitution.

The notion that America was an indivisible nation in which the states were necessarily subordinate to the supreme authority of the Union permeates his entire discourse in the case. His assertion that in the exercise of the powers committed to it, the "government of the union" may "legitimately control all individuals or governments within the American territory" is a good epitome of this notion.[73]

It is easy to understand why Marshall's opinion in the *Cohens* case impressed Beveridge as "one of the strongest and most enduring strands of that mighty cable woven by him to hold the American people together as a united and imperishable Nation." Beveridge's enthusiasm may be explained by the fact that he regarded it as "fortunate for the Republic" that the *Cohens* case afforded Marshall the opportunity "to assert the supremacy of the nation" at a time when the forces of disunion were rampant. He had in mind not only the growing opposition to the nationalist opinions of the Marshall Court, but also the bitter controversy over the Missouri Compromise of 1820. Together with his exposition in *McCulloch v. Maryland* two years earlier, Marshall's opinion in *Cohens v. Virginia* "was the most powerful answer that could be given, and from the source of greatest authority, to that defiance of the National Government and the threats of disunion then growing ever bolder and more vociferous. Marshall's utterances did not still those hostile voices, it is true, but they gave strength and courage to Nationalists and furnished to the champions of the Union arguments of peculiar force as coming from the supreme tribunal of the Nation." And as the biographer also of Lincoln, Beveridge may be pardoned for adding: "Could John Marshall have seen into the future he would have beheld Abraham Lincoln expounding from the stump to

[73] 6 Wheat. 264, 414.

the farmers of Illinois, in 1858, the doctrines laid down by himself in 1819 and 1821." [74]

But more immediately germane was the role Marshall assigned to the Supreme Court in maintaining national cohesion. The supremacy of the High Court was portrayed as the necessary bulwark of effective or binding national authority. Perhaps because Marshall saw the country as depending on the Court for its very survival, he was moved to say that the Court's failure to exert its power would be nothing short of "treason to the Constitution":

> It is most true that this Court will not take jurisdiction if it should not: but it is equally true, that it must take jurisdiction if it should. The judiciary cannot, as the legislature may, avoid a measure because it approaches the confines of the constitution. We cannot pass it by because it is doubtful. With whatever doubts, with whatever difficulties, a case may be attended, we must decide it if it can be brought before us. We have no more right to decline the exercise of jurisdiction which is given, than to usurp that which is not given. The one or the other would be treason to the constitution.[75]

VII

Justice Holmes was not the only one who used the centennial celebration of the day Marshall became Chief Justice of the United States to call attention to the influence of the ideas in *The Federalist* papers. Also speaking on "John Marshall Day," February 4, 1901, James Bradley Thayer took note of the extent to which Marshall borrowed from *The Federalist* when he expounded the doctrine of judicial review. After summarizing the argument in *Marbury v. Madison,* Thayer remarked: "This reasoning is mainly that of Hamilton, in his short essay of a few years before, in the

[74] Beveridge, *The Life of John Marshall,* IV, 343–344.

[75] 6 *Wheat.* 264, 404. Marshall's strongest condemnation of the asserted right of a state to refuse to be bound by a federal measure it deems to be unconstitutional is to be found in his private correspondence. "The idea that a state may constitutionally nullify an act of Congress is so extravagant in itself, and so repugnant to the existence of Union between the states, that I could with difficulty bring myself to believe it was serious[ly] entertained by any person. Even yet I scarcely know how to think it possible." John Marshall to Edward Everett, Nov. 3, 1830. (*Proceedings of the Massachusetts Historical Society.*)

Federalist." [76] He regretted that Marshall had not analyzed the
problem in *Marbury v. Madison* "after the fashion of his greatest opinions" and advanced several criticisms of the decision in
that case:

> . . . Absolutely settled as the general doctrine is to-day, and sound
> as it is when regarded as a doctrine for the descendants of British
> colonists, there are grave and far-reaching considerations—such,
> too, as affect to-day the proper administration of this extremely
> important power—which are not touched by Marshall, and which
> must have commanded his attention if the subject had been deeply
> considered and fully expounded according to his later method.
> His reasoning does not answer the difficulties that troubled Swift,
> afterward chief justice of Connecticut, and Gibson, afterwards
> chief justice of Pennsylvania, and many other strong, learned and
> thoughtful men; not to mention Jefferson's familiar and often
> ill-digested objections.
>
> It assumes as an essential feature of a written constitution
> what does not exist in any one of the written constitutions of
> Europe. It does not remark the grave distinction between the
> power of a federal court in disregarding the act of a co-ordinate
> department and the action of a federal court in dealing thus with
> the legislation of the local States; a distinction important in it-
> self, and observed under the written constitutions of Europe,
> which, as I have said, allow this power in the last sort of case,
> while denying it in the other.[77]

In saying these things, Thayer was repeating views he had set
forth some years earlier in the *Harvard Law Review*.[78] He had
then singled out for special praise Justice Gibson's refutation of
Marshall's logic in *Marbury v. Madison*. The 1893 article was
apparently conceived of by Thayer as an answer to the question
with which he began his discussion: "How did our American
doctrine, which allows to the judiciary the power to declare legislative Acts unconstitutional, and to treat them as null, come
about, and what is the true scope of it?" [79] Thayer then makes

[76] Thayer, *John Marshall*, p. 96.
[77] *Ibid.*, pp. 97–98.
[78] Thayer, "The Origin and Scope of the American Doctrine of Constitutional Law," VII *Harvard Law Review* 129 (1893). Reprinted in 1 *Selected
Essays on Constitutional Law* 503 (Chicago: Foundation Press, 1938).
[79] *Ibid.*

a number of points which may legitimately be regarded as an effort to answer Marshall's argument in *Marbury v. Madison:*

> So far as the grounds for this remarkable power are found in the mere fact of a constitution being in writing, or in judges being sworn to support it, they are quite inadequate. Neither the written form nor the oath of the judges necessarily involves the right of reversing, displacing, or disregarding any action of the legislature or the executive which these departments are constitutionally authorized to take, or the determination of those departments that they are so authorized. It is enough, in confirmation of this, to refer to the fact that other countries, as France, Germany, and Switzerland, have written constitutions, and that such a power is not recognized there.[80]

But for a fuller refutation of Marshall's conception of judicial power, Professor Thayer referred the reader to Justice Gibson's dissent in *Eakin v. Raub*.[81] He said that this famous dissenting opinion was "much the ablest discussion of the question which I have ever seen, not excepting the judgment of Marshall in Marbury v. Madison, which, as I venture to think, has been overpraised." [82] Gibson, too, seems to have believed that Marshall's performance in *Marbury v. Madison* had been lauded more than it deserved to be.

"It is not a little remarkable," observes the Pennsylvania justice at the start of his opinion, "that although the right in question has all along been claimed by the judiciary, no judge has ventured to discuss it, except Chief Justice Marshall, and if the argument of a jurist so distinguished for the strength of his ratiocinative powers be found inconclusive, it may fairly be set down to the weakness of the position which he attempts to defend." [83] While professedly dealing with the question whether the Pennsylvania Supreme Court was authorized by the constitution of that state to exercise the power of judicial review, Gibson undertakes to loosen all of the major links in the chain of argument wrought by Marshall. He begins with an attack on what

[80] 1 *Sel. Essays on Con. Law* 503, 504.
[81] 12 Sergeant and Rawle (Pennsylvania Supreme Court) 330 (1825).
[82] 1 *Sel. Essays on Con. Law* 503, n.2.
[83] *Eakin v. Raub*, 12 Sergeant and Rawle 330, 346.

is generally regarded as the fundamental postulate of Chief Justice Marshall's exposition of judicial power.

"Where the government exists by virtue of a *written* constitution," says Gibson, "the judiciary does not necessarily derive from that circumstance, any other than its ordinary and appropriate powers." Declaring that in the United States "the powers of the judiciary are divisible into those that are Political and those that are purely Civil," he insists that since American courts derive their authority from the common law tradition, they must confine themselves to the ordinary activity of courts—presumably, that of applying the law as they find it to the cases brought before them. Their rightful "business" is the "administration of distributive justice," and their power does not extend "to anything of a political cast whatever."

Assuming, then, that the "ordinary and essential powers of the judiciary" do not include "the annulling of an act of the legislature," what basis or justification is there for the exercise of such a power by the judiciary? Gibson denies that there is any "express grant" empowering the judiciary to control the decisions of the other branches of the government. He concedes that a constitution is "a law of superior obligation" and that in the event of conflict between the constitution and ordinary legislation, the legislative act "would have to give way." Yet he deems it a "fallacy" to use the possibility of such a "collision" as a reason for enabling the judiciary to set aside a law alleged to be contrary to the constitution.

The constitution and the *right* of the legislature to pass the act, may be in collision. But is that a legitimate subject for judicial determination? If it be, the judiciary must be a peculiar organ, to revise the proceedings of the legislature, and to correct its mistakes; and to what part of the constitution are we to look for this proud pre-eminence? Viewing the matter in the opposite direction, what would be thought of an act of assembly in which it should be declared that the Supreme Court had, in a particular case, put a wrong construction on the Constitution of the United States, and that the judgment should therefore be reversed? It would doubtless be thought a usurpation of judicial power. But it is by no means clear, that to declare a law void which has been enacted according to the forms prescribed in the constitution, is not a usurpation of legislative power.[84]

But Gibson did not rest his case against the doctrine of judicial review on the logical shortcomings of Marshall's reasoning in *Marbury v. Madison.* He had more weighty objections. In the main, he considered such a power in the judiciary to be entirely inconsistent with the separation of powers principle as well as with the belief in representative government. Particularly striking is his statement that judicial review depends on an extreme and unrealistic theory of constitutional checks:

> Every one knows how seldom men think exactly alike on ordinary subjects; and a government constructed on the principle of assent by all its parts, would be inadequate to its most simple operations. The notion of complication of counter checks has been carried to an extent in theory, of which the framers of the constitution never dreamt. When the entire sovereignty was separated into its elementary parts, and distributed to the appropriate branches, all things incident to the exercise of its powers were committed to each branch exclusively. The negative which each part of the legislature may exercise, in regard to the acts of the other, was thought sufficient to prevent material infractions of the restraints which were put on the power of the whole; for, had it been intended to interpose the judiciary as an additional barrier, the matter would surely not have been left in doubt.[85]

And a little later he adds: "The grant of a power so extraordinary ought to appear so plain, that he who should run might read."

In rejecting the need for the restraining hand of the judiciary to make effective the mandates of a Constitution, Gibson did not mean to claim that there was no danger that legislators might ignore constitutional limitations on their power. The peril was there, but we must look to public opinion and the ballot box for protection against legislative excess. Addressing himself to the contention that without judicial review the people would be denied the salutary benefits to be derived from a written con-

---

[84] *Ibid.,* p. 348.
[85] *Ibid.* pp. 351–352.

stitution and that the legislature would be "illimitable," Gibson said:

> But there is no magic or inherent power in parchment and ink, to command respect and protect principles from violation. In the business of government a recurrence to first principles answers the end of an observation at sea with a view to correct the dead reckoning; and for this purpose, a written constitution is an instrument of inestimable value. It is of inestimable value, also, in rendering its first principles familiar to the mass of people; for, after all, there is no effectual guard against legislative usurpation but public opinion, the force of which, in this country is inconceivably great. . . . Once let public opinion be so corrupt as to sanction every misconstruction of the constitution and abuse of power which the temptation of the moment may dictate, and the party which may happen to be predominant, will laugh at the puny efforts of a dependent power to arrest it in its course.[86]

When one thinks of the extent to which Marshall saw judicial review as being demanded by the necessities of a federal system, it is easy to imagine that he probably read with a smile of self-satisfaction the exception with which Gibson concludes his dissenting opinion in *Eakin v. Raub*. For Gibson makes it quite clear that his argument against the judicial "control" of the executive and the legislature does not apply to the function performed by the Supreme Court in subordinating the states to the "supremacy" of the Constitution. "By becoming parties to the federal constitution," he asserts, "the states have agreed to several limitations of their individual sovereignty, to enforce which, it was thought

---

[86] *Ibid.*, pp. 354–355. Gibson also rejects the idea that the oath taken by judges to support the Constitution is a sanction for their exercise of the right of judicial review. He expresses the matter this way: "The oath to support the constitution is not peculiar to the judges, but is taken indiscriminately by every officer of the government, and is designed rather as a test of the political principles of the man, than to bind the officer in the discharge of his duty: otherwise it were difficult to determine what operation it is to have in the case of a recorder of deeds, for instance, who, in the execution of his office, has nothing to do with the constitution. But granting it to relate to the official conduct of the judge, as well as every other officer, and not to his political principles, still it must be understood in reference to supporting the constitution, *only as far as that may be involved in his official duty;* and, consequently, if his official duty does not comprehend an inquiry into the authority of the legislature, neither does his oath." *Ibid.*, p. 353.

to be absolutely necessary to prevent them from giving effect to laws in violation of those limitations, through the instrumentality of their own judges." Citing the "supremacy" clause of the Constitution as authority for this proposition, he adds, "This is an express grant of a political power, and it is conclusive to show that no law of inferior obligation, as every state law must necessarily be, can be executed at the expense of the constitution, laws, or treaties of the United States." [87]

Putting aside, then, Gibson's concession that what has come to be called the "umpiring function" belongs legitimately to the Supreme Court, his basic quarrel with judicial review would seem to be that it makes it possible for the judiciary to meddle in spheres assigned by the Constitution to the representatives of the people. Such a power—the power to shape public policies through legislation or administration—is political, and not judicial. "Every power," declares Gibson, "by which one organ of the government is enabled to control another, or to exert an influence over its acts, is a political power." [88]

In advancing this criticism Gibson revealed, of course, that he did not share the conviction voiced by both Marshall and Hamilton that the judicial veto would protect society against the instability and injustice inhering in popular government. As a good Jeffersonian, Gibson no doubt resented the innuendo implicit in Hamilton's chief reason for opposing any scheme which would have joined judges with legislators in the review of legislation: "The members of the legislature will rarely be chosen with a view to those qualifications which fit men for the stations of judges; and as, on this account, there will be great reason to apprehend all the ill consequences of defective infor-

[87] *Ibid.*, p. 356.
[88] *Ibid.*, p. 346. Gibson had the courage to reverse himself, though the opportunity to do so did not come his way until twenty years later. While arguing a case before the Pennsylvania Supreme Court in March of 1846, one of the lawyers happened to remark: "That the courts possess the power to declare an act void is settled, Eakin v. Raub, . . . though it is said it must be a very clear case." At this point, Chief Justice Gibson interrupted to say: "I have changed that opinion for two reasons. The late Convention, by their silence, sanctioned the pretensions of the courts to deal freely with the acts of the legislature; and from experience of the necessity of the case." *Norris v. Clymer,* 2 Pa. St. Reports 277, 281.

mation, so, on account of the natural propensity of such bodies to party divisions, there will be no less reason to fear that the pestilential breath of faction may poison the fountains of justice." [89]

Ironically, the heart of Gibson's rejection of Marshall's theory of judicial review consists of objections which Hamilton sought to demolish in the course of defending "one court of supreme and final jurisdiction." Hamilton summarized those objections as follows:

> The authority of the proposed Supreme Court of the United States, which is to be a separate and independent body, will be superior to that of the legislature. The power of construing the laws according to the *spirit* of the Constitution, will enable that court to mould them into whatever shape it may think proper; especially as its decisions will not be in any manner subject to the revision or correction of the legislative body. This is as unprecedented as it is dangerous. In Britain, the judicial power, in the last resort, resides in the House of Lords, which is a branch of the legislative; and this part of the British government has been imitated in the State constitutions in general. The Parliament of Great Britain, and the legislatures of the several States, can at any time rectify, by law, the exceptionable decisions of their respective courts. But the errors and usurpations of the Supreme Court of the United States will be uncontrollable and remediless.[90]

Immediately after this resumé of the complaints against a supreme court independent of the Congress, Hamilton remarks, "This, upon examination, will be found to be made up altogether of false reasoning upon misconceived fact." One can be sure that John Marshall applauded—as indeed he did over and over again in the special language of constitutional discourse—the rebuttal framed by his fellow Federalist from New York:

> I admit . . . that the Constitution ought to be the standard of construction for the laws, and that wherever there is an evident opposition, the laws ought to give place to the Constitution. But this doctrine is not deducible from any circumstance peculiar to

[89] *The Federalist*, No. 81, p. 507.
[90] *Ibid.*, p. 506.

the plan of the convention, but from the general theory of a limited Constitution; and as far as it is true, is equally applicable to most, if not to all the State governments. There can be no objection, therefore, on this account, to the federal judicature which will not lie against the local judicature in general, and which will not serve to condemn every constitution that attempts to set bounds to legislative discretion.[91]

More than a century and a half after Marshall rendered his opinion in *Marbury v. Madison,* we are still debating both the legitimacy and the scope of the function he claimed for the Supreme Court. There may be many reasons for this situation, but the chief explanation is that the actual exercise of judicial power has inevitably entangled the High Court in the recurring differences of principle and policy which have divided the American people. It is, indeed, understandable why the responsibility of harmonizing the "conflicting principles" requiring constitutional adjudication has been described by Justice Frankfurter as the "agony" of a judge's "duty" [92] and by Chief Justice Warren as "the ordeal of judicial judgment." [93] The present Chief Justice has said of Marshall: "Perhaps the greatest contribution he made to our system of jurisprudence was the establishment of an independent judiciary through the principle of judicial review. In a case instituted the first year of his incumbency, he rooted this fundamental principle in American constitutional law as our original contribution to the science of law." [94] But it is also true that Marshall's responses to the great issues of his own day have continued to serve as useful guideposts for succeeding generations of judges.

[91] *Ibid.,* pp. 506–507.
[92] Frankfurter, *Of Law and Men,* p. 43.
[93] *Trop v. Dulles,* 356 U.S. 86, 104 (1958).
[94] Chief Justice Earl Warren, "Forward," to *Chief Justice John Marshall: A Reappraisal,* W. Melville Jones, ed. (Ithaca: Cornell University Press, 1956), p. XV.

6

"The Security of Property"

The controversy over the decision in *Cohens v. Virginia* tells us much about the main reason for the widespread dissatisfaction with the way the Supreme Court was wielding its power in the early decades of the nineteenth century. It was the Court's action in annulling state laws which was the principal provocation.

Seven years after *Marbury v. Madison* was decided, Marshall wrote an opinion which asserted the Court's right to hold state laws to be unconstitutional.[1] This notable decision was significant, however, for reasons other than its enunciation of the principle that the Court's authority as constitutional arbiter encompassed control of the behavior of state governments. It also exhibited the Chief Justice's high regard for private rights, particularly property. His social philosophy and personal interest were fused to produce a most powerful defense of the sanctity of private possessions. "No man in America," writes Beveridge, "could have followed with deeper anxiety the Yazoo controversy than John Marshall." [2]

But there was more than the pull of personal interest behind Marshall's opinion in *Fletcher v. Peck,* the first interpretation of the contract clause of the Constitution. This clause—which provides that "no State shall . . . pass any law impairing the obligation of contracts" [3]—is a product of the struggle between debtors and creditors during the period preceding the adoption

---

[1] *Fletcher v. Peck*, 6 Cranch 87 (1810).

[2] Beveridge, *The Life of John Marshall*, III, 582. Beveridge attributes Marshall's great concern with "the stability of contractual obligations" to his anxiety over the attacks on the title to the Fairfax Estate in Virginia, on which Marshall and his brother had claims.

[3] *Constitution*, Art. I, sec. 10.

of the Constitution. All one needs do is read Marshall's account of this conflict in his biography of Washington and one can immediately perceive the depth of the Chief Justice's bias in favor of the property owner. Recalling the conditions which prevailed in the country just before the Annapolis Convention of 1786, Marshall wrote:

> At length, two great parties were formed in every state, which were distinctly marked, and which pursued distinct objects, with systematic arrangement.
>
> The one struggled with unabated zeal for the exact observance of public and private engagements. By those belonging to it, the faith of a nation, or of a private man was deemed a sacred pledge, the violation of which was equally forbidden by the principles of moral justice, and of sound policy. The distresses of individuals were, they thought, to be alleviated by industry and frugality, not by a relaxation of the laws, or by a sacrifice of the rights of others. According to the stern principles laid down for their government, the imprudent and idle could not be protected by the legislature from the consequences of their own indiscretion; but should be restrained from involving themselves in difficulties, by the conviction that a rigid compliance with contracts would be enforced. They were consequently the uniform friends of a regular administration of justice, and of a vigorous course of taxation which would enable the state to comply with its engagements. By a natural association of ideas, they were also, with very few exceptions, in favor of enlarging the powers of the federal government, and of enabling it to protect the dignity and character of the nation abroad, and its interests at home. The other party marked out for itself a more indulgent course. Viewing with extreme tenderness the case of the debtor, their efforts were unceasingly directed to his relief. To exact a faithful compliance with contracts was, in their opinion, a measure too harsh to be insisted on, and was one which the people would not bear. They were uniformly in favor of relaxing the administration of justice, of affording facilities for the payment of debts, or of suspending their collection, and of remitting taxes.[4]

I

In this less than objective survey of past events, Marshall certainly made it clear that he frowned upon any interference with

[4] John Marshall, *The Life of George Washington*, V, 85–87.

the legal rights of private persons. He went on to deplore "this instability in principles which ought if possible to be rendered immutable." [5] It may be said that by his opinion in *Fletcher v. Peck*—an opinion which was delivered only three years after he had given the public his diagnosis of the social unrest in the decade which produced the Constitution—Marshall did much to help "render" the right of private property more "immutable." The case was an aftermath of the notorious Yazoo land frauds dating back to the 1790s.

In 1795 the legislature of Georgia disposed of more than 35,000,000 acres of highly desirable land by turning it over to four companies for the price of $500,000. When it was disclosed that every member of the legislature but one had accepted bribes from the lobbyists for the land companies, the public outcry forced a newly elected legislature to repeal the "give-away" statute a year later. But the land companies refused to comply with the rescinding act and continued to sell land to so-called "innocent" buyers. *Fletcher v. Peck* began as an attempt by one of these purchasers to recover the money he had paid to a speculator in the Georgia lands for a small tract. [6]

Considerable legal talent was employed by the land companies to vindicate their claims under the original grant by the Georgia legislature, including John Quincy Adams, Joseph Story, and Luther Martin. Among these high personages was Alexander Hamilton, whose counsel was sought by the New England–Mississippi Company, which had been organized for the purpose of protecting the interests of the "innocent purchasers." It was Hamilton's opinion that the rescinding act violated the contract clause of the Constitution, and he predicted that the Courts would hold so. His views were published in a pamphlet in 1799, and in it we read:

> Without pretending to judge of the original merits or demerits of the purchasers, it may be safely said to be a contravention of the first principles of natural justice and social policy,

[5] *Ibid.,* V, 87.
[6] There is considerable evidence that actually the case was "a friendly suit" arranged in order to bring it ultimately before the Supreme Court of the United States. For a fuller discussion of the background of the controversy and the litigation, see Beveridge, *The Life of John Marshall,* III, ch. 10.

without any judicial decision of facts, by a positive act of the legislature, to revoke a grant of property regularly made for valuable consideration, under legislative authority, to the prejudice even of third persons on every supposition innocent of the alleged fraud or corruption; and it may be added that the precedent is new of revoking a grant on the suggestion of corruption of a legislative body. Nor do I perceive sufficient ground for the suggestion of unconstitutionality in the first act.

In addition to these general considerations, placing the revocation in a very unfavorable light, the Constitution of the United States, article first, section tenth, declares that no state shall pass a law impairing the obligations of contract. This must be equivalent to saying no state shall pass a law revoking, invalidating, or altering a contract. Every grant from one to another, whether the grantor be a state or an individual, is virtually a contract that the grantee shall hold and enjoy the thing granted against the grantor, and his representatives. It, therefore, appears to me that taking the terms of the Constitution in their large sense, and giving them effect according to the general spirit and policy of the provisions, the revocation of the grant by the act of the legislature of Georgia may justly be considered as contrary to the Constitution of the United States, and therefore null. And that the courts of the United States, in cases within their jurisdiction, will be likely to pronounce it so.[7]

Much of Marshall's opinion in *Fletcher v. Peck* is an echo of the two points made by Hamilton. The very way in which the Chief Justice phrased the question in the case suggests that it was not the corruption of the legislature but its power to make the grant which interested him. "Did the then constitution of the state of Georgia prohibit the legislature to dispose of the lands, which were the subject of this contract, in the manner stipulated by the contract?" Finding that the Georgia legislature did possess the power to appropriate part of the public domain in the manner done by the act of 1795, the principal problem for the Court was, of course, whether the legislature violated the federal Constitution when it repealed the law a year later.

Before answering this question, Marshall called for restraint

[7] Quoted in Benjamin F. Wright, *The Contract Clause of the Constitution* (Cambridge: Harvard University Press, 1938), p. 22.

in declaring state laws unconstitutional. Saying that the question
whether a law is to be "pronounced" void is one of "much delicacy," he stated that such a declaration should never be made
in a "doubtful case." Though a court would be "unworthy of its
station" were it to refrain from doing its "duty," it ought not
to hold legislation to be invalid on "slight implication" or "vague
conjecture." Marshall's guide for the constitutional judge is
stated simply: "The opposition between the constitution and the
law should be such that the judge feels a clear and strong conviction of their incompatibility with each other." [8]

This call for judicial self-restraint was made by Marshall with
special reference to the attack on the 1795 law which had resulted in the land grab by the private companies. He saw no
reason for questioning the power of the Georgia legislature
to vote the grant. When he turned to the consideration of
the repealing act adopted in the following year, the Chief Justice showed no such restraint in exercising his power as a judge.
The clue to the outcome in the case is furnished by his attitude
toward the issue of corruption. It was to be "deplored" that
corruption "should find its way into the governments of our
infant republics and contaminate the very source of legislation,"
and that "impure motives" should influence the making of laws
or contracts. But it was not at all clear as to just how far courts
could go in examining such unfortunate circumstances. "It may
well be doubted," Marshall observed, "how far the validity of
a law depends upon the motives of its framers, and how far the
particular inducements, operating on members of the supreme
sovereign power of a State, to the formation of a contract by that
power, are examinable in a court of justice." After dwelling on
the difficulties inherent in any such attempt by courts to "control" the conduct of legislatures, he concluded that "it would be
indecent in the extreme" in a case involving a private contract
between two individuals for the Court "to enter into an inquiry
respecting the corruption of the sovereign power of a State."

Having thus removed the issue as to the legal consequences
raised by the influences and motives under which the original

[8] 6 Cranch 87, 128.

grant was made, Marshall went on to deal with the effect of the rescinding act on the rights and interests of the "innocent" purchasers. Conceding that the original grant may have been "infected with fraud," he emphasized that the law itself was a valid one and that the legislature could not, by a subsequent act of repeal, "annihilate" rights of parties who were not involved in the fraud.

Why, then, was the newly elected legislature of Georgia powerless to rescind the fraudulent act and thus wipe out rights which had been acquired under it? It is significant that among the reasons Marshall assigned for holding that the Georgia legislature could not do this, he mentioned first the objection that the new legislature was in effect usurping a function which belonged to the judiciary. "The Legislature of Georgia was a party to this transaction; and for a party to pronounce its own deed invalid, whatever cause may be assigned for its invalidity, must be considered as a mere act of power which must find its vindication in a train of reasoning not often heard in courts of justice." [9] Despite his show of deference to "the sovereign power of the State" exercised by the legislature, Marshall persisted in treating the legislature as if it were a private person, who had made a solemn and binding agreement in 1795 and a year later proceeded to break the agreement unilaterally. Nor was he impressed with the contention that, as he phrased it himself, "the real party, it is said, are the people, and when their agents are unfaithful, the acts of those agents cease to be obligatory." He had an unequivocal answer to this argument:

> It is, however, to be recollected that the people can act only by these agents, and that, while within the powers conferred on them, their acts must be considered as the acts of the people. If the agents be corrupt, others may be chosen, and if their contracts be examinable, the common sentiment, as well as the common usage of mankind, points out a mode by which this examination may be made, and their validity determined.
> If the Legislature of Georgia was not bound to submit its pretensions to those tribunals which are established for the security of property, and to decide on human rights, if it might claim to

[9] *Ibid.*, p. 132.

itself the power of judging in its own case, yet there are certain great principles of justice, whose authority is universally acknowledged, that ought not to be entirely disregarded.[10]

Marshall went on to explain that if the question posed by the action of the Georgia legislature in revoking a land grant were really a question of title, and if the legislature were going to deal with this question, it should do so on the basis of principles which would be followed by a judicial tribunal. The most important of these doctrines is that one who has paid for a good title should not be penalized for any defect in the title for which he is not to blame. If this doctrine were disregarded, "all titles would be insecure, and the intercourse between man and man would be very seriously obstructed." [11]

In the interest of making property and the titles to it more secure, Marshall repeatedly invokes universal principles of justice and equity, and this he does even before considering specific constitutional restrictions on the states. It is clear that he regarded the 1796 repeal of the previous year's grant as an act of naked power—something which only a government lost to all sense of limitation on its authority could contemplate doing. As he remarks, "If the legislature felt itself absolved from these rules of property which are common to all the citizens of the United States, and from those principles of equity which are acknowledged in all our courts, its act is to be supported by its power alone, and the same power may devest any other individual of his lands, if it shall be the will of the legislature so to exert it." [12]

Taking up next the argument that one legislature has the power to repeal a law passed by a former legislature, Marshall undertakes to refute it by saying that this principle applies only to what he terms "general legislation" and not to acts done under the former statute. "But, if an act be done under a law, a succeeding legislature cannot undo it. The past cannot be recalled by the most absolute power. Conveyances have been made." [13] In other words, the legal rights which stemmed from

[10] *Ibid.*, pp. 132–133.
[11] *Ibid.*, pp. 133–134.
[12] *Ibid.*, p. 134.
[13] *Ibid.*, p. 135.

any transfers of the land acquired under the original grant could not be disturbed by subsequent legislation. "When, then, a law is in its nature a contract, when absolute rights have vested under that contract, a repeal of the law cannot devest those rights; and the act of annulling them, if legitimate, is rendered so by a power applicable to the case of every individual in the community." [14]

II

It can be seen that the economic consequences of the outcome in *Fletcher v. Peck* were of prime concern to Marshall. The future welfare of all Americans was seemingly at stake, quite apart from what the Constitution might have to say on the subject. But the Chief Justice did finally come to grips with the constitutional issue; and when he did, it became obvious that to him the matter of chief importance was the idea that legislative power was subjected by the Constitution to restraints ultimately enforceable by the courts:

> To the legislature all legislative power is granted; but the question, whether the act of transferring the property of an individual to the public, be in the nature of the legislative power, is well worthy of serious reflection.
> It is the peculiar province of the legislature to prescribe general rules for the government of society; the application of those rules to individuals in society would seem to be the duty of other departments. How far the power of giving the law may involve every other power, in cases where the Constitution is silent, never has been, and perhaps never can be, definitely stated.[15]

Whatever Georgia might be free to do were she a separate sovereign, the pertinent consideration was that Georgia is a member of the "American union" and that Union "has a constitution the supremacy of which all acknowledge, and which imposes limits to the Legislatures of the several states, which none claim a right to pass." [16] Marshall then quotes the contract clause of the Constitution and proceeds to say that Georgia's rescinding act fell within this prohibition. To what sort of con-

[14] *Ibid.*
[15] *Ibid.*, pp. 135–136.
[16] *Ibid.*, p. 136.

tracts did this provision of the Constitution apply? More specifically, did it cover agreements entered into by a state itself?

From all that we know about the intent of the framers, it is evident that the contract clause was a restriction on the power of state legislatures to modify the terms of private contracts. In *Fletcher v. Peck,* Marshall rejects this view of the clause. He construes the clause as applying to all agreements, regardless of the parties to them. What made Marshall's opinion in that case so significant, therefore, is that it marked the beginning of the process by which the Court, under his leadership, was erecting the contract clause into an important check on policy-making in the states. He regarded this provision as one of the ways in which the framers of the Constitution undertook to protect society and property against the effects of private passions:

> Whatever respect might have been felt for the state sovereignties, it is not to be disguised that the framers of the constitution viewed, with some apprehension, the violent acts which might grow out of the feelings of the moment; and that the people of the United States, in adopting that instrument, have manifested a determination to shield themselves and their property from the effects of those sudden and strong passions to which men are exposed. The restrictions on the legislative power of the states are obviously founded in this sentiment; and the constitution of the United States contains what may be deemed a bill of rights for the people of each state.[17]

It is only after making this comment on the general motives of the framers of the Constitution that Marshall goes on to interpret the purpose of the clause in question. But interestingly enough—and the approach is characteristic of his methodology in constitutional interpretation—he unfolds his views of that purpose by means of a number of rhetorical questions. These questions are put by him in regard to the meaning of the section which forbids the states to adopt bills of attainder, *ex post facto* laws, and laws impairing the obligation of contracts. Here are the questions:

> A bill of attainder may affect the life of an individual, or may confiscate his property, or may do both.

[17] *Ibid.,* pp. 137–138.

In this form the power of the legislature over the lives and fortunes of individuals is expressly restrained. What motive, then, for implying, in words which import a general prohibition to impair the obligation of contracts, an exception in favor of the right to impair the obligation of those contracts into which the State may enter?

. . . . The Legislature is then prohibited [by the *ex post facto* provision] from passing a law by which a man's estate, or any part of it, shall be seized for a crime which was not declared, by some previous law, to render him liable to that punishment. Why, then, should violence be done to the natural meaning of words for the purpose of leaving to the legislature the power of seizing, for public use, the estate of an individual in the form of a law annulling the title by which he holds that estate? The court can perceive no sufficient grounds for making this distinction. This rescinding act would have the effect of an *ex post facto* law. It forfeits the estate of Fletcher for a crime not committed by himself, but by those from whom he purchased. This cannot be effected in the form of an *ex post facto* law, or bill of attainder; why, then, is it allowable in the form of a law annulling the original grant? [18]

His strained—and in some respects strange—reading of the constitutional clause in question only serves to make more conspicuous the dominant feature of Marshall's opinion in *Fletcher v. Peck*. At no point does the Chief Justice even attempt to prove that the framers of the Constitution meant to include public as well as private contracts within the prohibition of the clause. It was not the immediate result of the case, but rather the long-run effects of sustaining Georgia's rescinding act, which seems to have concerned him the most. But it would be superficial to attribute the decision in *Fletcher v. Peck* to Marshall's understandable sympathy for the land speculator.

When one takes Marshall at his word, as it were, it becomes plain that something far more vital for the American society was at stake. His insistence that the contract clause applied

[18] *Ibid.,* pp. 138–139. By the time Marshall made these remarks concerning the ban on *ex post facto* laws, it had already been established that the provision was limited to criminal matters and did not apply to retroactive legislation of a civil nature. In an opinion by Justice Samuel Chase, the Court held in 1798 that the prohibition on *ex post facto* laws applied exclusively to criminal legislation. *Calder v. Bull,* 3 Dallas 386.

to "contracts of every description" was more than a self-willed
act of reading meaning into words which is not there. It was
part and parcel of his larger campaign to build the Constitution
into a bulwark for the protection of the property owner. Moved
by such a purpose, he no doubt believed that it was as essential
—perhaps more so—to keep government from disturbing economic arrangements as it was to hold private persons to their
agreements. The depth of his conviction can be perceived more
clearly when it is remembered that he invoked "the general principles of our political institutions" as well as the "words of the constitution" in arriving at his conclusion:

> It is, then, the unanimous opinion of the court, that, in this
> case, the estate having passed into the hands of a purchaser for
> a valuable consideration, without notice, the state of Georgia was
> restrained, either by general principles which are common to our
> free institutions, or by the particular provisions of the constitu-
> tion of the United States, from passing a law whereby the estate of
> the plaintiff in the premises so purchased could be constitutionally
> and legally impaired and rendered null and void.[19]

The dual approach to constitutional questions implicit in
Marshall's statement just quoted has been explained quite differently. His reliance on "general principles," it has been suggested, was due to the fact that he was "uncertain as to precisely
why the repeal act was invalid." [20] Yet whatever doubts Marshall
may have entertained in 1810 concerning the exact scope of the
contract clause of the Constitution, his interpretations of that
clause in subsequent years merely confirm the impression left by
his opinion in *Fletcher v. Peck*—that the sanctity of contractual
obligations was an essential article of his social philosophy.
Groping for the strongest possible support for the Court's ruling,
he rested the decision on more than one basis, thus appearing
to be less than unequivocal. Nevertheless, it was apparent even
in 1810 that the contract clause itself was to serve as a vehicle
for realizing his larger goal. Something Justice Story quotes him

[19] 6 Cranch 87, 139.
[20] See Benjamin F. Wright, *op. cit.*, p. 34.

as saying about his attitude in 1787 discloses the source of his feeling about the great importance of the limitations on the states to be found in section 10 of Article I of the Constitution: "The questions, which were perpetually recurring in the State Legislatures, and which brought annually into doubt principles, which I thought most sacred; which proved that every thing was afloat, and that we had no safe anchorage ground; gave a high value in my estimation to that article of the Constitution, which imposes restrictions on the States." [21]

III

Time did not dim Marshall's memory or fears of legislative behavior typified by the assaults on private rights rampant in the 1780s. Quite the reverse. In his opinion in *Sturges v. Crowninshield*,[22] decided in 1819, we learn just what Marshall had in mind when he spoke of occurrences which seemed to assail "principles which I thought most sacred." This case came to the Court as an attack on "an act for the benefit of insolvent debtors and their creditors," which had been adopted by New York in 1811. In March of that year, Crowninshield gave Sturges two promissory notes which were to fall due in August. A month later, the legislature passed the statute which discharged debtors of any debts contracted prior to its adoption once they surrendered the property they had at the time of bankruptcy. Crowninshield failed to pay the notes, and Sturges sued him in the United States Circuit Court. The judges of that court were unable to agree and referred the questions to the Supreme Court.

Before he could address himself to the main issue in the case, it was necessary for Marshall to reconcile two seemingly conflicting provisions in the Constitution. These were the clause which prohibits the states from enacting "laws impairing the obligation of contracts" and the provision which gives Congress the power "to establish . . . uniform laws on the subject of bankruptcies throughout the United States." [23] Did the grant to Congress of the power to adopt bankruptcy laws take away from the

---

[21] Story, *A Discourse on the Life, Character, and Services of the Honorable John Marshall* (Boston: James Munroe and Company, 1835), p. 28.

[22] 4 Wheat. 122 (1819).

[23] *Constitution*, Art. I, sec. 8, par. 4.

states any authority to legislate on the subject of bankruptcy? Marshall disposes of this question rather quickly, mainly by arguing that not all of Congress' powers are exclusive. Some of the powers conferred on Congress by the Constitution are exclusive, such as the treaty making power, as is demonstrated by the provision which forbids the states to enter into treaties.[24] From this fact Marshall drew the inference that "the sense of the Convention" was that "the mere grant of a power to Congress, did not imply a prohibition on the States to exercise the same power." [25] But in the absence of any express prohibition on the states, how shall it be determined whether a power vested in Congress was meant to exclude the states from the same legislative field? Though the problem was complex, the criterion of constitutionality was clear: "Whenever the terms in which a power is granted to Congress, or the nature of the power, require that it should be exercised exclusively by Congress, the subject is as completely taken from the State Legislatures, as if they had been expressly forbidden to act on it." [26]

Applying this test of exclusiveness to the subject of bankruptcy, Marshall found that the constitutional provision in question did not necessarily deprive the states of the power to legislate on the same subject. Congress, if it chose in its "wisdom" to do so, could bar the states from enacting laws for the relief of bankrupts, but the mere possession by Congress of the power to adopt uniform laws on bankruptcy did not in itself exclude the states. As Marshall put it:

> . . . If, in the opinion of Congress, uniform laws concerning bankruptcies ought not to be established, it does not follow that partial laws may not exist, or that State legislation on the subject must cease. It is not the mere existence of the power, but its exercise, which is incompatible with the exercise of the same power by the States. It is not the right to establish these uniform laws, but their actual establishment, which is inconsistent with the partial acts of the States.[27]

[24] "No State shall enter into any Treaty, Alliance, or Confederation." *Constitution*, Art. I, sec. 10, par. 1.
[25] 4 Wheat. 122, 193.
[26] *Ibid.*
[27] *Ibid.*, p. 196.

Before concluding his discussion of the effect on the states of Congress' power over bankruptcies, the Chief Justice emphasized one point which he obviously regarded as the crux of the matter. Until Congress instituted a uniform policy on bankruptcies for the whole country, the states were free to adopt bankruptcy laws provided they contained "no principle" which was in conflict with the contract clause of the federal Constitution. This *caveat* brought Marshall to what he characterized as "the great question on which the cause must depend." That question was, of course, whether New York's bankruptcy law of 1811 violated the contract clause. Marshall describes the statute as an act which "liberates the person of the debtor, and discharges him from all liability for any debt previously contracted, on his surrendering his property in the manner it prescribes."

Assuming, then, that a state may come to the aid of the debtor to a certain extent, why could it be said that New York went too far? The answer to this question, says Marshall, depends on what is meant by the "obligation" of a contract and what will "impair" it. And as was his wont, he goes on to define the crucial terms with the implication that comprehension of their dictionary meaning will dispose of the constitutional issue. "It would seem difficult to substitute words," we are told, "which are more intelligible, or less liable to misconstruction, than those which are to be explained." And what do the key words mean? "A contract is an agreement in which a party undertakes to do, or not to do, a particular thing. The law binds him to perform his undertaking, and this is, of course, the obligation of his con-tract." In the case before the Court "the defendant [Crownin-shield] has given his promissory note to pay the plaintiff [Sturges] a sum of money on or before a certain day. The contract binds him to pay that sum on that day; and this is its obligation. Any law which releases a part of this obligation, must, in the literal sense of the word, impair it," all the more so when the law com-pletely discharges the debt.[28] Such is the practical import of the contract clause, and the Constitution embodies that simple and obvious meaning. "The words of the Constitution, then, are express, and incapable of being misunderstood. They admit

[28] *Ibid.*, p. 197.

of no variety of construction, and are acknowledged to apply to that species of contract, an engagement between man and man for the payment of money, which has been entered into by these parties." [29]

Curiously, however, after ascribing this clear and unmistakable meaning to the Constitution, Marshall concedes that the argument that the New York law does not fall within the prohibition of the contract clause merits serious attention. The core of the constitutional controversy was whether a debtor fulfilled his obligation to his creditors when he turned over to them whatever property he had at the time of bankruptcy, or whether the obligation to pay in full remained outstanding—so that he could be made to pay out of property or funds he might acquire later. The Constitution, says Marshall, barred the states from freeing the debtor from the obligation to use his "future acquisitions" in meeting his original commitment to the creditors:

> But it is not true that the parties have in view only the property in possession when the contract is formed, or that its obligation does not extend to future acquisitions. Industry, talents, and integrity, constitute a fund which is as confidently trusted as property itself. Future acquisitions are, therefore, liable for contracts; and to release them from this liability impairs their obligation.[30]

As he continued to explain the Court's attitude toward the effect of the contract clause upon the obligations of the debtor, Marshall inevitably found it necessary to deal with the history of the period during which the clause was written. He had to overcome the argument, as he himself summarized it, that "the prevailing evil of the times, which produced this clause in the Constitution, was the practice of emitting paper money, of making property which was useless to the creditor a discharge of his debt, and of changing the time of payment by authorizing distant instalments." The Court was told, that is to say, that the clause was intended to prevent the legislatures of the states from jeopardizing the interest of the creditor by legalizing paper money, compelling creditors to accept payment in kind, or by

[29] *Ibid.*, p. 198.
[30] *Ibid.*

enacting so-called "stay laws" for the benefit of the debtor. The nub of Marshall's reply is that the clause prohibits all impairments of the obligation of contracts, and not any one type of law having that effect. The states may undertake to legislate some relief for the bankrupt, but they may not erase the obligations the bankrupt has "entered into." By the time Marshall had disposed of the historical problem, it could be said that he had taken the argument regarding the silence of the framers on insolvency laws and turned it against those using it. He wrote:

> The argument drawn from the omission in the constitution to prohibit the States from passing insolvent laws admits of several satisfactory answers. It was not necessary, nor would it have been safe, had it even been the intention of the framers of the constitution to prohibit the passage of all insolvent laws, to enumerate particular subjects to which the principle they intended to establish should apply. The principle was the inviolability of contracts. This principle was to be protected in whatsoever form it might be assailed. To what purpose enumerate the particular modes of violation which should be forbidden, when it was intended to forbid all? Had an enumeration of all the laws which might violate contracts been attempted, the provision must have been less complete, and involved in more perplexity than it now is. The plain and simple declaration, that no State shall pass any law impairing the obligation of contracts, includes insolvent laws and all other laws, so far as they infringe the principle the Convention intended to hold sacred, and no farther.[31]

Nor was it to be assumed that the framers intended to stop the states from enacting any and all measures for the relief of the debtor. For one thing, it was not to be thought that the "illustrious patriots who framed our constitution" were so guilty of "excess of inhumanity" as to wish to perpetuate the practice of imprisoning debtors for life, or to restrain the states from ending imprisonment for debt. Furthermore, there is a difference between the obligation of a contract and the remedies for their enforcement. Though a state legislature may not tamper with

---

[31] *Ibid.*, pp. 199–200. Marshall stated that there may be some differences between insolvent and bankruptcy laws, but he maintained that the distinction is tenuous and, in any event, not significant for the purposes of the case.

the obligation of existing contracts, it might, in its "wisdom," decline to give the creditor the advantage of imprisoning the debtor in order to compel him to perform his contract. "Imprisonment is no part of the contract, and simply to release the prisoner does not impair its obligation." [32]

Returning to the historical argument, which had been pressed by the defenders of the New York bankruptcy law, the Chief Justice makes a rather revealing comment as to how the meaning of the Constitution is to be derived. The statement might well be regarded as the touchstone of the tradition of constitutional interpretation initiated by Marshall. It had been contended by counsel for Sturges that although the New York law might appear to be contrary to the words or letter of the contract clause, it did not violate its spirit. This was so, it was contended, because laws for the relief of debtors had been adopted by colonial and state legislatures and because the framers of the Constitution had in mind other types of infringements of the rights of creditors. Referring to the attempt to use history as the sole basis for discovering the meaning dictated by the "spirit" of a constitutional provision, rather than its literal sense, Marshall declared:

> Before discussing this argument, it may not be improper to premise that, although the spirit of an instrument, especially of a constitution, is to be respected not less than its letter, yet the spirit is to be collected chiefly from its words. It would be dangerous in the extreme to infer from extrinsic circumstances, that a case for which the words of an instrument expressly provide, shall be exempted from its operation. Where words conflict with each other, where the different clauses of an instrument bear upon each other, and would be inconsistent unless the natural and common import of words be varied, construction becomes necessary, and a departure from the obvious meaning of words is justifiable. But if, in any case, the plain meaning of a provision, not contradicted by any other provision in the same instrument, is to be disregarded, because we believe that the framers of that instrument could not intend what they say, it must be one in which the absurdity and injustice of applying the provision to the case, would be so monstrous, that all mankind would, without hesitation, unite in rejecting the application.[33]

[32] *Ibid.*, p. 201.
[33] *Ibid.*, pp. 202–203.

It is true, to be sure, that the "general distress" following the Revolution had led state legislatures to issue paper money, to require creditors to accept worthless lands and other property as tender in payment of debts, and to extend the time for collecting debts. But the contract clause is not to be judged solely in the light of these attacks on creditor rights. The Constitution forbids the states to "emit bills of credit" and to make anything but gold and silver a tender in payment of debts.[34] The presence in the Constitution of these express prohibitions merely shows that the "attention of the convention" was "particularly directed" to the immediate evils. But the insertion of the contract clause makes it equally clear that the framers were aware that the "mischief" might arise from other laws. They therefore were determined "to establish a great principle, that contracts should be inviolable." [35] Such is the "plain" and "obvious" intent of the clause:

> If, as we think, it must be admitted that this intention might actuate the convention; that it is not only consistent with, but is apparently manifested by, all that part of the section which respects this subject; that the words used are well adapted to the expression of it; that violence would be done to their plain meaning by understanding them in a more limited sense; those rules of construction, which have been consecrated by the wisdom of ages, compel us to say, that these words prohibit the passage of any law discharging a contract without performance.[36]

IV

Eight years after the decision in *Sturges v. Crowninshield,* there occurred an event which displayed even more dramatically Marshall's conviction that it was the duty of the Supreme Court to protect America's economic community against impairment of contractual obligations. It also suggests that he himself was probably prepared to go even further than the Court did in the *Sturges* case. Justice William Johnson said of the outcome in the *Sturges* case that "the judgement partakes as much of a compromise as of a legal adjudication." [37] It was perhaps because he was

[34] "No State shall . . . coin Money; emit Bills of Credit; make any thing but gold and silver Coin a Tender in Payment of debts." *Constitution,* Art. I, sec. 10.

[35] 4 Wheat. 122, 206.

[36] *Ibid.*

[37] *Ogden v. Saunders,* 12 Wheat. 213, 271, at 272 (1827).

writing in dissent—the only dissent on a constitutional question he
made public in the thirty-four years of his Chief Justiceship [38]—
that John Marshall was able to speak so uncompromisingly in
the 1827 case of *Ogden v. Saunders*. In it he maintains that the
limitation implicit in the contract clause forbids the states to
discharge debtors of agreements they entered into after the
statute was passed, as well as agreements formed before its adoption. "If his point of view had been that of the majority," observes
Benjamin F. Wright, "the decision, unless later reversed, would
have been as great a limitation upon state legislative power as
any of his period, perhaps the most sweeping." [39]

A majority of the Court—consisting of Justices Washington,
Johnson, Thompson, and Trimble—held that New York's insolvent law did not impair the obligation of future contracts, that
is to say, contracts made after the law was placed on the statute
books.[40] All four wrote opinions, but agreed on the essential
point, as stated by Justice Washington, that a law in operation at
the time a contract is entered into is "the law of the contract"—"a
part of the contract" which can be said to impair its obligation.[41]
Justice Johnson construed the prohibition on bills of attainder,
ex post facto laws, and laws impairing the obligation of contracts
as "a general provision against arbitrary and tyrannical legislation over existing rights, whether of person or property." [42] The

[38] In his only other dissenting opinion, Marshall took the position that
since a corporation is an impersonal entity lacking the organs of speech, it
can act or communicate its will only in writing. *Bank of United States v.
Dandridge*, 12 Wheat. 64, 90 (1827). The apologetic note with which Marshall
begins his opinion in this case suggests one reason for the infrequency of his
dissents: "I should now, as is my custom, when I have the misfortune to differ
from this Court, acquiesce silently in its opinion, did I not believe that the
judgment of the Circuit Court of Virginia gave general surprize to the profession, and was generally condemned." *Ibid.*, p. 90.

[39] Wright, *op. cit.*, p. 50. Professor Wright goes on to declare that had
Marshall's views in *Ogden v. Saunders* been adopted by the majority, the
decision "might have given to the Court a power of supervision over legislation
under the contract clause comparable with that developed late in the century
under the due process clause." *Ibid.*

[40] Strictly speaking, the majority decision was that New York's insolvent
law did not impair the obligation of future contracts between its own citizens,
but that it could not affect the rights of creditors who were citizens of other
states.

[41] 12 Wheat. 213, 259.

[42] *Ibid.*, p. 286. Johnson repudiated the doctrine that the ban on *ex post*

legislature was as free to set limits to "the will of the contracting parties" as respects bankruptcy as "in the instances of gaming debts, usurious contracts, marriage, brokerage bonds, and various others." [43]

In his dissenting opinion—in which he was joined by Justices Story and Duval—Marshall professed to see no difference between a law which frees a bankrupt from the obligation under agreements already in existence and a law which discharges him from the obligation of a contract into which he entered after the bankruptcy law was enacted by the legislature. But impressive as is the dogged persistence with which he sought to vindicate the inviolability of contracts, even more striking is his use of the occasion as another opportunity for expressing what he regarded as the correct view of the Court's function under the Constitution. "To say," Marshall remarks at the start of his opinion, "that the intention of the instrument must prevail; that this intention must be collected from its words; that its words are to be understood in that sense in which they are generally used by those for whom the instrument was intended; that its provisions are neither to be restricted into insignificance, nor extended to objects not comprehended in them, nor contemplated by its framers;—is to repeat what has been already said more at large, and is all that can be necessary." [44] He implies that what led the majority astray was their failure to adhere to this salutary method of interpreting the Constitution. They should have followed their "reasoning" in *Sturges v. Crowninshield;* he himself had "never yet seen cause for being dissatisfied" with that reasoning. Had they done so, they would have arrived at the inescapable conclusion that it was as harmful to allow legislatures freedom to disturb obligations assumed before the passage of such laws as obligations assumed after their passage. "When we consider the nature of our Union; that it is intended to make us, in a great measure, one people, as to commercial objects; that, so far as respects the intercommunication of individuals, the lines of separation between States are, in many respects, obliterated; it would not be matter of surprise,

---

facto laws applied only to criminal provisions, and called for its application to civil legislation.
   [43] *Ibid.,* p. 289.
   [44] *Ibid.,* p. 332.

if, on the delicate subject of contracts once formed, the interference of State legislation should be greatly abridged, or entirely
forbidden." [45]

So far as basic motivation is concerned, Marshall may be said
to have registered his main objection in the sentence just recalled.
But he takes twenty-two additional pages in which to support that
rationale. In the course of doing so, he once again reviews the
underlying purposes of the framers as they are to be deduced
from the language of the tenth section of the first article of the
Constitution. The resumé demonstrates how skillfully Marshall
could combine the interpretation of historical events, semantics,
and logic into a powerful argument for a particular constitutional
point of view. Noting that Section 10 of Article I contains restrictions on both retroactive and prospective legislation, he insists
that only the prohibitions on bills of attainder and *ex post facto*
laws refer to "pre-existing" situations. The prohibitions which
"relate to civil transactions of individuals" and the provisions
which forbid the states to make anything but gold and silver a
tender in payment of debts or to enact laws impairing the obligation of contracts are couched in general terms—"terms which
comprehend, in their ordinary signification, cases which occur
after, as well as those which occur before, the passage of the act."
These restrictions upon the states, Marshall stresses, "contemplate
legislative interference with private rights, and restrain that interference." The same "train of reasoning" which would confine the
application of the contract clause only to debts contracted before
the adoption of a bankruptcy law, he argues, would support
state legislation permitting the payment of future debts otherwise than in gold and silver. The one point made in defense of
the constitutionality of the New York law which seemed to offend
Marshall's sense of logical rigor the most, however, was the contention that a law discharging debtors from their obligations
under future contracts was to be regarded as a condition implied
in the contracts themselves.

The suggestion that, because of such legislation all future
contracts were to be construed as containing an "express stipulation" that they would lapse once the debtor became insolvent,

[45] *Ibid.*, p. 334.

disturbed Marshall greatly. He saw lurking in it grave dangers for society. "This is, unquestionably," he tersely affirms, "pressing the argument very far; and the establishment of the principle leads inevitably to consequences which would affect society deeply and seriously." [46] Once the "idea" was accepted that the states may introduce into contracts "a stipulation not admitted by the parties," the legislatures would be free to make any law a condition or implied stipulation of all subsequent contracts. "Thus, one of the most important features in the constitution of the United States," warns the Chief Justice, "one which the state of the times most urgently required, one on which the good and the wise reposed confidently for securing the prosperity and harmony of our citizens, would lie prostrate, and be construed into an inanimate, inoperative, unmeaning clause." [47]

In the process of elaborating his answer to the claim that certain legislative provisions may be made implied conditions of future contracts, Marshall is finally brought to the analogies represented by laws directed against frauds, usury, and excessive duration of contractual obligations. He is vehement in rejecting the suggestion that the existence of such statutes proves that legislatures have always been free to insert terms into contracts not actually agreed to by the parties to the contracts. This bit of refutation gives him an opportunity to argue as a disciple of the social compact theory of government and of natural rights.

v

But more illuminating than Marshall's kinship with the ideas of John Locke is the way in which he turns the Lockean concept of the origin of private rights into an argument for judicial review. The philosophic ground for the right of the legislature to regulate contracts in certain respects is summarized by him as follows:

> Contract, it is said, being the creature of society, derives its obligation from the law; and, although the law may not enter into the agreement so as to form a constituent part of it, still it acts externally upon the contract, and determines how far the principle of coercion shall be applied to it; and this being universally

[46] *Ibid.*, p. 338.
[47] *Ibid.*, p. 339.

understood, no individual can complain justly of its application to himself, in a case where it was known when the contract was formed.[48]

Speaking as a political theorist, Marshall seeks to counter this view by saying that the argument rests on a seriously mistaken hypothesis—a false notion as to the origin of human rights and of the relation of law to such rights. It simply is not true that contract "is the mere creature of society" and that it derives its obligation from "human legislation." It was significant that "we find no trace" in human history that the reason why men were held to their agreements was the result not of their commitments, but the coercion of society. On the contrary, "So far back as human research carries us," Marshall notes, "we find the judicial power, as a part of the executive, administering justice by the application of remedies to violated rights, or broken contracts." This old practice stemmed from the acceptance of "the idea of a pre-existing obligation on every man to do what he has promised on consideration to do." Marshall adds:

> . . . If, on tracing the right to contract, and the obligations created by contract, to their source, we find them to exist anterior to, and independent of society, we may reasonably conclude that those original and pre-existing principles are, like many other natural rights, brought with man into society; and, although they may be controlled, are not given by human legislation.
>
> In the rudest state of nature a man governs himself, and labors for his own purposes. That which he acquires is his own, at least while in his possession, and he may transfer it to another.[49]

Hence, the right to contract is enjoyed by men even before they enter society and is retained by them after becoming members of society.

What is the effect of society upon these rights? When men unite together and form a government, do they surrender their right to contract, as well as their right to enforce the observance of their contracts? For what purpose should they make this sur-

---

[48] *Ibid.*, p. 344.
[49] *Ibid.*, p. 345.

render? Government cannot exercise this power for individuals. It is better that they should exercise it for themselves. For what purpose, then, should the surrender be made? It can only be, that government may give it back again.[50]

There is only one "rational inference" that may be drawn from the evolution of human rights and of government. "Individuals do not derive from government their right to contract, but bring that right with them into society" and the "obligation is not conferred on contracts by positive law, but is intrinsic, and is conferred by the act of the parties." This historical and legal situation results, Marshall explains, from "the right which every man retains to acquire property, to dispose of that property according to his own judgment, and to pledge himself for a future act. These rights are not given by society, but are brought into it. The right of coercion is necessarily surrendered to government, and this surrender imposes on government the correlative duty of furnishing a remedy." [51]

Government may, then, regulate contracts in certain respects. Legislation may prescribe the manner in which contracts shall be evidenced and prohibit certain private arrangements altogether as being against public policy. Since the original and inherent right of individuals to bind themselves by contracts remains unimpaired, however, the important constitutional question is this: How far may government go in regulating the conditions to be embodied in contracts without disturbing the obligations of the parties to each other? To what extent, in other words, are private contracts subject to regulation by the coercive force of law? After quoting Blackstone—"a writer whose definitions especially have been the theme of almost universal panegyric"—to the effect that law is "a rule of civil conduct to be prescribed by the supreme power of a State," Marshall reminds us that in the United States the authority of government to lay down rules for the conduct of individuals is not an unlimited one:

> In our system, the legislature of a State is the supreme power, in all cases where its action is not restrained by the constitution of the United States. Where it is so restrained, the legislature

[50] *Ibid.*, p. 346.
[51] *Ibid.*, pp. 346–347.

ceases to be the supreme power, and its acts are not law. It is, then, begging the question to say, that, because contracts may be discharged by a law previously enacted, this contract may be discharged by this act of the legislature of New York; for the question returns upon us, Is this act a law? Is it consistent with, or repugnant to, the constitution of the United States? This question is to be solved only by the constitution itself.[52]

An irreverent contemporary critic of Marshall might well have retorted by suggesting that what the Chief Justice really meant to say was that it is the Supreme Court which must "solve" the question whether the New York statute was a constitutionally permissible "law." Had he been allowed to speak for the Court, Marshall would have held that though the Constitution recognizes the right of the states to control the subjects of contracts, it restrains their legislatures from interfering with the obligation assumed by men as "free agents."

It is neither "absurd" nor "self-contradictory" to depict the Constitution—whose "language is the language of restraint, not of coercion"—as guaranteeing the "inviolability" of contractual obligations while leaving the state governments free to concern themselves with the performance or enforcement of contracts. The seeming "self-contradiction" is to be explained simply by the fact that the Constitution created a system of government in which the local entities were to continue to exercise their historic powers, but under the limitations of the fundamental law of the nation.[53] And before concluding his forthright dissent, Marshall returns to the familiar theme of his contract clause opinions. The best way to comprehend the nature of the "restraint" imposed on the states by that clause is to recall the conditions it was intended by the framers of the Constitution to correct:

We cannot look back to the history of the times when the august spectacle was exhibited of the assemblage of a whole peo-

[52] *Ibid.*, pp. 347–348.
[53] "Our country exhibits the extraordinary spectacle of distinct, and, in many respects, independent governments over the same territory and the same people. The local governments are restrained from impairing the obligation of contracts, but they furnish the remedy to enforce them, and administer that remedy in tribunals constituted by themselves." *Ibid.*, pp. 350–351.

ple by their representatives in Convention, in order to unite thirteen independent sovereignties under one government, so far as might be necessary for the purposes of union, without being sensible of the great importance which was at that time attached to the tenth section of the first article. The power of changing the relative situation of debtor and creditor, of interfering with contracts, a power which comes home to every man, touches the interest of all, and controls the conduct of every individual in those things which he supposes to be proper for his own exclusive management, had been used to such an excess by the State legislatures, as to break in upon the ordinary intercourse of society, and destroy all confidence between man and man. The mischief had become so great, so alarming, as not only to impair commercial intercourse, and threaten the existence of credit, but to sap the morals of the people, and destroy the sanctity of private faith. To guard against the continuance of the evil was an object of deep interest with all the truly wise, as well as the virtuous, of this great community, and was one of the important benefits expected from a reform of the government.[54]

[54] *Ibid.*, pp. 354–355.

7

"Rights Which Are Protected by the Constitution"

Paradoxically, the best-known of Marshall's contract clause opinions did not concern the rights of persons engaged in business dealings. It is, of course, his opinion in the famous *Dartmouth College* case.[1] "The decision in that case," James Kent said, "did more than any other single act proceeding from the authority of the United States to throw an impregnable barrier around all rights and franchises derived from the grant of government; and to give solidity and inviolability to the literary, charitable, religious and commercial institutions of our country."[2]

Granted that Kent's estimate was really a contemporary judgment—and came from one of the Chief Justice's most avid admirers—it is nevertheless true that the principle enunciated by Marshall in the *Dartmouth College* case proved to be of great value for America's corporate structure. As Benjamin F. Wright has written, "In the *Dartmouth College* case, for the first time, a corporate charter was held to be a contract. And that ruling, with the rapid growth of the corporate form of industrial organization, made possible a breadth of application for the clause which would have astonished most, if not all, of those who voted for

[1] *Trustees of Dartmouth College v. Woodward*, 4 Wheat. 518 (1819).
[2] Kent, *Commentaries*, 12th ed., I, 418.

146

its adoption in 1787 and 1788." [3] Yet it is both ironic and instructive—the late Thomas Reed Powell might have termed it a "vagary" of constitutional interpretation [4]—that it was in the very same *Dartmouth College* case where future lawmakers were able to find a suggestive formula for escaping the worst effects of Marshall's conservative doctrine. It was Justice Story who, in his separate opinion concurring in the Chief Justice's views, indicated a way out should legislatures wish to retain the power to modify corporate privileges.[5]

I

The *Dartmouth College* case was the climax to a long-smoldering feud between the Board of Trustees and the president of the college, John Wheelock, son of the college's founder, Eleazar Wheelock.[6] Originating in rather obscure theological differences and personal animosities, the controversy eventually arrayed political forces within as well as outside the state. It was Eleazar Wheelock who had secured a royal charter in 1769 reorganizing into Dartmouth College the school he had established in 1754 for the education of Indians. Under that charter the college was to be governed by a board of twelve trustees, who were given the power to name their successors. In 1816 the New Hampshire legislature amended the charter in several important respects. The name of the college was changed to Dartmouth University, the number of trustees was increased to twenty-one, the new members of the board were to be named by the Governor, and a board of overseers was to supervise the acts of the trustees. A majority of the old Board of Trustees refused to accept the new

[3] Wright, *The Contract Clause of the Constitution*, pp. 39–40.

[4] See Powell, *Vagaries and Varieties in Constitutional Interpretation* (New York: Columbia University Press, 1956).

[5] Justice Story quoted a dictum from a Massachusetts case: "We are also satisfied that the rights legally vested in this or in any corporation cannot be controlled or destroyed by any subsequent statute, *unless* a power for that purpose be reserved to the legislature by the act of incorporation." *Wales v. Stetson*, 2 Mass. 14. The italics were supplied by Story. For a concise summary of the ways in which the states have used their power to repeal, alter, or amend charter provisions, see Wright, *op. cit.*, pp. 168–178.

[6] For a fuller account of the background of the case, see John M. Shirley, *The Dartmouth College Causes and the Supreme Court of the United States* (St. Louis: G. I. Jones and Co., 1879), and Beveridge, *The Life of John Marshall*, IV, ch. V.

charter and instituted legal action to recover the property of the college.

The effort of the Dartmouth trustees to vindicate their rights under the 1769 charter produced one of the most dramatic battles in our constitutional history. Because of Marshall's approach to the case, it has always seemed that the decision was of particular significance for commercial corporations. But it is one of the ironies of that struggle that, as Edward S. Corwin has suggested, no such furor would have arisen had the case been concerned with an ordinary business—"say a gas company." For then the "universal view of bench and bar in 1819" would probably have been that legislative alterations of the original terms of corporate charters violated the contract clause as that clause had been construed in *Fletcher v. Peck.*[7]

As it was, eminent lawyers and judges of the day could be found on both sides of the controversy. The Superior Court of New Hampshire, the state's highest tribunal, sustained the right of the legislature to change the charter of the college. It is a mark of the doubts and difficulties raised by the litigation that the case had to be argued twice before New Hampshire's Supreme Court, and that the Supreme Court of the United States postponed decision for nearly a year after hearing the case. Though acknowledging that the contract clause in the federal Constitution embraced all contracts relating to private property, Chief Justice William M. Richardson rested the New Hampshire court's decision, in the main, on the view that "a distinction is to be taken between particular grants by the Legislature of property or privileges to individuals for their own benefit, and grants of power and authority to be exercised for public purposes." Dartmouth College was a public corporation and its charter was therefore subject to modification by the legislature.

Richardson rejected the claim urged by the lawyers for the college, among them Daniel Webster, that the charter was a contract protected by the contract clause of the federal Constitution. The clause, Richardson said, was intended "to protect private rights of property and embraces all contracts relating to

---

[7] Corwin, *John Marshall and the Constitution*, p. 168.

private property," but was not intended "to limit the power of the states, in relation to their own public officers or servants, or their own civil institutions . . . nor grants of power and authority, by a State to individuals, to be exercised for purposes merely public." The college, "all of whose franchises are exercised for public purposes," is not a private, but a public corporation, subject to control by the legislature. Perhaps no other statement in Richardson's opinion discloses the state court's basic attitude as clearly as this one sentence: "The office of trustee of *Dartmouth College* is, in fact, a public trust, as much so as the office of governor, or of judge of this court." [8]

The appeal to the Supreme Court of the United States was argued in March of 1818. Daniel Webster and Joseph Hopkinson appeared in behalf of the old board of trustees, Webster giving the principal argument. Strangely enough, much of Webster 's presentation dealt with the bill of rights in the New Hampshire constitution. In his discussion of the federal Constitution, he placed his heaviest stress on the view that the college was a private corporation, whose charter of 1769 conferred on the original incorporators rights which the legislature could not abrogate.

When the arguments were over, Marshall announced that some of the Justices had not yet come to a decision and that the case would be continued. In the ensuing months, the friends of Dartmouth College carried on a campaign designed to assist the Justices who were beset by doubts to resolve them in behalf of the college. Chancellor Kent was won over to the cause and was persuaded to use his influence with certain members of the Supreme Court. The other side became sufficiently alarmed to employ the services of William Pinkney, one of the most distinguished lawyers of the day. However, on the second of February, 1819, as Pinkney was about to move for a reargument, Marshall, pretending not to see the lawyer, announced that the Court had reached a decision and began to read his opinion.

II

Even before relating the circumstances which brought the case to the Supreme Court, Chief Justice Marshall speaks of the

[8] 1 New Hampshire Rep. 111, 132, 117, 119.

"delicacy" of the constitutional issue facing the Court. But the paragraph is more than a confession of judicial humility; it prepares the way for the unique manner in which the decision was fashioned:

> This court can be insensible neither to the magnitude nor delicacy of this question. The validity of a legislative act is to be examined; and the opinion of the highest law tribunal of a State is to be revised: an opinion which carries with it intrinsic evidence of the diligence, of the ability, and the integrity with which it was formed. On more than one occasion, this Court has expressed the cautious circumspection with which it approaches the consideration of such questions; and has declared, that, in no doubtful case, would it pronounce a legislative act to be contrary to the constitution. But the American people have said, in the constitution of the United States, that "No State shall pass any bill of attainder, *ex post facto law,* or law impairing the obligation of contracts." In the same instrument they have also said, "that the judicial power shall extend to all cases in law and equity arising under the constitution." On the judges of this Court, then, is imposed the high and solemn duty of protecting, from even legislative violation, those contracts which the constitution of our country has placed beyond legislative control; and, however irksome the task may be, this is a duty from which we dare not shrink.[9]

From this statement of "cautious circumspection" Marshall moves immediately to a review of the origins of the royal charter establishing Dartmouth College and the attempt of the legislature to reform the institution. This recital leads him to conclude that "It can require no argument to prove that the circumstances of this case constitute a contract." [10] He then goes on to examine the question whether the charter, as a "complete and legitimate

---

[9] 4 Wheat. 518, 625.

[10] Marshall seeks to justify his assertion that the charter is a contract in the following words: "An application is made to the crown for a charter to incorporate a religious and literary institution. In the application, it is stated that large contributions have been made for the object, which will be conferred on the corporation, as soon as it shall be created. The charter is granted, and on its faith the property is conveyed. Surely in this transaction every ingredient of a complete and legitimate contract is to be found." *Ibid.,* p. 627.

John Marshall, by Chester Harding.
(Boston Athenaeum, photograph by G. M. Cushing)

Richmond March 27.

My dear Sir

I have a nephew a son of Major
Taylor who is at school in Kentucky under the direction of my brother Doctor
Marshall. He has written to me for some
books which I cannot procure here neither
& send them could not without leave to
afford to be conveyed from this to —
I take the liberty to ask the favor of you
to purchase them for me in Philadel phia
& have them with the bookseller packed up
to be delivered to the order of Doctor Marshall.
The books I wish to purchase are Enumerating in
Latin, Longinus Liber & Demosthenes in Greek,
also Xenophon retreat of the 10.000.
Be so good as to send the bookseller receipt for
the money and it is to be charged in an even
ton account. I enclose the inclosed to defray
their purchase immediately remit the residue.

27 march 1819
Off Gen. Marshall
Sam A. Barcom — Corner 6' & Carpenter Street —

Letter from John Marshall to Bushrod Washington, March 27, 1819.
(Reproduced by courtesy of College of William and Mary, Williamsburg, Virginia)

Richmond March 27th

My dear Sir

I have a nephew a son of Major Taylor who is at school in Kentucky under the direction of my brother Doctor Marshall. He has written to me for some books which I cannot procure here & which if I had them could not without much difficulty be conveyed from this place. I take the liberty to ask the favor of you to purchase them for me in Philadelphia & leave them with the bookseller packed up to be delivered to the order of Doctor Marshall. The books I wish to purchase are Terence & Livy in Latin, Longinus, Thucydides & Demosthenes in Greek; also Exenophons retreat of the 10,000. Be so good as to send the booksellers receipt for the money, as it is to be inserted in an executors account. Should the inclosed be insufficient I will immediately remit the residue. I will thank you also to pay Delaplain four dollars for me & take his receipt for the same for the last half volume. I believe it is the third.

Great dissatisfaction has been given to the politicians of Virginia by our opinion on the bank question. They have no objection to a decision in favor of the bank, since the good patriots who administer the government wished it, & would probably have been seriously offended with us had we dared to have decided otherwise, but they required an obsequious, silent opinion without reason. That would have been satisfactory, but our heretical reasoning is pronounced most damnable. We shall be denounced bitterly in the papers & as not a word will be said on the other side we shall be undoubtedly condemned as a pack of consolidating aristocratics. The legislature & executive who have enacted the law but who have power & places to bestow will escape with impunity, while the poor court who have nothing to give & of whom nobody is afraid bears all the obloquy of the measure.

We are in great distress here for money. Many of our merchants stop—a thing which was long unknown & was totally unexpected in Richmond.

Farewell,
    I am dear Sir,

                        J. Marshall

The Honble, Bushrod Washington, Philadelphia

Philadelphia
Aug. 18, 1792

Sir

I am happy to be able, at length, to send you answers to the objections which were communicated in your letter of the 29th of July.

They have unavoidably been drawn in haste, too much so, to do perfect justice to the subject, and have been copied just as they flowed from my heart and pen, without revision or correction. You will observe, that here and there some severity appears. I have not fortitude enough always to hear with calmness, calumnies, which necessarily include me, as a principal Agent in the measures censured, of the falsehood of which, I have the most unqualified consciousness. I trust that I shall always be able to bear, as I ought, imputations of errors of judgment; but I acknowledge that I cannot be intirely patient under charges, which impeach the integrity of my public conduct. I feel that I merit them in no degree; and expressions of indignation sometimes escape me, in spite of every effort to suppress them. I rely on your goodness for the proper allowances.

With high respect and the most affectionate attachment, I have the honor to be

Sir

Your most obedient servant,
Alexander Hamilton

The President of the United States

Philadelphia Aug. 18. 1792

C +

Sir

 I am happy to be able, at length,
to send you, an answer to the objections, which were
communicated in your letter of the 29th of July.

 They have unavoidably been drawn
in haste, too much so, to do perfect justice to
the subject, and have been copied just as they
flowed from my heart and pen, without revision
or correction. You will observe, that here and there
some severity appears — I have not fortitude
enough always to hear with calmness, calumnies
which necessarily include me, as a principal
Agent in the measures censured; of the
falsehood of which, I have the most
unqualified consciousness. I trust that I
shall always be able to bear, as I ought,
imputations of errors of Judgment; but I
acknowlege that I cannot be intirely
patient under charges, which impeach the

integrity of my public motives or conduct. I feel, that I merit them in no degree; and expressions of indignation sometimes escape me, in spite of every effort to suppress them. I rely on your goodness for the proper allowance.

With high respect and the most affectionate attachment, I have the honor to be

Sir

Your most Obedient
& humble servant

Alexander Hamilton

The President of the United States

Letter from Alexander Hamilton to the President of the United States, August 18, 1792.
(*Reproduced from the Collections of the Library of Congress*)

Alexander Hamilton, by Ezra Ames. (*Union College, Schenectady, New York*)

contract," is protected by the Constitution of the United States. The analysis he pursues shows Marshall at his boldest as an inventor of constitutional theory—constitutional theory offered in support of deeply held economic and social precepts.

Marshall begins by making a concession to those who felt that the contract clause did not apply to the case. It was true that the framers of the Constitution did not intend to "render immutable" a state's civil or governmental institutions. The contract clause, in its "more limited sense," protects only contracts which concern "property, or some object of value, and confer rights which may be asserted in a court of justice." Marshall was assuming that all parties to the controversy accepted these propositions but disagreed only on their application.

The decision as to which of the rival boards of trustees was entitled to control Dartmouth College must, therefore, depend on the view to be taken of the royal charter and of the nature of the institution it created. The alternative views are presented by Marshall in such a way as to leave no doubt of the choice open to the Court. If the charter were merely a grant of "political power" which led to the establishment of a civil institution, and if the funds were "public property," the legislature of the State of New Hampshire would be free to modify the college's administration as it saw fit—"to act according to its own judgment, unrestrained by any limitation of its power imposed by the constitution of the United States." [11] But Marshall concludes that

[11] "If the act of incorporation be a grant of political power, if it create a civil institution to be employed in the administration of the government, or if the funds of the college be public property, or if the State of New Hampshire, as a government, be alone interested in its transactions, the subject is one in which the legislature of the State may act according to its own judgment, unrestrained by any limitation of its power imposed by the constitution of the United States.

"But if this be a private eleemosynary institution, endowed with a capacity to take property for objects unconnected with government, whose funds are bestowed by individuals on the faith of the charter; if the donors have stipulated for the future disposition and management of those funds in the manner prescribed by themselves; there may be more difficulty in the case, although neither the persons who have made these stipulations, nor those for whose benefit they were made, should be parties to the cause. Those who are no longer interested in the property, may yet retain such an interest in the preservation of their own arrangements, as to have a right to insist, that those

Dartmouth College was a "private eleemosynary institution, endowed with a capacity to take property for objects unconnected with government," whose funds were given by private individuals on the promise, implicit in the charter, that the college would be administered in accordance with its original provisions. In his attempt to distinguish between private and public corporations, Marshall was thus echoing the argument presented by Webster:

> There are diverse sorts of corporations; and it may be safely admitted, that the legislature has more power over some, than over other. Some corporations are for governmental and political arrangements; such for example as cities, counties, and the towns in New England. These may be changed and modified as public convenience may require, due regard being always had to the rights of property. . . . It [Dartmouth College] is an eleemosynary corporation. It is a private charity originally founded and endowed by an individual, with a charter obtained for it at his request, for the better administration of his charity. . . . A college is as much a private corporation as a hospital; especially a college founded as this was, by private bounty.[12]

To show the charter's "true character" Marshall traces the origin of the college in some detail. He emphasizes the fact that Dr. Eleazar Wheelock's success in establishing Dartmouth College was made possible by the generosity of private donors in England and by the gift of land by persons interested in having the college located in the area. The conclusion to be drawn from this history is that Dartmouth College was really endowed by private individuals for purposes contemplated by its founders. "It is, then, an eleemosynary, and as far as respects its funds, a private corporation." Though education is "an object of national concern" and a "proper subject of legislation," it does not follow that

arrangements shall be held sacred. Or, if they have themselves disappeared, it becomes a subject of serious and anxious inquiry, whether those whom they have legally empowered to represent them forever, may not assert all the rights which they possessed, while in being; whether, if they be without personal representatives who may feel injured by a violation of the compact, the trustees be not so completely their representatives in the eye of the law, as to stand in their place, not only as respects the government of the college, but also as respects the maintenance of the college charter." *Ibid.*, pp. 629–630.

[12] Taken from Webster's argument for the plaintiff in error, March 10 and 11, 1818. 4 Wheat. 518, 562–563.

every teacher becomes a "public officer" and that donations for the support of education become "public property."

Thus far in his analysis of the case, it is quite clear that the Chief Justice was voicing the individualist's view that the trustees of Dartmouth College were entitled to continue to exercise the rights vested in them as the successors of the persons whose initiative and bounty had led to the creation of the college. But of course the trustees were acting not as individuals, but as members of a corporate body. For all practical purposes, it was the corporation which served as the instrument for perpetuating the rights and interests of the donors and founders of the college. It was this equation of private rights with corporate privileges which made the constitutional theory embodied by Marshall in his opinion in the *Dartmouth College* case so serviceable to the modern industrial corporation. That theory required a certain conception of the corporation which is set forth by him at considerable length:

A corporation is an artificial being, invisible, intangible, and existing only in contemplation of law. Being the mere creature of law, it possesses only those properties which the charter of its creation confers upon it, either expressly, or as incidental to its very existence. These are such as are supposed best calculated to effect the object for which it was created. Among the most important are immortality, and if the expression may be allowed, individuality; properties, by which a perpetual succession of many persons are considered as the same, and may act as a single individual. They enable a corporation to manage its own affairs, and to hold property without the perplexing intricacies, the hazardous and endless necessity, of perpetual conveyances for the purpose of transmitting it from hand to hand. It is chiefly for the purpose of clothing bodies of men, in succession, with these qualities and capacities, that corporations were invented, and are in use. By these means, a perpetual succession of individuals are capable of acting for the promotion of the particular object, like one immortal being. But this being does not share in the civil government of the country, unless that be the purpose for which it was created. Its immortality no more confers on it political power, or a political character, than immortality would confer such power or character on a natural person. It is no more a State instrument, than a natural person exercising the same power would be. If, then, a natural person, employed by individuals in the education of youth, or for the government of a seminary in which youth is educated, would not become a public officer, or be considered as a member of the civil government, how is it, that this artificial being, created by law, for the purpose of being employed by the same individuals for the same purposes, should become a part of the civil government of the country? [13]

Corporations are usually established for purposes which the government deems good for the community, and it is this expected "benefit" to the public which is the "consideration" justifying the grant of the privileges. It is by incorporating under the charter that "public spirited individuals" can be secure in the knowledge that the funds they contribute will be used for the purposes they had in mind when they launched the institution. The grant, given as it was for adequate consideration, does not confer on government the right to alter the charter of the corporation or to modify the administration of the funds. "From the fact, then, that a charter of incorporation has been granted, nothing can be inferred which changes the character of the institution or transfers to the government any new power over it." [14] Nor does the mere act of incorporation transform the college into a civil or governmental institution. Dartmouth College was created for purely private purposes and, whatever public good may come from it, was not designed by the donors and founders for the special benefit of New Hampshire, but was the result of having an institution of learning in the area: "The particular interests of New Hampshire never entered into the minds of the donors, never constituted a motive for their donation. The propagation of the Christian religion among the savages, and the dissemination of useful knowledge among the youth of the country, were the avowed and sole objects of their contributions." [15]

[13] *Ibid.*, pp. 636–637.
[14] *Ibid.*, p. 638.
[15] *Ibid.*, p. 640. Marshall recalls that even the choice of the particular location for the college was purely fortuitous: "Even the site of the college was selected, not for the sake of New Hampshire, but because it was 'most subservient to the great ends in view,' and because liberal donations of land were offered by the proprietors, on condition that the institution should be

III

Marshall finally reaches the one question about which, he acknowledges, "more doubt" has been expressed than on any of the other issues he has discussed. This was the question whether the charter of 1769 may be considered a contract in the light of the fact that the original donors of money and land were no longer able to challenge the revisions the legislature was seeking to make. Indeed, neither the founders of the college nor the "fluctuating" students—no one of whom has "a vested interest in the institution which can be asserted in a court of justice"—were in a position to object to the changes in the charter wrought by the legislature. As Marshall himself paraphrases the argument, "The trustees alone complain, and the trustees have no beneficial interest to be protected." Was the charter nevertheless a contract protected by the Constitution, or did the contract clause apply only to contracts in which the parties had a beneficial or vested interest?

After giving assurance that the Court had "bestowed" on this problem "the most deliberate consideration," the Chief Justice proceeds to say that the contributions of money and land were not for the benefit or "profit" of the donors or founders but for the broad educational mission they had in mind. The "immortal being created by the Crown" was the instrument for achieving and perpetuating the original design. It therefore followed that it is the corporation which must be regarded as the continuing "representative" of the rights and interests of the donors and founders. In Marshall's words, "The corporation is the assignee of their rights, stands in their place, and distributes their bounty, as they would themselves have distributed it, had they been immortal." [16] Though not of the usual variety, its charter is nevertheless a contract not to be altered by the legislature.

But before announcing that the Court found even such a contract to be protected by the Constitution against impairment by the legislatures of the states, the Chief Justice makes two concessions to the facts of history which, at first glance, would

there established. The real advantages from the location of the college, are, perhaps, not less considerable to those on the west, than to those on the east side of the Connecticut river." *Ibid.*

[16] *Ibid.*, p. 642.

appear to undermine the basis for the Court's conclusion. It turns out, however, that these concessions serve his larger purpose. Marshall is forced to admit that Parliament, as a legally unlimited legislative body, would have been free to modify the provisions of the charter of 1769. "According to the theory of the British Constitution," he writes, "their parliament is omnipotent. To annul corporate rights might give a shock to public opinion, which that government has chosen to avoid; but its power is not questioned." [17] In short, though "the perfidy of the transaction would have been universally acknowledged," there is no question that Parliament could have rescinded the charter. Regardless of Parliament's potential power over the charter, at the time it was granted "it would have been deemed sacred by all." Moreover, nothing had happened since 1769 to change the character of the charter as embodying private rights entitled to be exercised perpetually. "In reason, in justice, and in law, it is now what it was in 1769." [18]

Turning next to the question whether the Constitution of the United States protected such a contract against legislative tinkering, Marshall admits that it was entirely conceivable that the men who drafted that document did not have in mind the charters of eleemosynary and educational institutions when they wrote the contract clause. He puts it this way: "It is more than possible, that the preservation of rights of this description was not particularly in the view of the framers of the constitution, when the clause under consideration was introduced into that instrument." The framers were no doubt chiefly concerned with the sort of contract impairments common to the age. Still, there was a way of interpreting the clause so as to find room in it for the protection of such contracts as the charter of Dartmouth College.

> It is not enough to say, that this particular case was not in the mind of the Convention, when the article was framed, nor of the American people, when it was adopted. It is necessary to go farther, and to say that, had this particular case been suggested, the language would have been so varied, as to exclude it, or it would have been made a special exception. The case, being within

---

[17] *Ibid.*, p. 643.
[18] *Ibid.*

the words of the rule, must be within its operation likewise, unless there be something in the literal construction so obviously absurd, or mischievous, or repugnant to the general spirit of the instrument, as to justify those who expound the constitution in making it an exception.[19]

Then comes a series of rhetorical questions which clearly point the path of reasoning Marshall was to pursue in attributing to the Constitution, though it says nothing on the subject, an intention to free corporate charters from legislative control:

> In the absence of all authority of this kind, is there, in the nature and reason of the case itself, that which would sustain a construction of the constitution, not warranted by its words? Are contracts of this description of a character to excite so little interest, that we must exclude them from the provision of the constitution, as being unworthy of the attention of those who framed the instrument? Or does public policy so imperiously demand their remaining exposed to legislative alteration, as to compel us, or rather permit us to say, that these words, which were introduced to give stability to contracts, and which in their plain import comprehend this contract, must yet be so construed, as to exclude it? [20]

What, then, made Marshall so sure that the framers of the Constitution would have included college charters within the protection of the contract clause had the matter occurred to them? Dartmouth College, as a private charitable institution, was founded for purposes with which those men were in complete sympathy. All institutions organized for the advancement of learning were alike, and those who wrote the Constitution may be assumed to have intended to facilitate the growth of such institutions. And where is the evidence? Marshall finds it in the provision of the Constitution which authorizes Congress to promote the arts and sciences: "Congress shall have the power to promote the Progress of Science and useful Arts, by securing for limited Times to Authors and Inventors the exclusive Right to their respective Writings and Discoveries." [21]

[19] *Ibid.*, pp. 644–645.
[20] *Ibid.*, p. 645.
[21] *Constitution*, Art. I, sec. 8, par. 8.

Before concluding, Chief Justice Marshall discusses the effect of the American Revolution on private rights, particularly property. "It is too clear to require the support of argument," he states emphatically, "that all contracts and rights respecting property remained unchanged by the revolution." But this view of the Revolution raised a rather important question as to the effect of the struggle upon the authority of the newly independent states to regulate property rights. If it were true, as Marshall concedes, that "the powers of government" were transferred from King and Parliament to "the people of New Hampshire," did it not logically follow that the legislature of the state had the legal right to dissolve or modify private contracts, in the same way as did the government of Great Britain? Marshall disposes of this complex and subtle problem in political and legal theory rather cavalierly. He merely asserts that until the federal Constitution was adopted, New Hampshire's power to repeal charters was subject to the restrictions in its own constitution; quickly adding, "but the constitution of the United States has imposed this additional limitation, that the Legislature of a State shall pass no act 'impairing the obligation of contracts.' " In other words, the difference between the position of Parliament and that of the New Hampshire legislature, with respect to the rights of property, is that the state legislatures are subject to constitutional limitations on the power to pass laws.

It would thus appear, in the final analysis, that Marshall was able to reason his way to the invalidation of the New Hampshire act changing the charter of Dartmouth College by a rather "forced construction" of the contract clause. Let it be noted at once, however, that according to the Chief Justice it would be a "forced construction" of the Constitution not to infer from the provision authorizing Congress to advance the arts and sciences an intent to safeguard the charters of institutions of learning from being tampered with by legislatures.[22]

---

[22] Marshall's exact words were: "If the insignificance of the object [the security of 'ordinary contracts between man and man'] does not require that we should exclude contracts respecting it from the protection of the constitution; neither, as we conceive, is the policy of leaving them subject to legislative alteration so apparent, as to require a forced construction of that instrument in order to effect it." 4 Wheat. 518, 647.

Having found the Constitution spacious enough to include purposes not explicitly envisioned, Marshall could go on to say that it was unconstitutional for New Hampshire to adopt a law which, in effect, substituted "the will of the State . . . for the will of the donors." [23] Practically speaking, the state had destroyed the charter of 1769, an instrument by means of which the founders, Marshall stressed, had "contracted for a system, which should, as far as human foresight can provide, retain forever the government of the literary institution they had formed, in the hands of persons approved by themselves." [24]

IV

Even Thomas Jefferson was drawn into the controversy over Dartmouth College. On June 6, 1816, Governor William Plumer, who at the time was also leader of the Jeffersonians in New Hampshire, sent a message to the legislature outlining the basic issue posed by the dispute. "All literary institutions, like everything human, if not duly attended to," he declared, "are subject to decay." He condemned in particular the provision of the royal charter which vested in the Board of Trustees the power to perpetuate itself:

> This last principle is hostile to the spirit and genius of a free government. Sound policy therefore requires that the mode of election should be changed and that Trustees in future should be elected by some other body of men. . . . The College was formed for the public good, not for the benefit or emolument of its Trustees; and the right to amend and improve acts of incorporation of this nature has been exercised by all governments, both monarchical and republican. [25]

When Jefferson wrote to Plumer to thank him for sending along a copy of the message, he took the occasion to repeat sen-

---

[23] *Ibid.*, p. 652. "The whole power of governing the college is transferred from trustees appointed according to the will of the founder, expressed in the charter, to the executive of New-Hampshire. The management and application of the funds of this eleemosynary institution, which are placed by the donors in the hands of trustees named in this charter, and empowered to perpetuate themselves, are placed by this act under the control of the government of the State." *Ibid.*

[24] *Ibid.*, p. 653.

[25] Quoted in Corwin, *John Marshall and the Constitution*, pp. 156–157.

timents which show that Plumer's remonstrance to the legislature echoed some of the Virginian's deepest convictions: "The idea that institutions established for the use of the nation cannot be touched nor modified, even to make them answer their end . . . is most absurd. . . . Yet our lawyers and priests generally inculcate this doctrine, and suppose that preceding generations held the earth more freely than we do; had a right to impose laws on us, unalterable by ourselves; . . . in fine, that the earth belongs to the dead and not the living." [26]

A fundamentally opposite point of view is, of course, implicit in Marshall's opinion in the *Dartmouth College* case. In the next to the last paragraph of that opinion, the Chief Justice succeeds in summing up the long and winding course of the decision in one sentence. The Court decided the case as it did, he informs us, because it was "of opinion, on general principles, that in these private eleemosynary institutions, the body corporate, as possessing the whole legal and equitable interest, and completely representing the donors, for the purpose of executing the trust, has rights which are protected by the constitution." [27] Marshall shared Webster's view that the principles enunciated by the Court would "affect" not Dartmouth College alone, but all institutions of learning. This appeal to the Court was made by Webster near the close of his argument, on March 11, 1819. It is part of his eloquent peroration:

> The case before the Court is not of ordinary importance nor of every day occurrence. It affects not this college, but every college, and all the literary institutions of the country. They have flourished hitherto, and have become in a high degree respectable and useful to the community. They have all a common principle of existence, the inviolability of their charters. It will be a dangerous, a most dangerous expedient, to hold these institutions subject to the rise and fall of popular parties, and the fluctuations of public opinion. If the franchise may be at any time taken away, or impaired, the property also may be taken away or its use perverted. Benefactors will have no certainty of effecting the ob-

[26] Thomas Jefferson to William Plumer, July 21, 1816. *The Writings of Thomas Jefferson*, Washington, ed., VII, 19.
[27] 4 Wheat. 518, 654.

ject of their bounty; and learned men will be deterred from de-
voting themselves to the service of such institutions, from the
precarious title of their offices. Colleges and halls will be deserted
by all better spirits, and become a theatre for the contention of
politics. Party and faction will be cherished in the places conse-
crated to piety and learning. These consequences are neither remote nor possible only. They are certain and immediate.[28]

In an age when more and more of America's business activities
were coming to be conducted in corporate form, the doctrine of
the inviolability of charters was bound to be of importance to
corporate interests. Their resistance to legislative attempts to
alter their privileges was given constitutional sanction. Yet it is
not easy to assess the ultimate economic impact of Marshall's
opinion in the *Dartmouth College* case. That judicial concern for
the security of property and credit helped foster the atmosphere
in which American business flourished is clear enough.[29]

But the relation between Marshall's apotheosis of property
rights conferred by corporate charters and the burst of capitalist
activity in the United States is sometimes discussed as if the
causal connection between the two phenomena were direct and
inescapable.[30] The coincidence lends itself to what might be
called over-intellectualized treatment at the expense of more

[28] 4 Wheat. 518, 598–599.

[29] One of the best descriptions of the economic roots of Marshall's legal
philosophy will be found in the essay by Joseph Dorfman, "John Marshall:
Political Economist," reprinted in *Chief Justice John Marshall: A Reappraisal*,
W. Melville Jones, ed., pp. 125–144, particularly pp. 126–127.

[30] Marshall has also been blamed for the corruption of state legislatures
during the heyday of business expansion. The doctrine that a corporation's
charter was an inviolable contract made charters so valuable, it has been
suggested, that business promoters were encouraged to stop at nothing to
secure favorable privileges. A rather picturesque recent statement of this view
is that of Professor Wallace Mendelson: "Conservative tradition insists that
by putting the sanctity of 'contracts' above other considerations of ethics and
public welfare, Marshall and his associates promoted economic stability. Would
it not be more accurate to suggest rather that they encouraged the flagrant corruption of state politics and reckless waste of natural resources that marked
the nineteenth century? Surely judicial protection of fraud in the Yazoo land
scandal paved the way for the Robber Barons and their Great Barbecue at the
expense of the American people." *Capitalism, Democracy, and the Supreme
Court* (New York: Appleton-Century-Crofts, 1960), pp. 24–25.

attention to the natural forces at work in American society. When
the admiration for the Chief Justice is added to a penchant for
sweeping generalization, the result is the kind of exaggerated
claim we read in Beveridge. After noting that at first interest in
the *Dartmouth College* case was confined to New Hampshire
and Massachusetts, Beveridge quotes a contemporary judgment
about the importance of the decision which he sees as fully confirmed by subsequent events. "Perhaps no judicial proceedings
in this country ever involved more important consequences . . .
than the case of Dartmouth College," *The North American Review* had observed in 1820.[31] Beveridge's elaboration of this estimate is as follows:

> Important, indeed, were the "consequences" of the Dartmouth
> decision. Everywhere corporations were springing up in response
> to the necessity for larger and more constant business units and
> because of the convenience and profit of such organizations.
> Marshall's opinion was a tremendous stimulant to this natural
> economic tendency. It reassured investors in corporate securities
> and gave confidence and steadiness to the business world. It is un-
> deniable and undenied that America could not have been de-
> veloped so rapidly and solidly without the power which the law
> as announced by Marshall gave to industrial organization.[32]

Beveridge then suggests an even more significant consequence of
the *Dartmouth* decision:

> One result of his opinion was, for the period, of even higher
> value than the encouragement it gave to private enterprise and
> the steadiness it brought to business generally; it aligned on the
> side of Nationalism all powerful economic forces operating
> through corporate organization. A generation passed before rail-
> way development began in America; but Marshall lived to see the
> first stage of the evolution of that mighty element in American
> commercial, industrial, and social life; and all of that force, ex-
> cept the part of it which was directly connected with and under
> the immediate influence of the slave power, was aggressively and
> most effectively Nationalist.

[31] Quoted in Beveridge, *The Life of John Marshall*, IV, 276.
[32] *Ibid.*

That this came to be the fact was due to Marshall's Dartmouth opinion more than to any other single cause. The same was true of other industrial corporate organizations.[33]

Even more intriguing is the question as to what would have been the result of Marshall's *Dartmouth* opinion had America's lawmakers failed to take advantage of the escape route suggested by Justice Story. It is impossible to tell, that is to say, what the impact of Marshall's doctrine would have been had legislatures refrained from inserting clauses retaining the right to change or even to repeal charter provisions in the future. So widespread had this practice become that to many it began to look as if the principle that a charter is a contract had no practical value. Speaking in 1885, with the so-called *Granger* cases in mind,[34] one New England lawyer summed up the declining importance of the *Dartmouth College* case in a single grim if colorful comment: "This historic cause has been embalmed in spices, and laid carefully away upon a shelf, like the corpse of an Egyptian king." He called attention to a "very anomalous" situation:

[33] *Ibid.,* IV, 276–277. In arriving at this conclusion, Beveridge seems to have been influenced by the views of an eminent American historian and a distinguished legal scholar from England. "John Fiske does not greatly exaggerate," writes Beveridge, "in his assertion that the law as to corporate franchises declared by Marshall, in subjecting to the National Constitution every charter granted by a State 'went farther, perhaps, than any other in our history toward limiting State sovereignty and extending the Federal jurisdiction.' " (Beveridge was quoting from Fiske's *Essays, Historical and Literary*.) And again: "Sir Henry Sumner Maine has some ground for his rather dogmatic statement that the principle of Marshall's opinion 'is the basis of credit of many of the great American Railway Incorporations,' and 'has . . . secured full play to the economical forces by which the achievement of cultivating the soil of the North American Continent has been performed.' " (Beveridge was quoting from Maine's *Popular Government*.) *Ibid.,* IV, 277.

[34] 94 U.S. 113 to 186 (1877). Justices Field and Strong dissented in all these cases. The leading case was *Munn v. Illinois,* in which the Court, speaking through Chief Justice Morrison R. Waite, sustained the constitutionality of an Illinois law prescribing maximum rates for grain elevators. Waite rested the decision on the concept of business or property "clothed with a public interest," which he defined as follows: "When, therefore, one devotes his property to a use in which the public has an interest, he, in effect, grants to the public an interest in that use, and must submit to be controlled by the public for the common good, to the extent of the interest he has thus created. He may withdraw his grant by discontinuing the use; but, so long as he maintains the use, he must submit to the control." 94 U.S. 113, 126.

After the Supreme Court of the United States, in an important case, ably argued, and carefully considered, has given a solemn construction to a constitutional provision, as affording a perpetual guarantee of the permanence of corporate charters in their original integrity, the protection so assured has turned out to be practically useless, and corporations are as fully at the mercy of State Legislatures as though the *Dartmouth College* case had never been decided.[85]

Taken together, however, Marshall's contract clause opinions continued to serve as a fruitful source of ideas for those who were interested in giving constitutional protection to the rights claimed by the property owner and the business corporation in the United States. The least that can be said is that these opinions contributed substantially to the creation of the attitude which equated constitutional liberty with freedom from governmental restraint for the rights of property. One of the more perceptive assessments of their significance has come from the pen of Benjamin F. Wright— an assessment cast in terms of economic as well as political theory: "No group of his [Marshall's] cases so well illustrates his conservatism as does that concerned with the contract clause. By employing a far broader conception of contract than had been prevalent in 1787, and by combining this conception with the principles of eighteenth century natural law, he was able to make of the contract clause a mighty instrument for the protection of the rights of private property."[36]

[85] Aldace F. Walker, "A Legal Mummy, or the Present Status of the Dartmouth College case," an address delivered at the annual meeting of the Vermont Bar Association, Montpelier, Vt., Oct. 28, 1885. (Manuscript in the Harvard Law Library.) Mr. Walker described the actual status of the case as follows: "The result, therefore, is that the Dartmouth College case has been practically nullified; the protection given to corporations thereby has become nugatory to every intent; and although the question arising in their favor under the constitutional clause is still frequently raised, the cases are very rare, if not wholly non-existent, in which a decision can be obtained adjudging void any conceivable legislative interference whatever." *Ibid.*

[36] Wright, *op. cit.*, p. 28.

8

"Intended to Endure
for Ages to Come"

Perhaps no other facet of Marshall's work on the Supreme Court
reveals him to have been a conscious disciple of the Hamiltonian
brand of nationalism as distinctly as do the opinions in which he
vindicates the authority of the central government in the face of
formidable assertions of their rights by the states. By construing
liberally the undefined powers the Constitution delegates to
Congress, he unleashed a range of constitutional possibilities for
national control of American life far beyond the horizons he
himself was able to see. Of no pronouncement is this true more
than of his imposing opinion in the famous case of *McCulloch
v. Maryland*.[1]

"If we regard at once the greatness of the questions at issue in
the particular case, the influence of the opinion, and the large
method and clear and skillful manner in which it is worked
out, there is nothing so fine as the opinion in *McCulloch v.
Maryland*." This was the considered judgment of James Bradley
Thayer, a judgment he voiced on the occasion of the centenary
of Marshall's accession to the Chief Justiceship.[2] The *McCulloch*
opinion has also been described as "perhaps the most celebrated
judicial utterance in the annals of the English speaking world." [3]
And Beveridge says that it has "so decisively influenced the growth

[1] 4 Wheat. 316 (1819).
[2] Thayer, *John Marshall*, p. 85.
[3] William Draper Lewis, *Great American Lawyers* (Philadelphia: John C.
Winston Co., 1907), II, 363.

of the Nation that, by many, it is considered as only second in importance to the Constitution itself." [4]

So fulsome and universal has been the praise which posterity has heaped upon Marshall's achievement in *McCulloch v. Maryland* that some might suppose the case was the occasion for the announcement of new principles which were being boldly stated for the first time. Actually, of course, the case was concerned with issues which divided the nation's leaders at the very inception of the Republic. Indeed, Marshall readily acknowledges that the questions before the Court were not new. In the background lurked the great political and constitutional differences between Hamilton and Jefferson, the conflict over economic policy, the issue of "loose" versus "strict" construction of the Constitution, and even the danger that the continuing antagonism between Nation and States might some day erupt into outright civil war. That Chief Justice Marshall was profoundly convinced that the case before the Court was fraught with fateful consequences for the American people is evident in the opening sentences of his opinion:

> In the case now to be determined, the defendant, a sovereign State, denies the obligation of a law enacted by the legislature of the Union, and the plaintiff, on his part, contests the validity of an act which has been passed by the legislature of that State. The constitution of our country, in its most interesting and vital parts, is to be considered; the conflicting powers of the government of the Union and of its members, as marked in that constitution, are to be discussed; and an opinion given, which may essentially influence the great operations of the government. No tribunal can approach such a question without a deep sense of its importance, and of the awful responsibility involved in its decision. But it must be decided peacefully, or remain a source of hostile legislation, perhaps of a hostility of a still more serious nature; and if it is to be so decided, by this tribunal alone can the decision be made. On the Supreme Court of the United States has the constitution of our country devolved this important duty.[5]

However "majestic"—as Beveridge has characterized them— these words happen to be, they also summarize, quite accurately

---

[4] Beveridge, *The Life of John Marshall,* IV, 168.
[5] 4 Wheat. 316, 400–401.

and simply, the precise issue before the Court.[6] Thirty years after Hamilton had persuaded both President and Congress that there was ample authority under the Constitution to establish a national bank, the State of Maryland was asking the Marshall Court to rule that no such power existed. On the other hand, should the Court hold that the bank had been lawfully created, Maryland was demanding the right to tax its operations anyway.

Thus did the Court find itself in the unenviable position of having to pass on the validity of one of the most far-reaching economic measures of the Washington Administration, a measure which was supported by a precedent-setting gloss upon the Constitution advanced by the legislative and executive branches of the government. Important financial and business arrangements flowed from the action of Congress in creating the first National Bank. With his characteristic concern for the security of property, Marshall takes note of the grave economic issue at stake: "An exposition of the constitution, deliberately established by legislative acts, on the faith of which an immense property has been advanced, ought not to be lightly disregarded." [7] The same anxiety was voiced by Webster at the very start of his argument for the bank. "The mere discussion of such a question may most essentially affect the value of a vast amount of private property." [8]

I

Acting on the proposals embodied in Hamilton's "Report on a National Bank," Congress, in February 1791, established the Bank of the United States, giving it a twenty-year charter. But in 1811 it refused to renew the charter. Because of the financial

[6] Beveridge, *op. cit.* IV, 290. Where Beveridge was impressed by the high literary appeal of the trenchant words with which Marshall opens his opinion in *McCulloch v. Marylad*, Charles G. Haines discerned a much more strategic motive. "As was his custom when issues of grave political import were involved," Professor Haines has written, "Marshall began by the making of assumptions on seriously contested points which resolved the questions in dispute in favor of the federal government." More specifically, the opening comments were Marshall's way of rejecting the argument "frequently asserted by the States, particularly from 1810 to 1816, that the Supreme Court did not have jurisdiction in such a case." Haines, *The Role of the Supreme Court in American Government and Politics*, p. 354.

[7] 4 Wheat. 316, 401.

[8] *Ibid.*, p. 322.

upheaval following the War of 1812,[9] however, Congress was induced to incorporate the second Bank of the United States in 1816, the institution against which Andrew Jackson was to aim his wrath not too many years later. Following the dissolution of the first National Bank in 1811, there sprang up numerous state banks. Albert Gallatin, who served as Secretary of the Treasury from the start of Jefferson's first administration until May 1813, described the effect of the dissolution of the first National Bank as follows:

> The creation of new state banks . . . was a natural consequence of the dissolution of the Bank of the United States. And, as is usual under such circumstances, the expectation of great profits gave birth to a much greater number than was wanted. . . . That increase took place on the eve of and during a war which did nearly annihilate the exports and both the foreign and coasting trade. And, as the salutary regulating power of the Bank of the United States no longer existed, the issues were accordingly increased much beyond what the other circumstances already mentioned rendered necessary.[10]

These state banks resented and resisted the competition and policies of the local branches of the National Bank when it was reestablished in 1816. The legislatures of several states responded to these pressures by enacting laws intended to hamper the operations of the second Bank of the United States. By then the bank had come to be widely blamed for the economic distress in the years after the war. In 1818 the Maryland legislature adopted a statute requiring banks not chartered by itself to print their notes on special paper to be purchased from the state, or as a substitute, to pay an annual tax of $15,000. McCulloch, the cashier of the Baltimore branch of the bank, refused to comply with these provisions, and when the state courts found against him, he took the case to the Supreme Court.

When the issues were joined before the Supreme Court of

---

[9] For a fuller account of the conditions which impelled Congress to recharter the bank, see Bray Hammond, *Banks and Politics in America* (Princeton: Princeton University Press, 1957), ch. 9; also Beveridge, *op. cit.*, IV, ch. IV.

[10] Quoted in Hammond, *op. cit.*, p. 227.

the United States at its February term in 1819, some of the most towering legal minds in the country found themselves urging on the High Court fundamentally conflicting conceptions of the Constitution. Daniel Webster, William Pinkney, and Attorney General William Wirt spoke in behalf of the bank. Luther Martin, Maryland's Attorney General—who as a delegate to the Constitutional Convention of 1787 had refused to sign the Constitution—Joseph Hopkinson, and Walter Jones argued in behalf of Maryland. The notable presentation of these six distinguished lawyers required nine days to be completed.[11] Yet Marshall was able to deliver his opinion for the Court only three days later—a circumstance which certainly would seem to lend support to Beveridge's conjecture that the Chief Justice had prepared it long before the case was argued. Writes Beveridge:

> Since it is one of the longest of Marshall's opinions and, by general agreement, is considered to be his ablest and most carefully prepared exposition of the Constitution, it seems not unlikely that much of it had been written before the argument. The Court was very busy every day of the session and there was little, if any, time for Marshall to write this elaborate document. The suit against McCulloch had been brought nearly a year before the Supreme Court convened; Marshall undoubtedly learned of it through the newspapers; he was intimately familiar with the basic issue presented by the litigation; and he had ample time to formulate and even to write out his views before the ensuing session of the court. He had, in the opinions of Hamilton and Jefferson, the reasoning on both sides of this fundamental controversy. It appears to be reasonably probable that at least the framework of the opinion in McCulloch *vs.* Maryland was prepared by Marshall when in Richmond during the summer, autumn, and winter of 1818–19.[12]

However plausible the biographer's suspicion may be, it must not be permitted to obscure two rather striking facts about Marshall's opinion in *McCulloch v. Maryland*. In the first place, the opinion was essentially a restatement of the convictions and theories which the Chief Justice had been expressing for decades. On

[11] Feb. 22–27 and March 1–3, 1819.
[12] Beveridge, *op. cit.*, IV, 290.

the other hand, though this fact does not necessarily refute Beveridge, the opinion is replete with evidence of obvious borrowing from the arguments of counsel, particularly those of Webster and Pinkney. It was Webster who had observed that he thought the case for the constitutionality of the National Bank had been practically "exhausted" by Alexander Hamilton.

> This question [whether Congress had the power to incorporate a national bank] arose early after the adoption of the constitution, and was discussed and settled, as far as legislative decision could settle it, in the first Congress. The arguments drawn from the constitution in favor of this power, were stated, and exhausted, in that discussion. They were exhibited, with characteristic perspicuity and force, by the first Secretary of the Treasury, in his report to the President of the United States.[13]

But Marshall, unlike Webster, proceeded to deal with the question with a patience and spirit of elucidation that might have been bestowed on it had it been raised for the first time. Before doing so, he remarks that he would not want to give the impression that "were the question entirely new, the law would be found irreconcilable with the constitution." [14] It is a measure of the importance he was attaching to the fundamental issues raised by the litigation that even before taking up the question whether Congress had the constitutional power to incorporate the bank, Marshall first undertakes to lay to rest the erroneous conception of the Union on which the lawyers for Maryland had built their case. He understood their position to be that the Constitution was to be regarded "not as emanating from the people, but as the act of sovereign and independent States." This is the way he paraphrased their argument: "The powers of the general government, it has been said, are delegated by the States, who alone are truly sovereign; and must be exercised in subordination to the States, who alone possess supreme dominion." [15]

Marshall's polite rejoinder is that "It would be difficult to sustain this proposition." But it may be surmised that he meant to say that it would be "impossible" to prove this theory. He then

[13] 4 Wheat. 316, 322–323.
[14] *Ibid.*, p. 402.
[15] *Ibid.*

reviews the process by which the Constitutional Convention of
1787 was assembled and the process by which the document was
ratified.

As Marshall saw it, the issue was whether the Constitution
was a compact among the states or an instrument of government
ordained by the people of the United States. It was true that the
members of the Convention which drafted the Constitution were
chosen by the state legislatures, but the resolution transmitting
the document to the Congress recommended that the Constitution "be submitted to a convention of delegates, chosen in each
state by the people thereof, . . . for their assent and ratification."
The "people" subsequently assembled in conventions and ratified
the Constitution. The fact that they met in their respective states
—"And where else should they have assembled?"—is of no significance. "No political dreamer was ever wild enough," declares
the Chief Justice, "to think of breaking down the lines which
separate the States, and of compounding the American people
into one common mass." [16] The fact that the people deliberated
within the confines of their respective states did not transform
their action in adopting the Constitution into a decision of the
state governments.

What inference is to be drawn, then, from the circumstance
that the Constitution was ratified by popularly elected conventions? Marshall does not take long in answering this question and
in showing its relevance for the problem posed by the attack on the
constitutionality of the Bank of the United States. "From these conventions," he writes, "the constitution derives its whole authority."
Quoting from the Preamble to the Constitution he goes on to say:

> The government proceeds directly from the people; is "or-
> dained and established" in the name of the people; and is declared
> to be ordained, "in order to form a more perfect union, estab-
> lish justice, ensure domestic tranquility, and secure the blessings
> of liberty to themselves and to their posterity." The assent of the
> States, in their sovereign capacity, is implied in calling a Con-
> vention, and thus submitting that instrument to the people. But
> the people were at perfect liberty to accept or reject it, and their
> act was final. It required not the affirmance, and could not be

[16] *Ibid.*, p. 403.

negatived, by the State governments. The constitution, when thus adopted, was of complete obligation, and bound the State sovereignties.[17]

Speaking as a believer in popular sovereignty, Marshall rejects the argument that the American people had already surrendered the power to govern to the states and had no more to give. "But, surely, the question whether they may resume and modify the powers granted to government does not remain to be settled in this country," he observes tersely. Just as the people were "competent" to form a "league" by the Articles of Confederation, they were equally competent to transform the league into a more "effective government, possessing great and sovereign powers, and acting directly on the people." There then follows the important passage which discloses the reason for the Chief Justice's historical digression: "The government of the Union, then (whatever may be the influence of this fact on the case,) is, emphatically, and truly, a government of the people. In form and in substance it emanates from them. Its powers are granted by them, and are to be exercised directly on them, and for their benefit." [18]

The rest of Marshall's opinion in *McCulloch v. Maryland* might be described as an attempt to demonstrate the practical consequences of the proposition that the American people are the ultimate source of the authority vested by the Constitution in the federal government. Having shown that the government of the Union is indeed "a government of the people," he could go on to examine the scope of its power. Though it may be "acknowledged by all" that the central government established by the Constitution has only those powers actually granted to it, the question as to the "extent" of these "enumerated" or "delegated" powers "is perpetually arising, and will probably continue to arise as long as our system shall exist." When the powers asserted by the States and the national government appear to be

---

[17] *Ibid.,* pp. 403–404.

[18] *Ibid.,* pp. 404–405. For a succinct and provocative analysis of the various theories as to the nature of the American Union, see Alpheus T. Mason, "The Nature of our Federal Union Reconsidered," *Political Science Quarterly,* vol. LXV, no. 4 (Dec. 1950), pp. 502–521. See also Martin Diamond, "The Federalist's View of Federalism," in *Essays in Federalism* (Institute for Studies in Federalism, Claremont Men's College, 1961), pp. 21–66.

in conflict, what must be done is to delineate the jurisdiction of
the two governments. So far as the reach of federal authority
is concerned, the most important principle to keep in mind is
that the central government is "supreme" when it acts within its
lawful province.

"If any one proposition could command the universal assent
of mankind," the Chief Justice proclaims solemnly, "we might
expect it would be this—that the government of the Union, though
limited in its powers, is supreme within its sphere of action. This
would seem to result necessarily from its nature. It is the government of all; its powers are delegated by all; it represents all, and
acts for all." [19] When "the Nation" acts within its proper domain,
it can "bind its component parts," the states. Nor is the "supremacy" of national authority "left to mere reason"—it is commanded
by the "supremacy" clause of the Constitution.[20]

II

At last Marshall was ready to deal with the question whether
Congress, whose laws were "supreme" throughout the United
States, had the necessary authority under the Constitution to
charter the National Bank. He acknowledges immediately that
"Among the enumerated powers we do not find that of establishing a bank or creating a corporation." But the absence of the
specific power to charter banks did not mean that Congress might
not infer the right to do so from one or more of its delegated
powers. After all, there was a fundamental difference between the
Constitution and the Articles of Confederation. Unlike the Articles of Confederation, the Constitution contains no bars to
"incidental or implied powers." It does not demand that "every
power granted shall be expressly or minutely described." Marshall
was here contrasting the Constitution with the section of the
Articles of Confederation providing: "Each state retains its
sovereignty, freedom and independence, and every Power, Juris-

[19] *Ibid.*, p. 405.

[20] "But this question is not left to mere reason: the people have in express
terms, decided it, by saying, 'This constitution, and the laws of the United
States, which shall be made in pursuance thereof,' 'shall be the supreme Law
of the Land,' and by requiring that members of the State legislatures, and
the officers of the executive and judicial departments of the States, shall take
the oath of fidelity to it." *Ibid.*, pp. 405–406.

diction and right, which is not by this confederation expressly delegated to the United States, in Congress assembled." [21]

It was significant that not even the Tenth Amendment—framed by men who had "experienced the embarrassments" resulting from the inclusion of the crippling little adverb "expressly" in the Articles—did not confine the general government to powers explicitly granted.[22] The answer to the question whether a particular power has been delegated to the central government or denied to the states must, therefore, depend on "a fair construction of the whole instrument."

So the way to ascertain the full range of Congress' powers under the Constitution is to look at the document in its entirety. This theory leads Marshall to enunciate his now famous distinction between a mere legal code and the true nature of the American Constitution:

> A constitution, to contain an accurate detail of all the subdivisions of which its great powers will admit, and of all the means by which they may be carried into execution, would partake of the prolixity of a legal code, and could scarcely be embraced by the human mind. It would probably never be understood by the public. Its nature, therefore, requires, that only its great outlines should be marked, its important objects designated, and the minor ingredients which compose those objects be deduced from the nature of the objects themselves. That this idea was entertained by the framers of the American constitution, is not only to be inferred from the nature of the instrument, but from the language. Why else were some of the limitations, found in the ninth section of the 1st article, introduced? It is also, in some degree, warranted by their having omitted to use any restrictive term which might prevent its receiving a fair and just interpretation. In considering this question, then, we must never forget, that it is *a constitution* we are expounding.[23]

The Constitution may not speak of banks, but it does confer on the central government certain "great powers." Among them

[21] *Articles of Confederation*, Art. II. *Documents of American History*, Henry Steele Commager, ed. (New York: Appleton-Century-Crofts, 1963), p. 111.

[22] "The powers not delegated to the United States by the Constitution, nor prohibited by it to the States, are reserved to the States respectively, or to the people." *Constitution*, Amendment X.

[23] 4 Wheat. 316, 407.

is the power to tax, to borrow money, to regulate commerce, to declare war, and to raise and support armies and navies. "The sword and the purse, all the external relations, and no inconsiderable portion of the industry of the nation, are entrusted to its government." [24] Moreover, it is reasonable to assume that a government endowed with such powers—"on the due execution of which the happiness and prosperity of the Nation so vitally depend"—was meant to be free to choose the necessary "means" for putting those powers into practical effect. With the help of a few rhetorical questions, Marshall then presents his conception of the extent to which the promotion of the national interest may demand that Congress be permitted wide latitude in the choice of the best means for effectuating the great purposes of the Constitution:

> Throughout this vast republic, from the St. Croix to the Gulph of Mexico, from the Atlantic to the Pacific, revenue is to be collected and expended, armies are to be marched and supported. The exigencies of the nation may require that the treasure raised in the north should be transported to the south, that raised in the east conveyed to the west, or that this order should be reversed. Is that construction of the constitution to be preferred which would render these operations difficult, hazardous, and expensive? Can we adopt that construction, (unless the words imperiously require it) which would impute to the framers of that instrument, when granting these powers for the public good, the intention of impeding their exercise by withholding a choice of means? If, indeed, such be the mandate of the constitution, we have only to obey; but that instrument does not profess to enumerate the means by which the powers it confers may be executed; nor does it prohibit the creation of a corporation, if the existence of such a being be essential to the beneficial exercise of those powers.[25]

Maryland's lawyers had advanced the interesting argument that Congress was without power to charter banks because the creation of corporations was an attribute of sovereignty not possessed by the national legislature. Marshall has a double answer

[24] *Ibid.*
[25] *Ibid.*, pp. 408–409.

to this contention—one based on reason and the other on the nature of legal sovereignty in the United States. If Congress were restrained from using corporations because they are not specifically mentioned in the Constitution, the same logic could be used to deny it the authority to pass other laws it deems necessary for the execution of its powers. And as for the question of sovereignty, it was important to bear in mind that the authority to govern the American people is shared by two governments, and that it is not the exclusive prerogative of the states. "In America, the powers of sovereignty are divided between the government of the Union, and those of the States. They are each sovereign, with respect to the objects committed to it, and neither sovereign with respect to the objects committed to the other." [26] There was a difference, after all, between creating a banking corporation and the exercise of such "substantive and independent powers" as the powers to wage war, regulate commerce, or levy taxes. Such powers could not be "implied" as "incidental" to other powers:

> The power of creating a corporation, though appertaining to sovereignty, is not, like the power of making war, or levying taxes, or of regulating commerce, a great substantive and independent power, which cannot be implied as incidental to other powers, or used as a means of executing them. It is never the end for which other powers are exercised, but a means by which other ob-

[26] Marshall continued: "We cannot comprehend that train of reasoning which would maintain that the extent of power granted by the people is to be ascertained not by the nature and terms of the grant, but by its date. Some State constitutions were formed before, some since that of the United States. We cannot believe that their relation to each other is in any degree dependent upon this circumstance. Their respective powers must, we think, be precisely the same as if they had been formed at the same time. Had they been formed at the same time, and had the people conferred on the General Government the powers contained in the constitution, and on the States the whole residuum of power, would it have been asserted that the government of the Union was not sovereign with respect to those objects which were intrusted to it, in relation to which its laws were declared to be supreme? If this could not have been asserted, we cannot well comprehend the process of reasoning which maintains, that a power appertaining to sovereignty cannot be connected with that vast portion of it which is granted to the general government, so far as it is calculated to subserve the legitimate objects of that government." *Ibid.*, pp. 410–411.

jects are accomplished. . . . The power of creating a corporation is never used for its own sake, but for the purpose of effecting something else. No sufficient reason is, therefore, perceived, which it may not pass as incidental to those powers which are expressly given, if it be a direct mode of executing them.[27]

Thus as Hamilton had done in *The Federalist*,[28] so Marshall defends Congress' need for the exercise of considerable discretion if it is to give the country effective government. Like Hamilton, he is quick to point out that Congress' freedom to effectuate its powers does not depend on "general reasoning." In addition to the seventeen express powers it confers on Congress, the Constitution also gives it the specific authority "to make all Laws which shall be necessary and proper for carrying into Execution the foregoing Powers, and all other Powers vested by this Constitution in the Government of the United States, or in any Department or Officer thereof." [29]

III

In his elaborate analysis of the "necessary and proper" clause, Marshall undertakes to prove that its intended effect was to broaden and facilitate, rather than to restrict, Congress' freedom of action in deciding how best to carry out the powers delegated to it.[30] Counsel for Maryland had contended that although the clause was inserted to make clear Congress' right to pass laws, to be deemed constitutional such laws must be shown to be absolutely "necessary" in the execution of the enumerated powers. As Marshall rephrases their argument, "the word 'nec-

---

[27] *Ibid.*, p. 411. Marshall furnishes several illustrations of the distinction he sought to make: "No contributions are made to charity for the sake of an incorporation, but a corporation is created to administer the charity; no seminary of learning is instituted in order to be incorporated, but the corporate character is conferred to subserve the purposes of education. No city was ever built with the sole object of being incorporated but is incorporated as affording the best means of being well governed." *Ibid.*

[28] See above, pp. 68–71.

[29] *Constitution*, Art. I, sec. 8, par. 18.

[30] Marshall presents two principal reasons which led the Court to this conclusion: "1st. The clause is placed among the powers of Congress, not among the limitations on those powers. 2d. Its terms purport to enlarge, not to diminish the powers vested in the government. It purports to be an additional power, not a restriction on those already granted." 4 Wheat. 316, 419–420.

essary' is considered as controlling the whole sentence, and as limiting the right to pass laws for the execution of the granted powers, to such as are indispensable, and without which the power would be nugatory. That it excludes the choice of means, and leaves to Congress, in each case, that only which is most direct and simple." [31]

The Chief Justice emphatically rejects the reading of "necessary" as connoting "physical necessity" and offers what he regarded as a much more commonsense view. "If reference be had to its use, in the common affairs of the world, or in approved authors," he explains, "we find that it [the word "necessary"] frequently imports no more than that one thing is convenient, or useful, or essential to another." [32] Not only is this meaning justified by "common usage" but there is evidence that the framers of the Constitution appreciated that the word "necessary" did not have a "fixed" meaning and that necessity is a matter of degree. When they wished to restrict action to that which was "indispensably necessary," they knew how to say so, as is evident in the provision prohibiting a state from taxing imports or exports "except what may be absolutely necessary for executing its inspection laws." [33] A word like "necessary" belongs to that class of terms which have "various senses" and their meaning in a particular situation can be gathered only if "the subject, the context, the intention of the person using them," are taken into account.

Originating in such practical considerations, the "necessary and proper" clause was obviously designed to leave Congress free to choose from among available alternatives those measures which it would find convenient and appropriate. In other words, it is the nature of the Constitution as a document for an unchartered future which is the key to the meaning of the clause:

[31] *Ibid.*, p. 413.

[32] Among the other synonyms Marshall suggests for "necessary" are: "needful," "requisite," "essential," "conducive to." *Ibid.*

[33] Marshall compares the permissive language of the "necessary and proper" clause with the provision that "No State shall, without the Consent of the Congress, lay any Imposts or Duties on Imports or Exports, except what may be absolutely necessary for executing its inspection Laws." *Constitution*, Art. I, sec. 10, par. 2.

The subject is the execution of those great powers on which the welfare of a nation essentially depends. It must have been the intention of those who gave these powers, to insure, as far as human prudence could insure, their beneficial execution. This could not be done by confining the choice of means to such narrow limits as not to leave it in the power of Congress to adopt any which might be appropriate, and which were conducive to the end. This provision is made in a constitution intended to endure for ages to come, and, consequently, to be adapted to the various *crises* of human affairs. To have prescribed the means by which government should, in all future time, execute its powers, would have been to change, entirely, the character of the instrument, and give it the properties of a legal code.[34]

By way of illustrating the practical value of the "necessary and proper" clause, the Chief Justice cited several significant developments. Among them was the enactment of a federal criminal code punishing those who violate federal laws, the use by Congress of its power to "establish post offices and post roads" as the basis for legislation making it an offense to rob the mails, and laws punishing persons who falsify court records or commit perjury. This recital led Marshall to raise one of his unique rhetorical questions: "If the word 'necessary' means 'needful,' 'requisite,' 'essential,' 'conducive to,' in order to let in the power of punishment for the infraction of law; why is it not equally comprehensive when required to authorize the use of means which facilitate the execution of powers of government without the infliction of punishment?" [35]

Marshall speaks of the "baneful influence" which the "narrow construction" of the Constitution would have "on all the operations of the government." The practical effect of such construction can only be to render "government incompetent to its great

---

[34] 4 *Wheat.* 316, 415.

[35] *Ibid.*, p. 418. Marshall sought to fortify his argument for incidental powers by pointing out that since Congress is specifically authorized to punish some crimes, the strict constructionists could logically argue that where the power to punish is not expressly given it is denied. As he says, "Congress is empowered 'to provide for the punishment of counterfeiting the securities and current coin of the United States,' and to define and punish piracies and felonies committed on the high seas, and offenses against the law of nations." *Ibid.*, p. 419. See *Constitution*, Art. I, sec. 8, clauses 6 and 10.

objects." But such a result was not intended by the American people. "The good sense of the public has pronounced, without hesitation," observes Marshall, "that the power of punishment appertains to sovereignty, and may be exercised whenever the sovereign has a right to act, as incidental to his constitutional powers. It is a means for carrying into execution all sovereign powers, and may be used, although not indispensably necessary. It is a right incidental to the power, and conducive to its beneficial exercise." [36]

All of this argumentation and all of these illustrations were intended to emphasize an important principle in the interpretation of the Constitution. The principle is that so long as the laws enacted by Congress are appropriately related to the powers vested in it and are not forbidden by the Constitution, Congress enjoys wide discretion in devising the particular instruments for the carrying out of those powers. Or, to put it another way, Congress is free to use its "best judgment" when it undertakes to embody in legislation the great purposes of the Constitution which are reflected in the powers it delegates to the national government. Marshall's formulation of this canon of construction is thus finally cast in terms of the relation between means and ends:

> We admit, as all must admit, that the powers of the government are limited, and that its limits are not to be transcended. But we think the sound construction of the Constitution must allow to the national legislature that discretion, with respect to the means by which the powers it confers are to be carried into execution, which will enable that body to perform the high duties assigned to it, in the manner most beneficial to the people. Let the end be legitimate, let it be within the scope of the constitution, and all means which are appropriate, which are plainly adapted to that end, which are not prohibited, but consist with the letter and spirit of the constitution, are constitutional.[37]

Judged by such criteria, there could be no doubt that a banking corporation might be deemed by Congress to be "a convenient, a useful, and essential instrument" for the government's "fiscal operations." The history of corporations, especially their use in

[36] 4 Wheat. 316, 418.
[37] *Ibid.*, p. 421.

"that government from which we have derived most of our legal principles and ideas," supports the soundness of the Constitution in "wisely" refraining to specify all the means for effectuating the powers of the government. All who have been "concerned in the administration of our finances" have recognized this role of banks, and even some "statesmen of the first class" who opposed the first National Bank had come to change their minds.[38]

Inasmuch as the use of banks for achieving the federal government's "legitimate objects" would seem to be an "appropriate" means for managing its fiscal affairs, and since it is not prohibited by the Constitution, whether or not it was necessary to charter the National Bank was a question to be decided by Congress, and not by the courts. In the course of emphasizing this point, Marshall takes occasion to set forth an important guide for the exercise of the power of judicial review:

> Were its [the bank's] necessity less apparent, none can deny its being an appropriate measure; and if it is, the degree of its necessity, as has been very justly observed, is to be discussed in another place. Should Congress, in the execution of its powers, adopt measures which are prohibited by the constitution; or should Congress, under the pretext of executing its powers, pass laws for the accomplishment of objects not entrusted to the government; it would become the painful duty of this tribunal, should a case requiring such a decision come before it, to say that such an act was not the law of the land. But where the law is not prohibited, and is really calculated to effect any of the objects entrusted to the government,

---

[38] Marshall might have been thinking of James Madison, who opposed Hamilton's plan for the creation of the National Bank. When Madison vetoed a bank bill in 1815 because he disapproved of its particular form, he took occasion to say that in his judgment the constitutionality of Congress' power to establish banks had been recognized by repeated actions of the legislative, executive, and judicial branches of the Government—so much so, indeed, that it might be said to have received the "concurrence of the general will of the nation." *Messages and Papers of the Presidents*, James D. Richardson, ed. (Washington: Bureau of National Literature and Art, 1903), I, 555. Some years later, Madison explained that he had accepted the constitutionality of the bank "in pursuance of my early and unchanged opinion, that, in the case of a Constitution as of a law, a course of authoritative expositions sufficiently deliberate, uniform, and settled, was an evidence, of the public will necessarily overruling individual opinions." *The Writings of James Madison*, Gaillard Hunt, ed., IX, 442, 443.

to undertake here to inquire into the degree of its necessity, would
be to pass the line which circumscribes the judicial department,
and to tread on legislative ground. This court disclaims all pretensions to such a power.[39]

IV

Having thus defended the Court's "unanimous and decided"
opinion that the law incorporating the Bank of the United States
was "a law made in pursuance of the constitution and is a part
of the supreme law of the land," Marshall proceeds to deal with
the question whether the State of Maryland could tax a branch
of the bank. Two difficulties had to be overcome before this
question could be answered. The Chief Justice concedes, in the
first place, that the power to tax is of such "vital importance"
that the states must be assumed to have retained that power even
though the Constitution endows the national government with
the power to tax. Secondly, while the Constitution does limit
the taxing authority of the states in some respects, there is no
provision forbidding them to tax federally chartered institutions.
According to Marshall, it is the "paramount character of the constitution" which is at the basis of the provision prohibiting the
states from taxing imports and exports. This same principle also
restrains the states from exercising their power to tax in any way
that is "in its nature incompatible with and repugnant to" laws
passed by Congress.

Marshall makes it plain that what he meant by the "paramount character of the constitution" was that the Constitution
and laws made in pursuance of it were superior to the constitution and laws of any state. In other words, the exemption of the
operations of the National Bank from the reach of Maryland's
taxing power stemmed from the "great principle" that "the constitution and the laws made in pursuance thereof are supreme;
that they control the constitution and laws of the respective
States, and cannot be controlled by them." The "supremacy" of
the federal Constitution is a principle "which so entirely pervades
the constitution, is so intermixed with the materials which com-
pose it, so interwoven with its web, so blended with its texture,

---

[39] 4 Wheat. 316, 423.

as to be incapable of being separated from it, without rending it into shreds." [40]

From the "axiom" about the Constitution's supremacy, Chief Justice Marshall draws certain inferences—or "corollaries" as he calls them—on the basis of which Maryland's claim to tax the National Bank was categorically rejected. These "propositions" are summarized by him as follows: "That a power to create implies a power to preserve. . . . That a power to destroy, if wielded by a different hand, is hostile to, and incompatible with these powers to create and to preserve. . . . That, where this repugnancy exists, that authority which is supreme must control, not yield to that over which it is supreme." [41]

It is evident from the very outset of his discussion of the validity of the Maryland tax that Marshall would set it aside on the basis of two weighty considerations. One was his view of the power to tax as a potential weapon of destruction, and the other was his conception of sovereignty in the United States. These are matters which inevitably call for "construction." Yet they had to be kept in mind if the constitutional problem posed by Maryland's attempt to use one of its legitimate powers to interfere with a function authorized by Congress was going to be settled correctly. The Chief Justice writes:

> That the power of taxing it [the bank] by the States may be exercised so as to destroy it, is too obvious to be denied. But taxation is said to be an absolute power, which acknowledges no other limits than those expressly prescribed in the constitution, and like sovereign power of every other description, is trusted to the discretion of those who use it. But the very terms of this argument admit that the sovereignty of the State, in the article of taxation itself, is subordinate to, and may be controlled by the constitution of the United States. How far it has been controlled by that instrument must be a question of construction. In making this construction, no principle not declared, can be admissible, which would defeat the legitimate operations of a supreme government. It is of the very essence of supremacy to remove all obstacles to its action within its own sphere, and so to modify every power vested in sub-

[40] *Ibid.,* p. 426.
[41] *Ibid.*

ordinate governments, as to exempt its own operations from their own influence. This effect need not be stated in terms. It is so involved in the declaration of supremacy, so necessarily implied in it, that the expression of it could not make it more certain. We must, therefore, keep it in view while construing the constitution.[42]

This statement of "abstract truths" brings Marshall to apply what he calls "the test of the constitution" in refuting one of Maryland's principal contentions. In doing so, he also invokes an interesting theory of the political process to buttress his constitutional position. "The argument on the part of the State of Maryland," Marshall tells us, "is, not that the States may directly resist a law of Congress, but that they may exercise their acknowledged powers upon it, and that the constitution leaves them this right in the confidence that they will not abuse it." Under the Constitution each state retained its "original right" to tax people and property. Within the states, however, the dependence of legislators upon the support of their constituents furnishes protection against the abuse of the power to tax. But there was no reason for being confident that the power would not be abused once a state were permitted to tax the operations of federal instrumentalities.[43]

---

[42] *Ibid.*, p. 427.

[43] It may be of interest to recall, at greater length, Marshall's theory concerning the political safeguard against the abuse of the power to tax—a safeguard present within a state but not available if it were to tax federally chartered institutions: "It is admitted that the power of taxing the people and their property is essential to the very existence of government, and may be legitimately exercised on the objects to which it is applicable, to the utmost extent to which the government may chuse to carry it. The only security against the abuse of this power, is found in the structure of the government itself. In imposing a tax the legislature acts upon its constituents. This is in general a sufficient security against erroneous and oppressive taxation.

"The people of a State, therefore, give to their government a right of taxing themselves and their property, and as the exigencies of government cannot be limited, they prescribe no limits to the exercise of this right, resting confidently on the interest of the legislator, and on the influence of the constituents over their representative, to guard them against its abuse. But the means employed by the government of the Union have no such security, nor is the right of a State to tax them sustained by the same theory. Those means are not given by the people of a particular State, not given by the constituents of the legislature, which claims the right to tax them, but by the

Far-reaching as may be that portion of a state's sovereignty which enables it to tax people and property, it does not extend to the instrumentalities used by Congress in the execution of its powers. "They are given by all, for the benefit of all, and upon theory should be subjected to that government only which belongs to all." Marshall regarded it as "self-evident" that since taxation was an "incident" of sovereignty, a state's power to tax extends only to those objects over which it has jurisdiction and may not reach objects over which a state has no authority.[44] On the basis of the "soundest principles," therefore, it was clear that no single state could be permitted to tax the activities or instrumentalities employed by the government of all the people.

For Marshall it was unimportant that the Constitution did not restrain the states, in explicit terms, from taxing agencies which Congress might use in carrying out its powers. Such a limitation upon the states was to be inferred from the "supremacy" assigned to national laws. "It is of the very essence of supremacy," declares the Chief Justice, "to remove all obstacles to its action within its own sphere, and so to modify every power vested in subordinate governments as to exempt its own operations from their influence."

Nor was Marshall willing to have the right to tax federal instrumentalities depend upon the degree or the amount of the tax sought to be collected by a state. In refusing to consider the actual economic effects of the Maryland tax, he was simply following the lead of Webster and Pinkney. As counsel for the bank, they were careful not to confine their attack on the Maryland tax to its consequences for the financial operations of the fed-

people of all the States. They are given by all, for the benefit of all—and upon theory, should be subjected to that government only which belongs to all." *Ibid.,* pp. 428–429.

[44] "The sovereignty of a State extends to everything which exists by its own authority, or is introduced by its permission; but does it extend to those means which are employed by Congress to carry into execution powers conferred on that body by the people of the United States? We think it demonstrable that it does not. Those powers are not given by the people of a single State. They are given by the people of the United States, to a government whose laws, made in pursuance of the constitution, are declared to be supreme. Consequently, the people of a single State cannot confer a sovereignty which will extend over them." *Ibid.,* p. 429.

eral government. Pinkney argued that "there must be . . . an implied exception to the general taxing power of the states" and that the Supreme Court was not equipped to determine "what is an abuse and what is a legitimate use of the power." Pinkney wanted to know by what tests the Court could "ascertain *a priori* that a given amount of tax will crush the Bank?" He argued that such an inquiry did not fall within the competence of judges: "It is essentially a question of political economy, and there are always a vast variety of facts bearing upon it. The facts may be mistaken. Some important considerations belonging to the subject may be kept out of sight. They must all vary with times and circumstances." [45]

Anyone familiar with this argument of Pinkney's will be struck at once by the extent to which Marshall borrowed from it. Even Beveridge, with all his admiration for the "great" Chief Justice, had to acknowledge the debt: "To reproduce his [Pinkney's] address is to set out in advance the opinion of John Marshall stripped of Pinkney's rhetoric which, in that day, was deemed to be the perfection of eloquence." [46]

To Marshall the basic issue was not whether the states could be trusted not to abuse their power to tax. Under the division of powers between nation and states implicit in the Constitution, the states were completely without authority to tax institutions which owed their existence to laws intended to be "supreme" throughout the United States. As Marshall declares: "We find, then, on just theory, a total failure of this original right to tax the means employed by the government of the Union, for the execution of its powers." [47] Thus did the great exponent of implied national powers read into the Constitution a sweeping limitation upon the authority of the states. He justified the implied prohibition not merely as a principle essential to the maintenance of national supremacy. It was also the only criterion of interference with federal functions which the judiciary was capable of applying effectively:

[45] *Ibid.*, p. 392.
[46] Beveridge, *op. cit.*, IV, 287.
[47] 4 Wheat. 316, 430.

If we measure the power of taxation residing in a State, by the extent of sovereignty which the people of a single State possess, and can confer on its government, we have an intelligible standard, applicable to every case to which the power may be applied. We have a principle which leaves the power of taxing the people and property of a State unimpaired; which leaves to a State the command of all its resources, and which places beyond its reach, all those powers which are conferred by the people of the United States on the government of the Union, and all those means which are given for the purpose of carrying those powers into execution. We have a principle which is safe for the States, and safe for the Union. We are relieved, as we ought to be, from clashing sovereignty; from interfering powers; from a repugnancy between a right in one government to pull down what there is an acknowledged right in another to build up; from the incompatibility of a right in one government to destroy what there is a right in another to preserve. We are not driven to the perplexing inquiry, so unfit for the judicial department, what degree of taxation is the legitimate use, and what degree may amount to the abuse of the power. The attempt to use it on the means employed by the government of the Union, in pursuance of the constitution, is itself an abuse, because it is the usurpation of a power which the people of a single State cannot give.[48]

Marshall evidently believed that it is the very nature of taxation which demanded the principles he was inferring from the Constitution. The states were not to be allowed to use their historic right to tax in ways which would undermine the national government's position in the Union. In his now familiar words, "That the power to tax involves the power to destroy; that the power to destroy may defeat and render useless the power to create; that there is a plain repugnance, in conferring on one government a power to control the constitutional measures of another, which other, with respect to those very measures, is declared to be supreme over that which exerts the control, are propositions not to be denied." [49]

It may be true that taxation does not "necessarily and un-

[48] *Ibid.*
[49] *Ibid.*, p. 431.

avoidably destroy," but the possibility that the states might venture to impede the operations of the federal government through taxation was not to be discounted by invoking "the magic of the word *confidence.*" More was at stake than the attempt of a single state to tax a branch of the National Bank. If the concept of state power advocated by Maryland were to prevail, the whole character of the American constitutional system would be altered and the national government would find itself at the mercy of the states.[50]

The practical consequences were likely to be catastrophic. Looking to the future, Marshall foresaw the danger that the theory of concurrent powers urged by Maryland would subject the whole domain of federal activity to taxation by the states. Logically and inevitably, once their right to tax a banking institution chartered by Congress was recognized, the states would be free to control other federal operations:

> If the States may tax one instrument, employed by the government in the execution of its powers, they may tax any and every other instrument. They may tax the mail; they may tax the mint; they may tax patent rights; they may tax the papers of the customhouse; they may tax judicial process; they may tax all the means employed by the government, to an excess which would defeat all the ends of government. This was not intended by the American people. They did not design to make their government dependent on the States.[51]

v

The decision in *McCulloch v. Maryland* is the source for the American doctrine of intergovernmental tax immunity. Exactly a decade later, Marshall led the Court in laying down the principle that United States securities were exempt from state and

---

[50] "If we apply the principle for which the State of Maryland contends, to the constitution generally, we shall find it capable of changing totally the character of that instrument. We shall find it capable of arresting all the measures of the government, and of prostrating it at the foot of the States. The American people have declared their constitution, and the laws made in pursuance thereof, to be supreme; but this principle would transfer the supremacy, in fact, to the States." *Ibid.*, p. 432.

[51] *Ibid.*

local taxation.[52] The decision which he delivered in this case held that the tax which the City Council of Charleston had levied on interest-paying stocks owned by Weston, a private citizen, was in effect a burden on Congress' power to borrow money on the credit of the United States, and was therefore unconstitutional. Once again Marshall rested the immunity on two cardinal precepts—the principle of national supremacy and the doctrine that the states had absolutely no power to encroach upon the fields duly delegated to the federal government:

> The restraint is imposed by our Constitution. The American people have conferred the power of borrowing money on their government, and by making that government supreme, have shielded its action, in the exercise of this power, from the action of the local governments. The grant of the power is incompatible with a restraining or controlling power; and the declaration of supremacy is a declaration that no such restraining or controlling power shall be exercised.[53]

Shortly after the Civil War, the Supreme Court made the exemption reciprocal by ruling that the salaries of state officials were immune from federal taxation.[54] Yet the ironic fact about the evolution of intergovernmental tax immunity is that the court completely ignored Marshall's original premise when it converted the doctrine into one of mutual exemption. In *McCulloch v. Maryland,* the Chief Justice had been quite explicit in rejecting the idea that the considerations which justified the freedom of federal instrumentalities from state taxation would also support the immunity of state agencies from federal taxation. Wrote Marshall:

> It has also been insisted, that, as the power of taxation in the general and State governments is acknowledged to be concurrent, every argument which would sustain the right of the general government to tax banks chartered by the States, will equally sustain

[52] *Weston v. Charleston,* 2 Pet. 449 (1829). In 1842 a like immunity was extended to the salaries earned by persons holding federal office. *Dobbins v. Erie County,* 16 Pet. 435.
[53] 2 Pet. 449, 464.
[54] *Collector v. Day,* 11 Wall. 113 (1870).

the right of the States to tax banks chartered by the general government.

But the two cases are not on the same reason. The people of all the States have created the general government, and have conferred upon it the general power of taxation. The people of all the States, and the States themselves, are represented in Congress, and, by their representatives, exercise this power. When they tax the chartered institutions of the States, they tax their constituents; and these taxes must be uniform. But when a State taxes the operations of the government of the United States, it acts upon institutions created, not by their own constituents, but by people over whom they claim no control. It acts upon the measures of a government created by others as well as themselves, for the benefit of others in common with themselves. The difference is that which always exists, and always must exist, between the action of the whole on a part, and the action of a part on the whole—between the laws of a government declared to be supreme, and those of a government which, when in opposition to those laws, is not supreme.[55]

Before concluding his opinion in *McCulloch v. Maryland,* Chief Justice Marshall summarized the Court's decision in a way which implied that the inhibition being placed upon the states was not to be confined to the power of taxation. After saying that the Court had given the case its "most deliberate consideration," he suggested its potential significance in one sentence: "The result is a conviction that the States have no power, by

[55] 4 Wheat. 316, 435–436. Despite this unequivocal language, the Court which decided *Collector v. Day* relied in the main on *McCulloch v. Maryland* and *Dobbins v. Erie County.* Justice Samuel Nelson, who spoke for the Court, asked: ". . . if the means and instrumentalities employed by that government [federal] to carry into operation the power granted to it are necessarily, and, for the sake of self-preservation, exempt from taxation by the States, why are not those of the States depending upon their reserved powers for like reasons, equally exempt from Federation taxation?" 11 Wall. 113, 126. Nelson announced that henceforth state instrumentalities would be "equally exempt from Federal taxation." It was not until the 1930s that the Supreme Court began to resurrect the distinction between federal and state taxation originally formulated by Marshall and to discard some of the intergovernmental tax immunities. For a fuller discussion of this development, see S. J. Konefsky, *Chief Justice Stone and the Supreme Court* (New York: The Macmillan Company, 1945), ch. I.

taxation or otherwise, to retard, impede, burden, or in any manner control, the operations of the constitutional laws enacted by
Congress to carry into execution the powers vested in the general
government." [56]

[56] 4 Wheat. 316, 436. In one respect Marshall's opinion in *McCulloch v.
Maryland* is not quite as sweeping as it is sometimes depicted. By way of
dictum, he conceded that the states were free to tax the real property of the
National Bank—in common with other real property. "This opinion does
not deprive the States of any resources which they originally possessed. It
does not extend to a tax paid by the real property of the bank, in common
with the other real property within the State, nor to a tax imposed on the
interest which the citizens of Maryland may hold in this institution, in common with other property of the same description throughout the State. But
this is a tax [the Maryland tax] on the operations of the bank, and is, consequently, a tax on the operation of an instrument employed by the government of the Union to carry its powers into execution. Such a tax must be unconstitutional." 4 Wheat. 316, 436–437.

9

"Contests Respecting Power Must Arise"

On the occasion of the two-hundredth anniversary of John Marshall's birth, Justice Felix Frankfurter ventured to speak of the long-range effect of the great Chief Justice's achievement in molding the constitutional outlook of the American people. "There can be little doubt," the Justice told his distinguished audience at the Harvard Law School in 1955, "that Marshall saw and seized his opportunities to educate the country to a spacious view of the Constitution, to accustom the public mind to broad national powers, to counteract the commercial and political self-centeredness of States." [1] And some years earlier, the then Professor Frankfurter had undertaken to summarize the point of view from which Marshall was bound to approach the task of expounding the meaning of the commerce clause of the Constitution:

> Temperament, experience and association converged to make it easy for Marshall to use the commerce clause as a curb upon local legislation. Valley Forge made him a nationalist; ties of friendship and shared labors in the struggle for the Constitution confirmed his faith. Local government was associated in his mind with the petty bickerings of narrow ambition and a dangerous indifference to rights of property. The need of a strong central government, as the indispensable bulwark of the solid elements of the nation, was for him the deepest article of his political faith. [2]

[1] Frankfurter, "John Marshall and the Judicial Function," 69 Harvard Law Review, 767; reprinted in *Government under Law*, Sutherland, ed., p. 11.
[2] Frankfurter, *The Commerce Clause under Marshall, Taney and Waite*

Though the 1955 comment by Justice Frankfurter was no doubt offered as a general assessment of Marshall's fundamental contribution, it happens also to be a most apt description of the Chief Justice's exposition of the commerce clause of the federal Constitution. His opinion in *Gibbons v. Ogden*,[3] the first of these interpretations, certainly demonstrates that he was interested in arresting the "commercial self-centeredness" of the states. The case had been brought by those who were determined to break the monopoly which the legislature of New York had granted to Robert R. Livingston and Robert Fulton in the operation of steamboats on the navigable waterways of the state.

"No more impressive example of the great and permanent influence and value of Marshall's constitutional decisions exists," one commentator has written, "than in what is known as the New York Steamboat Case." [4] Edward S. Corwin has described it as Marshall's "profoundest, most statesmanlike opinion, from whose doctrines the Court has at times deviated, but only to return to them." [5] And Beveridge's encomium gives the impression that the biographer was running out of adjectives: "But few events in our history have had a larger and more substantial effect on the well-being of the American people than this decision, and Marshall's opinion in the announcement of it." And again:

> It is not immoderate to say that no other judicial pronouncement in history was so wedded to the inventive genius of man and so interwoven with the economic and social evolution of a nation

(Chapel Hill: University of North Carolina Press, 1937), p. 14. Professor Frankfurter hastened to add a *caveat* for those who would exaggerate the "conflict" between Marshall and his successor as Chief Justice in their respective interpretations of the commerce clause: "One of the classic plots in the writing of American history has been the clash of ideas attributed to Marshall and Taney. A strong central government on the one hand and states' rights on the other are the allegiances which have respectively enlisted the two sides. This kind of oversimplification of an extremely complicated interplay of forces has combined with the moral momentum which success confers upon the victorious antagonist to create the conventionalized picture of Marshall as the true believer and Taney as the false prophet." *Ibid.*

[3] 9 Wheat. (1824).
[4] *The Complete Constitutional Decisions of John Marshall*, John M. Dillon, ed. (Chicago: Callaghan and Company, 1903), p. 421.
[5] Corwin, *John Marshall and the Constitution*, p. 137.

and a people. After almost a century, Marshall's Nationalist theory of commerce is more potent than ever; and nothing human is more certain than that it will gather new strength as far into the future as forecast can penetrate.[6]

I

What is there about Marshall's opinion in *Gibbons v. Ogden* that might conceivably justify such laudatory appraisal? It is sometimes forgotten that in it Marshall had the seemingly uncomfortable task of having to reverse the opinion of a judge with whom he had considerable affinity. It was James Kent who led New York's highest court in sustaining the constitutionality of the laws under which Fulton and Livingston were given the exclusive right to navigate by steamboats. What makes Kent's *seriatim* opinion in the New York Court of Errors particularly interesting is that it affords a rather striking example of an approach to the interpretation of the commerce clause which stands in sharp contrast to that Marshall was to exhibit. It also makes quite explicit the two factors which were destined to exert such a powerful influence on the judicial adjustment of rival national and state claims in the regulation of commerce. In the first place, Kent sought to show that his conclusion—that the law granting Livingston and Fulton the exclusive privilege to ply the waters of the state by steam-driven vessels was a valid exercise of the state's power—was not

---

[6] Beveridge, *The Life of John Marshall*, IV, 446, 447. Beveridge believed that Marshall's opinion in *Gibbons v. Ogden*, by freeing the waterways of the nation from local impediments to navigation, served as an incalculable spur to the development of the American economy. It also gave "tremendous encouragement" to the subsequent building of railways and telephone and telegraph systems. "New York instantly became a free port for all America. Steamboat navigation of American rivers, relieved from the terror of possible and actual State-created monopolies, increased at an incredible rate; and because of two decades of restraint and fear, at abnormal speed.

"New England manufacturers were given a new life, since the transportation of anthracite coal—the fuel recently discovered and aggravatingly needed —was made cheap and easy. The owners of factories, the promoters of steamboat traffic, the innumerable builders of river craft on every navigable stream in the country, the farmer who wished to send his products to market, the manufacturer who sought quick and inexpensive transportation of his wares —all acclaimed Marshall's decision because all found in it a means to their own interests." *Ibid.*, IV, 446.

affected by his attitude toward the wisdom of the "policy" it embodied:

> This house, sitting in its judicial capacity as a court, has nothing to do with the policy or expediency of these laws. The only question here is, whether the legislature had the authority to pass them. If we can satisfy ourselves upon this point, or, rather, unless we are fully persuaded that they are void, we are bound to obey them, and give them the requisite effect.[7]

But besides the pull of a judge's social or economic predilections, there was also his conception of what Kent spoke of as "the nature of the federal system." In his view, the Constitution distributed power between nation and states in such a way as to leave both "supreme within their respective constitutional spheres." The notion that one government would be "supreme" over the other "would involve a contradiction." Courts should not tax their "sagacity" or "consciences" by deciding claims of state interference with national regulation on the basis of "theoretical difficulties" or "collisions" which might arise in the future. There was only one "safe rule" for courts to follow: "If any given power was originally vested in this state, if it has not been exclusively ceded to Congress, or if the exercise of it has not been prohibited to the states, we may then go on in the exercise of the power until it comes practically in collision with the actual exercise of some congressional power."[8]

Turning directly to the question as to the power to regulate commerce, Kent found that the commerce clause did not confer on Congress the exclusive right to deal with it. He wrote:

> This power is not, in express terms, exclusive and the only prohibition upon the states is, that they shall not enter into any treaty or compact with each other, or with a foreign power, nor lay any duty on tonnage, or on imports or exports, except what may be necessary for executing their inspection laws . . . the states are under no other constitutional restriction, and are, consequently, left in possession of a vast field of commercial regulation; all the internal commerce of the state by land and water remains entirely,

[7] *Livingston v. Van Ingen,* 9 Johnson's Reports 507, 572 (1812).
[8] *Ibid.*

and I may say exclusively, within the scope of its original sovereignty. The congressional power relates to external not internal
commerce, and it is confined to the regulation of that commerce.[9]

Most of Kent's opinion may be described as a series of variations
on one basic theme: "The states are under no other restrictions
than those expressly specified in the constitution, and such regulations as the national government may, by treaty, and by laws,
from time to time prescribe." It struck Kent as "inadmissible"
that a state should be "divested of a capacity to grant an exclusive privilege of navigating a steam-boat, within its own waters,
merely because we can imagine that congress, in the plenary exercise of its power to regulate commerce, may make some regulation inconsistent with the exercise of this privilege." State laws
were not to be upset because of the mere possibility that they
might be in conflict with a regulation which Congress might
adopt on the same subject in the future. Any such "doctrine"
would be a "monstrous heresy" and could be used to destroy the
"legislative power" of the states. Moreover, state judges were to
remember that "there is, fortunately, a paramount power in the
supreme court of the United States to guard against the mischiefs of collision." [10]

When the case reached the Supreme Court of the United
States in 1824, Chief Justice Marshall made it abundantly clear
that he viewed the "mischiefs of collision" quite differently from
the way they were seen by the widely respected Chancellor of New
York. It became the occasion for one of Marshall's major dis-
quisitions on the character of the American constitutional system.
In the course of developing this disquisition, he was able, once
again, to place the Court's official imprimatur upon his particular notions as to the underlying purposes of the Constitution.

Indeed, considering the extent to which the impetus for the
Constitution originated in dissatisfaction over the commercial
difficulties under the Articles of Confederation, the case was an
ideal vehicle for revealing Marshall's basic conception of the
"more perfect union." As one scholar has recently written, "It

[9] *Ibid.*, pp. 577–578.
[10] *Ibid.*, p. 578.

is impossible to read the correspondence of Madison, Hamilton, Mason, and others without perceiving the imperative necessity that they felt of committing the regulation of trade and commerce to a single national authority." [11] Hamilton's statement of the matter was perhaps most forceful of all:

> In addition to the defects already enumerated in the existing federal system, there are others of not less importance, which concur in rendering that system altogether unfit for the administration of the affairs of the Union.
>
> The want of a power to regulate commerce is by all parties allowed to be of the number. . . . It is indeed evident, on the most superficial view, that there is no object, either as it respects the interest of trade or finance, that more strongly demands a federal superintendence.[12]

Referring to the discussion by counsel [13] of the "political situation" of the country before the Constitution was adopted, Marshall remarks that the important fact is not that the states were independent in those days but that the Constitution changed that situation. As he put it:

> It has been said, that they [the states] were sovereign, were completely independent, and were connected with each other only by a league. This is true. But, when these allied sovereigns converted their league into a government, when they converted their Congress of Ambassadors, deputed to deliberate on their common concerns, and to recommend measures of general utility, into a Legislature, empowered to enact laws on the most interesting subjects, the whole character in which the States appear, underwent a change, the extent of which must be determined by a fair consideration of the instrument by which that change was effected.[14]

There it is; at the very outset of his opinion, the Chief Justice gives us the central tenet of his view of political power in the

[11] George L. Haskins, "Marshall and the Commerce Clause of the Constitution," reprinted in *Chief Justice John Marshall: A Reappraisal,* W. Melville Jones, ed., p. 149.

[12] *The Federalist,* No. 22, p. 191 (Wright, ed.).

[13] Daniel Webster and Attorney General William Wirt argued against the constitutionality of the steamboat monopoly. Thomas J. Oakley and Robert Emmet defended it.

[14] 9 Wheat. 1, 187.

American federal Republic. Issues as to the relative authority of nation and states to deal with a particular problem will be disposed of easily enough, he seems to be saying, if it is remembered that the Constitution created an actual government and that the Congress was vested with the coercive powers of a national legislature. And, as to the range or scope of the powers of the national legislature, it can best be understood by recalling the fundamental purposes or "objects" for which the Constitution was adopted. Once more Marshall repudiates a "strict" or "narrow" interpretation of those powers:

> If they [counsel] contend for that narrow construction which, in support of some theory not to be found in the constitution, would deny to the government those powers which the words of the grant, as usually understood, import, and which are consistent with the general views and objects of the instrument; for that narrow construction, which would cripple the government, and render it unequal for the object for which it is declared to be instituted, and to which the powers given, as fairly understood, render it competent; then we cannot perceive the propriety of this strict construction, nor adopt it as the rule by which the constitution is to be expounded. . . . We know of no rule for construing the extent of such powers, other than is given by the language of the instrument which confers them, taken in connexion with the purposes for which they were conferred.[15]

All of these even by then familiar Marshallian precepts were but preliminary to the gloss the Chief Justice was about to place upon the meaning of the commerce clause. He first quotes the exact language of the clause: "Congress shall have power to regulate commerce with foreign nations, and among the several States, and with the Indian tribes." [16] Then he makes a comment which may be seen as both a description of and justification for his particular approach to the process of constitutional interpretation: "The subject to be regulated is commerce: and our constitution being, as was aptly said at the bar, one of enumeration, and not of definition, to ascertain the extent of the power, it becomes necessary to settle the meaning of the word." [17]

[15] *Ibid.*, pp. 188–189.
[16] *Constitution*, Art. I, sec. 8, cl. 3.
[17] 9 Wheat. 1, 189.

And of course, the task of furnishing authoritative "definitions" of the powers conferred by the Constitution belonged to the Court for whom the Chief Justice was speaking. Though Marshall may not have "settled" the meaning of the crucial words in the commerce clause for all time, much of what he has to say in *Gibbons v. Ogden* has continued to be useful to both federal and state courts, not to mention Congress itself. In the circumstances of that historic case, Marshall's seeming exercise in semantics was designed to help justify the Supreme Court's resolution of a difficult and important practical problem.

II

Between 1798 and 1811, the legislature of New York had enacted, on five different occasions, laws granting to Livingston and Fulton the exclusive privilege of operating steamboats within the navigable waters of the state. Thomas Gibbons, whom the New York courts sought to restrain from running a steamboat between Elizabethtown, New Jersey, and New York City, claimed that his right to do so was protected by the Coasting License Act which Congress had adopted in 1793.[18] To quote Edward S. Corwin's incredibly succinct one-sentence summary of a complex case: "For a quarter of a century Robert R. Livingston and Robert Fulton and their successors had enjoyed from the Legislature of New York a grant of the exclusive right to run steamboats on the waters of the State, and in this case one of their licensees, Ogden, was seeking to prevent Gibbons, who had steamers in the coasting trade under an act of Congress, from operating them on the Hudson in trade between points in New York and New Jersey."[19]

There was thus posed for the Supreme Court the problem of resolving a conflict arising out of an attempt of a state to regulate a subject which had allegedly been assigned to the jurisdiction of the national government. It therefore became necessary to "define" the extent of Congress' power to regulate interstate commerce. Did commerce consist merely of the process of buying

[18] New York's attempt to maintain a monopoly in the use of steamboats induced a number of states to adopt retaliatory measures directed against New York shipping. For a brief discussion of what he characterizes as the resulting "commercial war"—as well as for a rather dramatic account of the complicated litigation—see Beveridge, *op. cit.*, IV, ch. VIII.

[19] Corwin, *op. cit.*, pp. 135–136.

and selling, or did it embrace navigation as well? Marshall's answer to this question may be said to have initiated the tradition of viewing "commerce" as a broad and practical conception:

> Commerce, undoubtedly, is traffic, but it is something more: it is intercourse. It describes the commercial intercourse between nations, and parts of nations, in all its branches, and is regulated by prescribing rules for carrying on that intercourse. The mind can scarcely conceive a system for regulating commerce between nations, which shall exclude all laws concerning navigation, which shall be silent on the admission of vessels of the one nation into the ports of the other, and be confined to prescribing rules for the conduct of individuals, in the actual employment of buying and selling, or of barter.
>
> If commerce does not include navigation, the government of the Union has no direct power over that subject, and can make no law prescribing what shall constitute American vessels, or requiring that they shall be navigated by American seamen. Yet this power has been exercised from the commencement of the government, has been exercised with the consent of all, and has been understood by all to be a commercial regulation. All America understands, and has uniformly understood, the word "commerce" to comprehend navigation. It was so understood, and must have been so understood, when the constitution was framed. The power over commerce, including navigation, was one of the primary objects for which the people of America adopted their government, and must have been contemplated in forming it. The convention must have used the word in that sense, because all have understood it in that sense; and the attempt to restrict it comes too late.[20]

But Marshall does not rest the proposition that commerce "comprehends" navigation on the common sense of the matter alone. He found support for it in the language of the Constitution itself. On the theory that "the exceptions from a power mark its extent," he goes on to maintain that the limitations on the power over commerce written into the ninth section of Article I show that Congress was meant to have the right to control navigation.[21] Further proof is furnished by the history of the embargo

[20] 9 Wheat. 1, 189–190.
[21] "No Preference shall be given by any Regulation of Commerce or

laws enacted by Congress. Marshall ends his exposition of the meaning of the word "commerce" on a note of absolute certainty: "The word used in the constitution, then, comprehends, and has been always understood to comprehend, navigation within its meaning; and a power to regulate navigation is as expressly granted as if that term had been added to the word 'commerce'." [22]

More significant, however, than the commentary on navigation is Marshall's analysis of the scope of the power over foreign and interstate commerce. "To what commerce does this power extend?" he asks, and answers by saying that the words in the commerce clause "comprehend every species of commercial intercourse between the United States and foreign nations." If commerce is to be seen as a "unit, every part of which is indicated by the term," so is commerce among the several states or interstate commerce. "Commerce among the States cannot stop at the external boundary line of each State, but may be introduced into the interior." The power to regulate commerce "among the several States" obviously extends to the regulation of commerce which "concerns more States than one," and not the "exclusively internal commerce" of a single state. "The genius and character of the whole government seem to be," declares Marshall, "that its action is to be applied to all the external concerns of the nation, and to those internal concerns which affect the States generally; but not to those which are completely within a particular State, which do not affect other States, and with which it is not necessary to interfere, for the purpose of executing some of the general powers of the government. The completely internal commerce of a State, then, may be considered as reserved for the State itself." [23] Furthermore, just as the country's commerce with foreign nations does not stop at the jurisdictional lines of the states, so

Revenue to the Ports of one State over those of another; nor shall Vessels bound to, or from, one State, be obliged to enter, clear or pay Duties in another." *Constitution*, Art. I, sec. 9, cl. 6. Commenting on the first part of this clause, Marshall says "the most obvious preference which can be given to one port over another, in regulating commerce, relates to navigation." And he was sure that the words in the second part "have a direct reference to navigation." 9 Wheat. 1, 191.

[22] 9 Wheat. 1, 193.

[23] *Ibid.*, p. 195.

the power of Congress over commerce among the several states must be exercised within their "territorial jurisdiction."

As Marshall saw it, there were purely practical considerations which justify the conception of commerce to which he was committing the Court. Referring to foreign commerce he observes:

> The commerce of the United States with foreign nations, is that of the whole United States. Every district has a right to participate in it. The deep streams which penetrate our country in every direction, pass through the interior of almost every state of the Union, and furnish the means of exercising this right. If Congress has the power to regulate it, that power must be exercised wherever the subject exists. If it exists within the States, if a foreign voyage may commence or terminate at a port within a state, then the power of Congress may be exercised within a State.[24]

And moving on to describe commerce within the United States, he continues:

> This principle is, if possible, still more clear, when applied to commerce "among the several States." They either join each other, in which case they are separated by a mathematical line, or they are remote from each other, in which case other States lie between them. What is commerce "among" them; and how is it to be conducted? Can a trading expedition between two adjoining States, commence and terminate outside of each? And if the trading intercourse be between two States remote from each other, must it not commence in one, terminate in the other, and probably pass through a third? Commerce among the States must, of necessity, be commerce with the States. . . . The power of Congress, then, whatever it may be, must be exercised within the territorial jurisdiction of the several States.[25]

When Marshall turned from the discussion of the subject to which the commerce power relates to examine the question as to just how far Congress can go in exercising that power, it became evident that he was using the occasion to set down the broadest possible conception of the federal commerce power. The only restrictions on the power which exist, he says repeatedly, are those explicitly set forth in the Constitution itself. As one rereads

[24] *Ibid.*
[25] *Ibid.*, pp. 195–196.

the terse paragraph in which is to be found his famous delineation of the far-reaching dimensions of Congress' power under the
commerce clause, it is indeed easy to understand why it proved so
exceedingly suggestive to later generations. It has continued to encourage those who have had to find constitutional pegs on which
to support federal efforts to cope with the economic and techno-
logical transformations of American society.[26] The much quoted
passage reads as follows:

> We are now arrived at the inquiry—What is this power?
>
> It is the power to regulate; that is, to prescribe the rule by
> which commerce is to be governed. This power, like all others
> vested in Congress, is complete in itself, may be exercised to its
> utmost extent, and acknowledges no limitations, other than are
> prescribed in the Constitution. . . . If, as has always been under-
> stood, the sovereignty of Congress, though limited to specified ob-
> jects, is plenary as to those objects, the power over commerce with
> foreign nations, and among the several States, is vested in Congress
> as absolutely as it would be in a single government, having in its
> constitution the same restrictions on the exercise of the power as
> are found in the constitution of the United States. The wisdom
> and the discretion of Congress, their identity with the people, and
> the influence which their constituents possess at elections, are, in
> this, as in many other instances, as that, for example, of declaring
> war, the sole restraints on which they have relied, to secure them
> from its abuse. They are the restraints on which the people must
> often rely solely, in all representative governments.[27]

III

Yet the immediate issue in *Gibbons v. Ogden* did not concern
the ultimate reach of Congress' power to regulate interstate and
foreign commerce. Nor could it be disposed of by a neat bit of
verbalization in the form of a definition. Only by seeing the case
from the point of view of the states can the much more difficult
and perplexing constitutional question posed by the litigation be
appreciated.

That question has to do with the effect upon the powers of

[26] One of the best and most succinct recent analyses of Marshall's influence
in this regard can be found in the article by George L. Haskins, cited above,
note 11, p. 197.

[27] 9 Wheat. 1, 196–197.

the states stemming from the grant to Congress of the power to regulate foreign and interstate commerce. Putting it another way, it might be asked: Just how much authority to legislate on commerce was left with the states after the Constitution vested in Congress the power to regulate commerce with "foreign nations . . . and among the several States"? As might be expected, the answer to this general question pressed on the Court by Oakley and Emmet—as part of their defense of the exclusive privilege granted to Livingston and Fulton—is quite different from that advanced by Webster and Wirt in their attack on the constitutionality of the steamboat monopoly. It was Webster who sought to persuade the Court to accept the view that in conferring on Congress the power to regulate commerce among the states, the Constitution meant to give it complete power and to bar the states from the field. There was no "general concurrent power" over commerce, he insisted. Marshall found "great force" in this argument and disclosed that the Court was "not satisfied that it has been refuted." The aim of the grant to Congress, Webster maintained, was to rescue commerce "from the embarrassing and destructive consequences resulting from the legislation of so many different States, and to place it under the protection of a uniform law." Recalling the "perpetual jarring and hostility of commercial regulations" which prevailed under the Articles of Confederation, he told the Court that "It is apparent from the prohibitions on the power of the States" that "the general concurrent power was not supposed to be left with them." But Webster had also acknowledged that not all local regulations which might affect commerce lay within the exclusive control of Congress. Such laws as those undertaking to regulate ferries, bridges, and turnpikes, as well as quarantine measures, were characterized by him as "rather regulations of police than of commerce in the constitutional understanding of that term." But over the "high branches" of commerce, Congress' power was exclusive.[28]

Daniel Webster once described Marshall's opinion in *Gibbons v. Ogden* as "little else than a recital of my argument." [29] However

[28] *Ibid.*, pp. 11, 14, 19.
[29] Quoted by Charles Warren, *The Supreme Court in United States History* (Boston: Little, Brown, and Company, 1922; 1937 ed.), I, 610.

much Webster may have exaggerated the extent to which the Chief Justice borrowed from him, the influence of his notable argument in the case is quite apparent. But Marshall's summary of the oral argument in behalf of New York is also both accurate and fair—a fine example of what James Bradley Thayer has characterized as his "candid allowance for all that was to be said upon the other side." [30] The Chief Justice writes:

> But it has been urged with great earnestness, that, although the power of Congress to regulate commerce with foreign nations, and among the several States, be co-extensive with the subject itself, and have no other limits than are prescribed in the constitution, yet the States may severally exercise the same power, within their respective jurisdictions. In support of this argument, it is said, that they possessed it as an inseparable attribute of sovereignty, before the formation of the constitution, and still retain it, except so far as they have surrendered it by that instrument; that this principle results from the nature of the government, and is secured by the tenth amendment; that an affirmative grant of power is not exclusive, unless in its own nature it be such that the continued exercise of it by the former possessor is inconsistent with the grant, and that this is not of that description.[31]

He understood the opposite view to be that "full power to regulate a particular subject implies the whole power, and leaves no residuum; that a grant of the whole is incompatible with the existence of a right in another to any part of it."

Immediately after giving these brief summaries of the extensive presentations to the court, Marshall makes an observation which well epitomizes the ironic character of constitutional argumentation in the United States. "Both parties have appealed to the constitution, to legislative acts, and judicial decisions; and have drawn arguments from all these sources, to support and illustrate the propositions they respectively maintain." [32] Though Marshall does not make a completely unequivocal choice between the mutually contradictory inferences drawn from the same "sources," he certainly seems to favor the view which would

[30] Thayer, *John Marshall,* p. 58.
[31] 9 Wheat. 1, 197–198.
[32] *Ibid.,* p. 198.

have excluded the states from the field. The apparent ambiguity, it has been suggested, was due less to "unconscious confusion of thought" and probably more to the fact that "while . . . he [Marshall] saw in the commerce clause an opportunity to protect the national interest against state interferences even in the absence of Congressional action, he was not yet prepared to transmute this possibility into constitutional doctrine."[33]

From whatever motive, Marshall refused to say whether the commerce clause, by its own force, rendered a state constitutionally powerless to enact a statute such as New York's monopoly law. Instead, he chose to rule that the law was in conflict with the federal Coasting License Act of 1793. At the moment, all he was willing to say was that a state may not regulate commerce while Congress has undertaken to do so. "In discussing the question whether this power is still in the States," writes Marshall, "we may dismiss from it the inquiry whether it has been surrendered by the mere grant to Congress, or is retained until Congress shall exercise the power." Since Congress had already legislated on the subject of navigation, it was unnecessary to pass on the broader constitutional problem. "We may dismiss that inquiry because it has been exercised, and the regulations which Congress deemed it proper to make are now in full operation." Having thus declined to grapple with the constitutional issue as framed by the eminent lawyers who had argued the case, Marshall professed to see a much simpler and narrower question to be determined by the Court: "The sole question is, can a State regulate commerce with foreign nations and among the States, while Congress is regulating it?" [34]

As part of their argument that the mere grant to Congress of the power to regulate foreign and interstate commerce did not necessarily deprive the states of all authority over such commerce, counsel for Aaron Ogden contended that logically such a view would deny to the states the power to tax. In rejecting this position, Marshall tries to show that there was no "analogy" between the power over commerce and the taxing power:

[33] Frankfurter, *The Commerce Clause under Marshall, Taney and Waite,* p. 18.
[34] 9 Wheat. 1, 200.

Although many of the powers formerly exercised by the States, are transferred to the government of the Union, yet the State governments remain, and constitute a most important part of our system. The power of taxation is indispensable to their existence, and is a power which, in its own nature, is capable of residing in, and being exercised by, different authorities at the same time. . . . Congress is authorized to lay and collect taxes, etc., to pay the debts, and provide for the common defence and general welfare of the United States. This does not interfere with the power of the States to tax for the support of their own governments; nor is the exercise of that power by the States, an exercise of any portion of the power that is granted to the United States. In imposing taxes for State purposes they are not doing what Congress is empowered to do. Congress is not empowered to tax for those purposes which are within the exclusive province of the States. When, then, each government exercises the power of taxation, neither is exercising the power of the other. But, when a State proceeds to regulate commerce with foreign nations, or among the several States, it is exercising the very power that is granted to Congress, and is doing the very thing which Congress is authorized to do. There is no analogy, then, between the power of taxation and the power of regulating commerce.[35]

This distinction between the power of taxation and the power over commerce was an integral part of the logic employed by Marshall in answering the contention that the framers of the Constitution did not intend to make the authority to regulate commerce an exclusive power of the national government. A good deal of stress was placed by him on the inference to be drawn from the fact that the states are forbidden to tax imports and exports.[36] On the premise that exceptions to the exercise of a power prove the existence of the power, it was maintained by the lawyers for the steamboat monopoly that but for the prohibition of such exactions, the states would be able to impose duties on imports and exports. By the same token, a state might regulate foreign and interstate commerce unless specifically forbidden to do so by the Constitution.

[35] *Ibid.*, pp. 198–200.
[36] "No State shall, without the Consent of the Congress, lay any Imposts or Duties on Imports or Exports, except what may be absolutely necessary for executing its inspection Laws." *Constitution*, Art. I, sec. 10, cl. 2.

Marshall's rejoinder to this argument is clear and emphatic. He readily concedes that the states would have been free to tax imports and exports were they not expressly restrained from doing so by the Constitution. But the proposition that it therefore follows that they could also regulate foreign and interstate commerce "cannot be admitted." It was manifest that the right to tax imports and exports is "a branch of the taxing power," as are duties on tonnage.[37] Marshall's use of the general language of the Constitution to "document" his particularized reading of its important clauses is quite striking:

> . . . The constitution, then, considers these powers [Congress' powers in the field of taxation and commerce] as substantive, and distinct from each other; and so places them in the enumeration it contains. The power of imposing duties on imports is classed with the power to levy taxes, and that seems to be its natural place. But the power to levy taxes could never be considered as abridging the right of the States on that subject; and they might, consequently, have exercised it by levying duties on imports or exports, had the constitution contained no prohibition on this subject. This prohibition, then, is an exception from the acknowledged power of the States to levy taxes, not from the questionable power to regulate commerce.[38]

Still more crucial—especially from the standpoint of the development of future doctrines—was Marshall's distinction be-

---

[37] "No State shall, without the Consent of the Congress, lay any Duty of Tonnage." *Constitution*, Art. I, sec. 10, cl. 3. Commenting on this prohibition on the states, Marshall points out that as men who were familiar with the provocations which brought on the Revolution, the framers of the Constitution appreciated that a right to impose tonnage duties did not imply the power to regulate commerce. "It is true, that duties may often be, and in fact often are, imposed on tonnage, with a view to the regulation of commerce; but they may be also imposed with a view to revenue; and it was, therefore, a prudent precaution, to prohibit the States from exercising this power. The idea that the same measure might, according to circumstances, be arranged with different classes of power, was no novelty to the framers of our constitution. Those illustrious statesmen and patriots had been, many of them, deeply engaged in the discussions which preceded the war of our revolution, and all of them were well read in those discussions. The right to regulate commerce, even by the imposition of duties, was not controverted; but the right to impose a duty for the purpose of revenue, produced a war as important, perhaps, in its consequences to the human race, as any the world has ever witnessed." 9 Wheat. 1, 202.

[38] 9 Wheat. 1, 201-202.

tween the regulation of commerce entrusted to Congress and local regulations which might have an incidental or "remote influence" on commerce. Like inspection laws—which are designed to "improve the articles before they become part of foreign or interstate commerce"—such state regulations "form a portion of that immense mass of legislation which embraces everything within the territory of a State not surrendered to the General Government." Besides inspection laws, such legislation is exemplified by quarantine and health laws, laws regulating the purely "internal commerce of a State," and regulations of turnpike roads and ferries. Regarding such local regulations—which are to be considered as part of a state's "system of police"—Marshall says that since "no direct general power" over them is vested in Congress, the power remains with the states. Yet it is "obvious" that in the exercise of its "express powers," Congress may undertake to deal with matters to which a state might seek to apply its own powers. Such conflicts are unavoidable in the American federal Union. "In our complex system, presenting the rare and difficult scheme of one general government, whose action extends over the whole, but which possesses only certain enumerated powers; and of numerous State governments, which retain and exercise all powers not delegated to the Union, contests respecting power must arise."[39]

IV

Marshall devoted more than half of his fifty-three-page opinion to this general analysis before turning to the question as to why New York's steamboat monopoly legislation was in conflict with the law passed by Congress for the licensing of ships engaged in the coastal trade. The important issue, as framed by the Chief Justice, was whether the New York law was in "collision" with an act of Congress by depriving "a citizen of a right to which that act entitles him." Whatever may have been the asserted legal basis for the statutes adopted by New York on the subject of steamboat navigation, if they were found to collide with a law validly enacted by Congress, "the acts of New York must yield to the law of Congress." Marshall rejects any suggestion that when a measure adopted by a state in the exercise of its "acknowledged

[39] *Ibid.*, pp. 204–205.

sovereignty" comes into conflict with a law passed by Congress, the two laws are to be regarded "like opposing powers." The Constitution recognizes no such equality between federal and state actions: "But the framers of our constitution foresaw this state of things, and provided for it, by declaring the supremacy not only of itself, but of the laws made in pursuance of it. The nullity of any act inconsistent with the constitution, is produced by the declaration, that the constitution is the supreme law." [40]

Accordingly, no state may interfere with the movement of vessels which have been licensed by Congress to engage in the coasting trade. However propelled and whether carrying passengers or merchandise, such vessels are free to ply the waterways of the United States. Since the federal power over commerce includes the right to regulate navigation, the method or "principle" by which boats are operated does not, in any way, curtail Congress' control of shipping. Steamboats were entitled, states Marshall quite explicitly, "to the same privileges, and can no more be restrained from navigating waters, and entering ports which are free to such vessels, [vessels "using sails"] than if they were wafted on their voyage by the winds, instead of being propelled by the agency of fire." He continues: "The one element may be as legitimately used as the other, for every commercial purpose authorized by the laws of the Union; and the act of a State inhibiting the use of either to any vessel having a license under the act of Congress, comes, we think, in direct collision with that act."[41]

Even Beveridge—avid admirer of the eminent Chief Justice though he was—permitted himself to say that in *Gibbons v. Ogden*, Marshall is at times "diffuse, prolix, and indirect," and that the opinion suffers from "excessive length" and "over-explanation." [42] Yet these seeming defects of style are such in a superficial sense only. Actually, they may be seen as a clue to Marshall's basic strategy as an interpreter of the Constitution. They were the characteristics of a judge who was determined to use constitutional cases as so many opportunities for disseminat-

[40] *Ibid.*, pp. 210–211.
[41] *Ibid.*, p. 221.
[42] Beveridge, *op. cit.*, IV, 434, 437, 439.

ing ideas, and a way of thinking about them, which would help to propagate his conception of the governmental system ordained by the Constitution. His method, admittedly verbose and repetitious, was part and parcel of a larger design. Indeed, he himself was not unaware of these shortcomings, as the apologetic note on which he ends clearly shows.[43] The apology, however, merely leads him into a stern peroration, in which we are once again reminded that the Chief Justice's ultimate aim was to "preserve" sound principles of constitutional interpretation:

> Powerful and ingenious minds, taking, as postulates, that the powers expressly granted to the government of the Union, are to be contracted by construction, into the narrowest possible compass, and that the original powers of the States are retained, if any possible construction will retain them, may, by a course of well digested, but refined and metaphysical reasoning, founded on these premises, explain away the constitution of our country, and leave it, a magnificent structure, indeed, to look at, but totally unfit for use. They may so entangle and perplex the understanding, as to obscure principles, which were before thought quite plain, and induce doubts where, if the mind were to pursue its own course, none would be perceived. In such a case, it is peculiarly necessary to recur to safe and fundamental principles to sustain those principles, and, when sustained, to make them the tests of the arguments to be examined.[44]

Marshall's opinion in *Gibbons v. Ogden* was far from being an unequivocal statement of the nationalism with which his name has come to be identified. It was left to Justice William Johnson

[43] "The Court is aware that, in stating the train of reasoning by which we have been conducted to this result, much time has been consumed in the attempt to demonstrate propositions which may have been thought axioms. It is felt that the tediousness inseparable from the endeavor to prove that which is already clear, is imputable to a considerable part of this opinion. But it was unavoidable. The conclusion to which we have come, depends on a chain of principles which it was necessary to preserve unbroken; and, although some of them were thought nearly self-evident, the magnitude of the question, the weight of character belonging to those from whose judgment we dissent, and the argument at the bar, demanded that we should assume nothing." 9 Wheat. 1, 221-222. Beveridge's conjecture was that the remark about "the weight of character belonging to those from whose judgment we dissent" was Marshall's way of "placating" James Kent. *The Life of John Marshall*, IV, 441.
[44] 9 Wheat. 1, 222.

—whose biographer has described him as the "first dissenter" on the Supreme Court [45]—to give the completely uncompromising answer to the fundamental question in the case, an answer which might have come more appropriately from Marshall. Johnson, in his vigorous concurring opinion, maintained that the power of Congress "must be exclusive" and that the very "grant of this power carries with it the whole subject, leaving nothing for the State to act upon." He could not accept the specific ground for the decision—the conclusion that the state law sanctioning a monopoly in the operation of steamboats was contrary to the policy embodied in the federal Coasting License Act. "If there was any one object riding over every other in the adoption of the constitution," Justice Johnson declared, "it was to keep the commercial intercourse among the States free from all invidious and partial restraints." [46] As Beveridge has written: "So it turned out that the first man appointed for the purpose of thwarting Marshall's Nationalism, expressed, twenty years after his appointment, stronger Nationalist sentiments than Marshall himself was, as yet, willing to avow openly." [47]

[45] Donald G. Morgan, *Justice William Johnson, The First Dissenter* (Columbia, S.C.: University of South Carolina Press, 1954).

[46] 9 Wheat. 1, 222, 227, 231.

[47] Beveridge, *op. cit.,* IV, 444.

10

"A Power Which No State Ought to Exercise"

Whatever hesitation Marshall may have had in placing the invalidity of the steamboat monopoly on a straightforward constitutional ground, any such doubts vanished completely by the time he came to pen his other great commerce clause opinion three years later.[1] As Edward S. Corwin has noted, "the principle of the exclusiveness of Congress's power to regulate commerce among the States and with foreign nations, which is advanced by way of *dictum* in Gibbons *vs.* Ogden, becomes in Brown *vs.* Maryland a ground of decision." [2]

But perhaps one reason Marshall could speak with greater force in *Brown v. Maryland* was that the issue confronting the Court was more clearly delineated by the case itself. The conflict between state and federal powers was more obvious, and the need for exclusive national dominion seemed more urgent. Another factor making the Court's task easier was that it was able to invoke a specific constitutional prohibition,[3] in addition to the generality of the commerce clause.

A Maryland law required importers of goods from foreign countries to secure a license from the state before they could sell the imported products. The license fee was $50.[4] Brown and his

[1] *Brown v. Maryland,* 12 Wheat. 419 (1827).

[2] Corwin, *John Marshall and the Constitution,* p. 142.

[3] "No State shall, without the Consent of the Congress, lay any Imposts or Duties on Imports or Exports, except what may be absolutely necessary for executing its inspection Laws." *Constitution,* Art. I, sec. 10, cl. 2.

[4] The provision in question read as follows: "And be it enacted, that all

partners were convicted in a Baltimore court for importing and selling some dry goods without first having obtained a license authorizing them to do so.

I

After the briefest kind of statement of the case—just one paragraph, to be exact—Marshall presents the single constitutional problem to be resolved by the Court. "The cause depends entirely, on the question," he states, "whether the Legislature of a State can constitutionally require the importer of foreign articles to take out a license from the State before he shall be permitted to sell a bale or package so imported." But before moving into the heart of the controversy, he pauses long enough on the preliminaries to summarize certain principles of constitutional interpretation by which the Court must be guided.

In view of the outcome, it is ironic that Marshall should begin by remarking that "It has been truly said that the presumption is in favor of every legislative act, and that the whole burden of proof lies on him who denies its constitutionality." We are told that those who attacked the validity of the Maryland statute had taken "upon themselves" the burden of demonstrating that it violated the commerce clause as well as the provision forbidding the states to tax imports. Maryland's lawyers, on the other hand, contended that the Constitution forbade only such state measures as might be considered direct duties or taxes on imports and exports. How, then, should the Court approach the problem of interpreting constitutional clauses which lend themselves to such clashing readings?

"In performing the delicate and important duty of construing clauses in the constitution of our country, which involve conflicting powers of the government of the Union and of the re-

importers of foreign articles or commodities, of dry goods, wares, or merchandise, by bale or package, or of wine, rum, brandy, whisky, and other distilled spirituous liquors, etc. and other persons selling the same by wholesale, bale or package, hogshead, barrel, or tierce, shall, before they are authorized to sell, take out a license, as by the original act is directed, for which they shall pay fifty dollars; and in case of neglect or refusal to take out such license, shall be subject to the same penalities and forfeitures as are prescribed by the original act to which this is a supplement." 12 Wheat. 419, 436.

spective States," writes the Chief Justice, "it is proper to take a view of the literal meaning of the words expounded, of their connexion with other words, and of the general objects to be accomplished by the prohibitory clause, or by the grant of power." [5]

Presumably guided by the last-mentioned rule of construction, Marshall devotes several pages to an examination of the "meaning" of the words in the Constitution which prohibit the states from imposing "imposts or duties on imports or exports." As is true of similar semantic exercises in other of his opinions, the discussion of words becomes a vehicle for unfolding the underlying purposes of particular constitutional provisions. One of his main conclusions is that, although an impost or duty on imports is ordinarily collected from the importer before he is permitted to take possession of the commodities, the exaction would be no less an impost or duty if it were levied after the articles had already come into the country.[6]

To bolster the argument that payments by the importer— even after his products had entered the United States—might actually be a duty on those articles, Marshall points to the "exception" to be found in the very provision of the Constitution which forbids the states to tax imports or exports. A state is not to place any duties on imports or exports "except what may be absolutely necessary for executing its inspection laws." Since inspection can take place only after goods have "landed" in a port, it is obvious that the framers of the Constitution were determined to keep the states from burdening imports or exports with taxes, whether imposed before or after the goods had come into the country. Marshall takes this little proposition and converts it into a theory for gathering the meaning of the Constitution:

> If it be a rule of interpretation to which all assent, that the exception of a particular thing from general words, proves that,

[5] *Ibid.*, p. 437.

[6] "'A duty on imports,' then, is not merely a duty on the act of importation, but is a duty on the thing imported. It is not, taken in its literal sense, confined to a duty levied while the article is entering the country, but extends to a duty levied after it has entered the country." *Ibid.*, pp. 437–438.

in the opinion of the lawgiver, the thing excepted would be within the general clause had the exception not been made, we know no reason why this general rule should not be as applicable to the constitution as to other instruments. If it be applicable, then this exception in favor of duties for the support of inspection laws, goes far in proving that the framers of the constitution classed taxes of a similar character with those imposed for the purposes of inspection, with duties on imports and exports, and supposed them to be prohibited.[7]

But the dictionary and logical inference were not the only tools by which it could be demonstrated that the framers of the Constitution intended to preclude the states from taxing importers of foreign articles. The conclusion to be drawn from the "narrow" or "literal interpretation of the words" in the pertinent provision, Marshall suggests, is made inescapably clear when one recalls the "objects" of the prohibition in question:

> From the vast inequality of the different States of the Confederacy, as to commercial advantages, few subjects were viewed with deeper interest, or excited more irritation, than the manner in which the several States exercised, or seemed disposed to exercise, the power of laying duties on imports. From motives which were deemed sufficient by the statesmen of that day, the general power of taxation, indispensably necessary as it was, and jealous as the States were of any encroachment on it, was so far abridged as to forbid them to touch imports or exports, with the single exception which has been noticed. Why are they restrained from imposing these duties? Plainly, because, in the general opinion, the interest of all would be best promoted by placing that whole subject under the control of Congress. Whether the prohibition to "lay imposts, or duties on imports or exports" proceeded from an apprehension that the power might be so exercised as to disturb that equality among the States which was generally advantageous, or that harmony between them which it was desirable to preserve, or to maintain unimpaired our commercial connexions with foreign nations, or to confer this source of revenue on the government of the Union, or whatever other motive might have induced the prohibition, it is plain that the object would be as completely defeated by a power to tax the article in the hands of the importer

[7] *Ibid.*, p. 438.

the instant it was landed, as by a power to tax it while entering the port.[8]

From a practical standpoint, there was no difference between the power to stop the sale of foreign commodities and the power to keep them from entering the country. "No goods would be imported if none could be sold." Once a state was permitted to tax articles in the hands of the importer, such a power could be used to levy "light" duties as well as "very heavy" duties.

II

As he had done eight years earlier in *McCulloch v. Maryland*, Marshall articulates a view of governmental power under the American federal system which presupposes a total lack of authority in the states to deal with matters which have been placed within the national sphere. When called on to resolve conflicts between the respective powers of nation and state, the Court is concerned with the question whether the particular power is possessed by the government claiming it, and not with the amount or extent of the tax. Said Marshall: "Questions of power do not depend on the degree to which it may be exercised. If it may be exercised at all, it must be exercised at the will of those in whose hands it is placed. If the tax may be levied in this form by a State, it may be levied to an extent which will defeat the revenue by impost, so far as it is drawn from importations into the particular State." [9]

It was true that all power was capable of being abused, but that hazard is no argument against the exercise of a particular power. Marshall also agreed that no state "would act so unwisely" as to lessen or kill its own trade. But the Court should not be expected to decide the case on such an optimistic ground. Replying to the contention that no state would be "so blind to its own interests" as to tax imports to the point of hurting its own commerce, the Chief Justice's answer was as blunt as it was succinct: "Yet the framers of our constitution have thought this a power which no State ought to exercise." [10]

But even if it were assumed that a state would not pursue a

[8] *Ibid.*, pp. 438–439.
[9] *Ibid.*, p. 439.
[10] *Ibid.*, p. 440.

tax policy which might jeopardize its own interests, there was
always the danger that it would ignore the needs of other states.
Indeed, this possibility was one of the "mischiefs" the framers had
in mind when they prohibited the states from taxing imports.
Marshall's statement of the practical consequences of allowing a
state to impose duties on the importer shows the extent to which
his interpretations of the commerce clause were shaped in the
shadow, as it were, of the commercial irritations under the Confederation:

> A duty on imports is a tax on the article which is paid by the
> consumer. The great importing States would thus levy a tax on the
> non-importing States, which would not be less a tax because their
> interest would afford ample security against its ever being so heavy
> as to expel commerce from their ports. This would necessarily pro-
> duce countervailing measures on the part of those States whose
> situation was less favorable to importation. For this, among other
> reasons, the whole power of laying duties on imports was, with a
> single and slight exception, taken from the States. When we are
> inquiring whether a particular act is within this prohibition, the
> question is not, whether the State may so legislate as to hurt itself,
> but whether a particular act is within the words and mischief of
> the prohibitory clause. It has already been shown, that a tax on the
> article in the hands of the importer, is within its words; and we
> think it too clear for controversy, that the same tax is within its
> mischief. We think it unquestionable, that such a tax has precisely
> the same tendency to enhance the price of the article, as if im-
> posed upon it while entering the port.[11]

One of Maryland's principal contentions was that if the prohibition of state taxes on imports were to be construed as denying to a state the right to exact payments after foreign articles
had already been brought into the country, the states would be
deprived of an important source of revenue. Marshall understood the argument to be, as he expressed it, that "entering the
country is the point of time when the prohibition ceases, and the
power of the State to tax commences." Though he thought there
was "great reason" in the position that the constitutional prohi-

[11] *Ibid.*

bition should not be pushed to the point of destroying the power of taxation retained by the states, he could not agree that the point at which the state may tax imports "is the instant that the articles enter the country." [12]

There were no fixed or "universal" criteria for determining, in a particular situation, when the ban on import duties operates, and when the right of a state to tax persons and property within its borders begins. Nevertheless, there was one general rule for dealing with this admittedly "perplexing" problem—the rule which came in time to be known as the "original package" doctrine. The passage in which Marshall sets forth this formula became sufficiently significant in later adjudications to merit quotation at some length:

> The constitutional prohibition on the States to lay a duty on imports, a prohibition which a vast majority of them must feel an interest in preserving, may certainly come in conflict with their acknowledged power to tax persons and property within their territory. The power, and the restriction on it, though quite distinguishable when they do not approach each other, may yet, like the intervening colours between white and black, approach so nearly as to perplex the understanding, as colours perplex the vision in marking the distinction between them. Yet the distinction exists, and must be marked as the cases arise. Till they do arise, it might be premature to state any rule as being universal in its application. It is sufficient for the present to say, generally, that, when the importer has so acted upon the thing imported, that it has become incorporated and mixed up with the mass of property in the country, it has, perhaps, lost its distinctive character as an import,

---

[12] "It may be conceded, that the words of the prohibition [the prohibition on the state not to tax imports] ought not to be pressed to their utmost extent; that in our complex system, the object of the powers conferred on the government of the Union, and the nature of the often conflicting powers which remain in the States, must always be taken into view, and may aid in expounding the words of any particular clause. But, while we admit that sound principles of construction ought to restrain all Courts from carrying the words of the prohibition beyond the object the constitution is intended to secure; that there must be a point of time when the prohibition ceases, and the power of the State to tax commences; we cannot admit that this point of time is the instant that the articles enter the country. It is, we think, obvious, that this construction would defeat the prohibition." *Ibid.*, p. 441.

and has become subject to the taxing power of the State; but while remaining the property of the importer, in his warehouse, in the original form or package in which it was imported, a tax upon it is too plainly a duty on imports to escape the prohibition in the constitution.[13]

Brown and his partners had been indicted, Marshall emphasizes, for failing to obtain permission from the state to import a package of foreign goods—before that product had become part of the "general mass" of property sold in Maryland. They were thus being penalized for exercising a privilege they had already been granted by the federal government—presumably under the tariff laws. By paying a duty to the United States, the importer has "purchased" not only the right to import, but to sell throughout the country. Marshall also rejects the argument that the license fee imposed by Maryland was merely an exercise of the state's power to tax occupations. He suggests that acceptance of this theory would be an example of "varying the form without varying the substance," since the ultimate impact of the levy would be not on the importer, but on the process of importing goods. "So, a tax on the occupation of an importer is . . . a tax on importation. It must add to the price of the article, and be paid by the consumer, or by the importer himself, in like manner as a direct duty on the article itself would be made. This the

[13] *Ibid.*, pp. 441-442. Later in the opinion—by way of demonstrating that the Maryland tax was on a product before it had become part of the "general mass of property" subject to taxation by the state—Marshall supplies some additional details on his "original package" concept. We read: "This indictment is against the importer, for selling a package of dry-goods in the form in which it was imported, without a license. This state of things is changed if he sells them, or otherwise mixes them with the general property of the State, by breaking up his packages, and traveling with them as an itinerant peddler. In the first case, the tax intercepts the import, as as import, on its way to become incorporated with the general mass of property, and denies it the privilege of becoming so incorporated until it shall have contributed to the revenue of the State. It denies to the importer the right of using the privilege which he has purchased from the United States, until he shall have also purchased it from the State. In the last cases, the tax finds the article already incorporated with the mass of property by the act of the importer. He has used the privilege he had purchased, and has himself mixed them up with the common mass, and the law may treat them as it finds them. The same observations apply to plate, or other furniture used by the importer." *Ibid.*, p. 443.

State has not a right to do, because it is prohibited by the constitution." [14]

It does not follow, however, that because they may not tax imported articles while still in the original packages, the states are rendered helpless to deal with problems which may arise from the presence of foreign articles in their midst. In the exercise of its police power, a state would be free to adopt regulations designed to safeguard the health and safety of its inhabitants. Such regulations might even be thought of as "inspection laws."

III

All but four of the fourteen-page decision in *Brown v. Maryland* were given over to this elaborate analysis of the provision, in Article I, section 10, taking from the states the power to place duties on imports and exports. So completely did Marshall demolish the case for the right of the states to license and tax importers, that the subsequent discussion of the objection based on the commerce clause, brief though it is, comes as something of an anticlimax. One impatient with the Chief Justice's habit of reiteration might even say that it was sheer redundancy. His opinions in *McCulloch v. Maryland* and *Gibbons v. Ogden* are cited, and the whole concluding section is pervaded by the tone of one who obviously felt that it was a little too late in the day for such issues to be raised again.

Yet Marshall's exposition of the commerce clause in *Brown v. Maryland* serves as a useful resumé of important constitutional principles, principles which he himself, to be sure, had already fully articulated. In it will be found fresh evidence of the extent to which his interpretations of the Constitution were dictated by his attitude toward the events and forces which produced the document of 1787. Describing those events as a "great revolution," he goes on to explain the considerations which underlie the commerce clause in the following words:

> The oppressed and degraded state of commerce previous to the adoption of the constitution can scarcely be forgotten. It was regulated by foreign nations with a single view to their own interests; and our disunited efforts to counteract their restrictions were

[14] *Ibid.*, p. 444.

rendered impotent by want of combination. Congress, indeed, possessed the power of making treaties; but the inability of the Federal Government to enforce them had become so apparent as to render that power in a great degree useless. Those who felt the injury arising from this state of things, and those who were capable of estimating the influence of commerce on the prosperity of nations, perceived the necessity of giving the control over this important subject to a single government. It may be doubted whether any of the evils proceeding from the feebleness of the federal government, contributed more to that great revolution which introduced the present system, than the deep and general conviction, that commerce ought to be regulated by Congress. It is not, therefore, matter of surprise, that the grant should be as extensive as the mischief, and should comprehend all foreign commerce, and all commerce among the States. To construe the power so as to impair its efficacy, would tend to defeat an object, in the attainment of which the American public took, and justly took, that strong interest which arose from a full conviction of its necessity.[15]

Remarking that the "truth" of the principles concerning the scope of Congress' power to regulate commerce which had been formulated in *Gibbons v. Ogden* was "proved by facts continually before our eyes," the Chief Justice interprets the earlier decision as having "demonstrated" the proposition that the commerce power reaches into the "interior" of a state.[16] Since the federal power over commerce may be exercised within the territory of a state, it follows that Congress may permit the sale of products brought into a state from foreign countries. Sale is a major "ingredient" of commercial intercourse, and it is the prospect of sale which gives "value" to the transactions involved in the importation of goods. "To what purpose," asks Marshall, "should

[15] *Ibid.*, pp. 445–446.

[16] It may be of interest to recall Marshall's own statement of the conception of the power to regulate commerce which he had enunciated in *Gibbons v. Ogden*. Speaking of that case in *Brown v. Maryland*, he writes: "What, then, is the just extent of a power to regulate commerce with foreign nations, and among the several States?

"This question was considered in the case of *Gibbons v. Ogden*, . . . in which it was declared to be complete in itself, and to acknowledge no limitations other than are prescribed by the constitution. The power is co-extensive with the subject on which it acts, and cannot be stopped at the external boundary of a State, but must enter its interior." *Ibid.*, p. 446.

the power to allow importation be given, unaccompanied with the power to authorize a sale of the thing imported?" This rhetorical query is, as might be expected, more of a declaration than a question, and it is immediately made clear that there can be but one answer. After saying, in several different ways, that the opportunity to sell the things imported is "indispensable" to the very existence of importation, Marshall adds: "Congress has a right, not only to authorize importation, but to authorize the importer to sell." [17]

There was more than one reason which made it essential that the privilege to import be construed to include the right to dispose of the things imported. Through one of his characteristic uses of rhetorical questions, Marshall makes it plain that for him considerations of morality as well as of good business required such a construction. Congress meant to deal "honestly and fairly" with the importer—"an intent as wise as it is moral." The importer's "contract" would be worthless unless he were afforded the opportunity to sell within the state. Moreover, any interference with the importer's right to sell would create embarrassments for the United States in its relations with other countries.

Nor could we depend on the hope that the "good sense" of the states would make them realize that such interferences would discourage commerce. "The constitution," retorts Marshall, "has not confided this subject to that good sense." He continues: "It is placed elsewhere. The question is, where does the power reside? Not, how far will it be probably abused? The power claimed by the State is, in its nature, in conflict with that given to Congress; and the greater or less extent in which it may be exercised does not enter into the inquiry concerning its existence." [18] Once it is admitted that the right to import "implies" the right to sell the goods which have been imported, any interference by a state with the privileges of the importer is in direct conflict with the federal power over the importation of foreign goods.[19]

[17] *Ibid.,* p. 447.
[18] *Ibid.*
[19] "Any penalty inflicted on the importer for selling the article in his character as importer, must be in opposition to the act of Congress which authorizes importation. Any charge on the introduction and incorporation of the articles into and with the mass of property in the country, must be hostile

Though the right of the states to tax persons and property within their territorial limits may be "sacred," that right may not be used "so as to obstruct the free course of a power given to Congress." In the practical exercise of the powers they retained after the Constitution was adopted, it was inevitable that the states should find themselves, from time to time, entering fields pre-empted for the federal government. But the principle of national supremacy leaves courts no choice except to uphold the primacy which the Constitution assigns to federal authority:

> It has been observed, that the powers remaining with the States may be so exercised as to come in conflict with those vested in Congress. When that happens, that which is not supreme must yield to that which is supreme. This great and universal truth is inseparable from the nature of things, and the constitution has applied it to the often interfering powers of the general and State governments as a vital principle of perpetual operation. It results, necessarily, from this principle, that the taxing power of the States must have some limits.[20]

Marshall saw no need for discussing further the proposition that the delegation of certain powers to the federal government inevitably restricts the authority of the states. He recalled that the problem had received "great attention" in *McCulloch v. Maryland* and that the principles enunciated in that case were

to the power given to Congress to regulate commerce, since an essential part of that regulation, and principal object of it, is to prescribe the regular means for accomplishing that introduction and incorporation." *Ibid.*, p. 448.

[20] *Ibid.* Marshall gave some examples of the "limits" on the taxing power of the States: "It cannot reach and restrain the action of the national government within its proper sphere. It cannot reach the administration of justice in the Courts of the Union, or the collection of the taxes of the United States, or restrain the operation of any law which Congress may constitutionally pass. It cannot interfere with any regulation of commerce. If the States may tax all persons and property found on their territory, what shall restrain them from taxing goods in their transit through the State from one port to another, for the purpose of re-exportation? The laws of trade authorize this operation, and general convenience requires it. Or what should restrain a State from taxing any article passing through it from one State to another, for the purpose of traffic? Or from taxing the transportation of articles passing from the State itself to another State, for commercial purposes? These cases are all within the sovereign power of taxation, but would obviously derange the measures of Congress to regulate commerce, and affect materially the purpose for which that power was given." *Ibid.*, p. 448–449.

"entirely applicable" to the constitutional issue posed in *Brown v. Maryland*.[21] Thus was foreign commerce given an immunity from taxation by the states as broad as that accorded to federal instrumentalities.

IV

No discussion of Marshall's exposition of the commerce clause would be complete without a reminder that the Chief Justice did not hew to an undeviating nationalistic line. Only two years after the seemingly sweeping decision in *Brown v. Maryland,* Marshall delivered an opinion vindicating the claim of a state which could just as well have come from the Court presided over by Roger Brooke Taney.[22] The case is *Willson v. Blackbird Creek Marsh Co.*,[23] and the decision was unanimous.

The dam which the Blackbird Creek Marsh Company had erected by authority of the Delaware legislature had resulted in the obstruction of navigation on the creek. When a vessel owned by Willson damaged the dam while trying to get around the obstruction, the company sued for damages in the Delaware courts. Chief Justice Marshall led the Supreme Court in sustaining the constitutionality of the Delaware law and in affirming the judgment of the Delaware Court of Appeals.

What sort of a constitutional question did this case pose for the Court? The problem was whether, by permitting the erection of an obstruction on a navigable creek, the Delaware law estab-

---

[21] *Ibid.*, p. 449. One dictum pronounced by Marshall in *Brown v. Maryland* was destined not to be honored by subsequent courts, though it was followed for a time. The Chief Justice had declared toward the end of his opinion: "It may be proper to add that we suppose the principles laid down in this case to apply equally to importation from a sister State." *Ibid.* It has been suggested that the chief reason this dictum was bound to be abandoned was that it would have cut too deeply into the revenues of the states. "In his eagerness to save national commerce from the particularism of the states, Marshall would have unduly contracted the available resources of the states' taxing power. He overreached himself. His doctrine was formally rejected in *Woodruff v. Parham* (8 Wall. 123) and that, too, at a time, in 1868, when the dominant mood of the country was nationalistic." Frankfurter, *The Commerce Clause under Marshall, Taney and Waite*, p. 37.

[22] For a discussion of the interpretation of the commerce clause by the Taney Court, see Carl B. Swisher, *Roger B. Taney* (New York: The Macmillan Company, 1935), ch. XIX.

[23] 2 Pet. 245 (1829).

lishing the Blackbird Creek Marsh Company conflicted with
Congress' power over navigable waters. No sooner has he stated
the question and described the creek "as in the nature of a high-
way, through which the tide ebbs and flows," than Marshall proceeds to say something about the purpose of the dam which
pretty much disposes of the case. He writes:

> The act of assembly by which the plaintiffs were authorized to
> construct their dam, shows plainly that this is one of those many
> creeks, passing through a deep level marsh adjoining the Delaware,
> up which the tide flows for some distance. The value of the prop-
> erty on its banks must be enhanced by excluding the water from
> the marsh, and the health of the inhabitants probably improved.
> Measures calculated to produce these objects, provided they do not
> come into collision with the powers of the general government,
> are undoubtedly within those which are reserved to the states. But
> the measure authorized by this act stops a navigable creek, and
> must be supposed to abridge the rights of those who have been
> accustomed to use it. But this abridgment, unless it comes in con-
> flict with the Constitution or a law of the United States, is an affair
> between the government of Delaware and its citizens, of which this
> Court can take no cognizance.[24]

Unlike the situations with which the Court was dealing in *Gibbons v. Ogden* and *Brown v. Maryland,* there was no specific
federal legislation to which Marshall could point as a basis for
showing a clash between federal and state authority. In the *Willson* case, the sole objection was that the Delaware statute en-
croached on the power of the federal government to regulate
commerce with foreign nations and among the several states. Yet
Congress had not exercised this power by enacting any law designed to stop the erection of local structures which might interfere with the movement of vessels on navigable waters. In the
absence of such regulations by Congress, the *Willson* decision is
plainly saying, the states were free to consult their own local
needs and interests in dealing with the problem. As Marshall
stated:

> If Congress had passed any act which bore upon the case; any
> act in execution of the power to regulate commerce, the object

[24] *Ibid.,* p. 250.

of which was to control state legislation over those small navigable creeks into which the tide flows, and which abound throughout the lower country of the middle and southern states; we should feel not much difficulty in saying that a state law coming in conflict with such act would be void. But Congress has passed no such act.[25]

The Court therefore concluded that, "under all the circumstances of the case," the Delaware law in question was not at variance with the power to regulate commerce "in its dormant state," or any legislation adopted by Congress.

When Marshall's commerce clause opinions are looked at with historical perspective, two highly significant results emerge rather clearly. Those opinions have continued to serve, in the first place, as a fruitful source of concepts for the process of drawing both negative and positive inferences from the essentially undefined language of the commerce clause. On the negative side, it may be said that Marshall's constructions of the clause were soon absorbed into the Court's basic theory of constitutional limitations on the states. Coming to have the force of precedent and bearing the prestige of their famous author, these early interpretations could always be turned to when the need was for restraining state and local governments in the name of the Constitution—especially where no explicit prohibitions were available. When the time came to initiate positive measures of national control over commerce and industry, Marshall's notions as to the broad range of Congress' power to regulate commerce were equally useful as guidelines. Contrary to the general impression, however, the jurisprudence pioneered by Marshall in the commerce field can be cited on both sides of the fundamental issue as to the effect on the states of the grant to Congress of the power over interstate and foreign commerce.

But there is a second, and no less important respect, in which the Supreme Court is indebted to the great Chief Justice—whenever it is considering the complexities arising from the fact that in the United States two governments exercise powers impinging on commerce and industry. In all of his utterances on the subject, Marshall placed on the Court itself the ultimate responsi-

[25] *Ibid.*, p. 252.

bility for resolving the conflicts between nation and state which are bound to occur in this field. His commerce clause opinions thus helped to authenticate the Supreme Court as the constitutional umpire or arbiter of the delicate political equilibrium contemplated by the framers of the Constitution when they created the "more perfect Union."

:

PART III

"We Must
Never Forget"

11

"An Axiom of Eternal Truth in Politics"

As co-architects of a distinctive vision of America's national destiny, Alexander Hamilton and John Marshall naturally shared common aspirations as well as common frustrations. Though neither man was a builder of formal systems of thought, both of them helped to fashion a point of view and a method of approach that have taken on the character of a veritable ideology. Nearly a century and a half later, that ideology still has its bitter detractors but also its passionate defenders.

It is probably a measure of the far-reaching significance of the issues with which Hamilton and Marshall were concerned that echoes of the battles in which they were key participants continue to be heard. The recurring clamor should serve to remind us of the important reason why those issues refuse to be stilled. In a fundamental sense, and in a society which has grown ever more diverse and complex, the issues continue to be of the variety which are not capable of permanent resolution.

Indeed, the very texture of the tradition initiated by Hamilton and Marshall helps make it forever pertinent for the people of the United States. Their unique outlook on national problems was, in essence, a remarkably coherent amalgam of economic, political, and legal ideas and values. What gave unifying force to the disparate elements of their creed and, at the same time, motive power for the unfathomable future, was their attitude toward the Constitution.

Yet the ironic fact about their joint contribution is that the

closing years of both Hamilton and Marshall were marred by
extreme pessimism over the fate of the nation's fundamental
charter. Unburdening himself to Gouverneur Morris just two
years before his fatal duel with Aaron Burr, Hamilton wrote:

> Mine is an odd destiny. Perhaps no man in the United States
> has sacrificed or done more for the present Constitution than my-
> self; and contrary to all anticipations of its fate, as you know from
> the very beginning. I am still laboring to prop the frail and worth-
> less fabric. Yet I have the murmurs of its friends no less than the
> curses of its foes for my reward. What can I do better than with-
> draw from the scene? Every day proves to me more and more, this
> American world was not made for me.[1]

Writing less than three years before his death, Marshall confessed like anxiety to Joseph Story:

> If the prospects of our country inspire you with gloom, how
> do you think a man must be affected who partakes of all your
> opinions and whose geographical position enables him to see a
> great deal that is concealed from you. I yield slowly and reluctantly
> to the conviction that our constitution cannot last. I had sup-
> posed that north of the Potomac a firm and solid government
> competent to the security of rational liberty might be preserved.
> Even that now seems doubtful. The case of the south seems to me
> to be desperate. Our opinions are incompatible with a united gov-
> ernment even among ourselves. The union has been prolonged
> thus far by miracles. I fear they cannot continue.[2]

---

[1] Hamilton to Morris, February 27, 1802. Hamilton, *Works,* Lodge, ed.,
X, 290.

[2] Marshall to Story, Richmond, September 22, 1832. *Proceedings of the
Massachusetts Historical Society* (Second Series, 1901), XIV, 351–352. Marshall's
meaning when he speaks of "the case of the south" can be gathered from a
letter he had sent Joseph Story several weeks earlier. Writing on the second
of August on a variety of subjects, the Chief Justice reported to his colleague,
"We are up to the chin in politics," and went on to include this comment:
"Things to the South wear a very serious aspect. If we can trust appearances
the leaders are determined to risk all the consequences of dismemberment.
I cannot entirely dismiss the hope that they may be deserted by their followers,—at least to such an extent as to produce a pause at the Rubicon.
They undoubtedly believe that Virginia will support them. I think they are
mistaken both with respect to Virginia and North Carolina. I do not think
either State will embrace this mad and wicked measure." Marshall to Story,
August 2, 1832. *Ibid.,* XIV, 350.

And a year later he strikes an even more somber note:

> The political world, at least our part of it, is surely moved *topsy-turvy*. What is to become of us and our constitution? Can the wise men of the East answer the question? Those of the South perceive no difficulty. Allow a full range to state rights and state sovereignty, and, in their opinion, all will go well.[3]

Poignant and purely personal though the bitterness voiced by Hamilton may appear to be, it would be superficial to think of it as reflecting nothing more than a man's disappointment over the collapse of his political ambitions. There is a sense in which his gloom, as well as that of Marshall, may be said to have been expressions of a much deeper discontent. Both Hamilton and Marshall had reason to wonder whether the whole system of beliefs and institutions they had striven so hard to foster was not doomed to disappear from the American landscape. Their reference to the Constitution was symbolic only; they were using the word as a synonym for their own set of social and political ideals.

Hamilton was too profound a student of historical forces not to appreciate that what Thomas Jefferson was later to call "the revolution of 1800" [4] not only spelled the eclipse of the Federalist Party, but also augured a drastic reversal of national trends. As John C. Miller, in his remarkably dispassionate biography of Hamilton, has recently written:

> The supreme irony of Hamilton's achievement is that the methods by which he sought to lay the economic foundations of the American union actually aggravated political sectionalism in the United States—the very eventuality he most dreaded. There are few instances in history that demonstrate more strikingly how the best-laid plans of statesmen can go awry. Hamilton dedicated himself to the cause of union; yet when he retired from the office of Secretary of the Treasury, the fissures between North and South had begun to assume menacing proportions. True, Hamilton did not bear the sole responsibility for this untoward and, for him, wholly unexpected development; and yet he, more than any other

[3] Marshall to Story, November 16, 1833. *Ibid.*, XIV, 358.
[4] Thomas Jefferson to Judge Spencer Roane, September 6, 1819. *The Works of Thomas Jefferson*, Ford, ed., XII, 135.

individual, was responsible for the policies which divided the American people and which led to the creation of political parties. It was his archrival, Thomas Jefferson, who united Americans and, until the imposition of the embargo of 1808, seemed on the point of making the United States a one-party state. If the American world were made for Thomas Jefferson, then Alexander Hamilton felt that he stood on foreign ground indeed.[5]

By 1832 Marshall, who had grown more conservative than ever—"ultra-conservative" his biographer tells us [6]—had come to be disturbed by the implications of the new democracy led by Andrew Jackson, whom the aging Chief Justice regarded as having been inspired by Jefferson's dangerous ideas. Writing to Justice Story on Christmas Day of that year, and referring to the growing crisis over nullification—a crisis precipitated by South Carolina's resistance to the tariff laws—the Chief Justice complained: "We are now gathering the bitter fruits of the tree even before that time planted by Mr. Jefferson." [7] At this time Marshall was par-

---

[5] Miller, *Alexander Hamilton: Portrait in Paradox* (New York: Harper and Brothers, 1959), p. XII (Introduction).

[6] Beveridge, *The Life of John Marshall*, IV, 471. The characterization occurs in the next to the last chapter, entitled "The Supreme Conservative." It is concerned in large part with Marshall's attitude toward the issues before the Virginia Constitutional Convention of 1829–30, to which he had been elected as a delegate. Marshall's political views are summarized by Beveridge as follows: "When he took his seat as a delegate to the Virginia Constitutional Convention of 1829–30, a more determined conservative than Marshall did not live. Apparently he did not want anything changed—especially if the change involved conflict—except, of course, the relation of the States to the Nation. He was against a new constitution for Virginia; against any extension of suffrage; against any modification of the County Court system except to strengthen it; against a free white basis of representation; against legislative interference with business." *Ibid.*, IV, 479. Beveridge calls attention to the contrasting and significant fact that Jefferson had "exposed the defects of Virginia's constitution" as early as 1816. The reference is to Jefferson's letter to Samuel Kercheval, dated July 12, 1816. Jefferson's lengthy letter will be found in P. L. Ford's edition of *The Works of Thomas Jefferson*, XII, 3–15.

[7] Marshall to Story, December 25, 1832, *Proceedings of the Massachusetts Historical Society* (Second Series), XIV, 354. It is a mark of Marshall's antagonism toward both Jefferson and Jackson that his condemnation of the Sage of Monticello should have been uttered at the very moment when Jackson—in his famous "Nullification Proclamation"—had threatened to use force against the nullifiers. Marshall's letter containing the jibe at Jefferson was in reply to one from Story, in which the latter had enclosed a copy of a speech delivered by Webster in Boston applauding President Jackson for

ticularly alarmed by the mounting defiance of the Court's authority, climaxed as it was by Jackson's notorious taunt: "John Marshall has made his decision; now let him enforce it!" [8]

Jackson's challenge to Marshall was an aftermath to the Supreme Court's decisions in the so-called *Cherokee Indian* cases.[9] In the first of these cases, Marshall's opinion for the majority held that the Court was without jurisdiction to decide the case. The Chief Justice announced the important doctrine that the relation of the Indians to the United States "resembles that of a ward to his guardian." [10] Although for some purposes the Indians had been treated by the government as a foreign nation, they were not to be regarded as a foreign state within the meaning of the provision in Article III of the Constitution, which confers original jurisdiction on the Supreme Court over cases to which a state of the Union or a foreign nation is a party.

The dramatic irony of this controversy lies in the fact that the decree which Jackson had declined to enforce was seeking to vindicate the power of the national government, including that of the President. The decision which evoked Georgia's outright defiance and Jackson's refusal to carry out the Court's order held unconstitutional a Georgia law under which a four-year prison

taking a stand against nullification and for his determination to preserve the Union. Jackson had issued the Proclamation on December 10, 1832. *Messages and Papers of the Presidents*, Richardson, ed., II, 640–656. Describing to Story the effect of Jackson's Proclamation on the "dominant party" in Virginia, Marshall has some sarcastic things to say: "Imitating the Quaker who said the dog he wished to destroy was mad, they said Andrew Jackson had become a Federalist, even an ultra Federalist. To have said he was ready to break down and trample on every other department of government would not have injured him, but to say that he was a Federalist,—a convert to the opinions of Washington, was a mortal blow under which he is still staggering." Marshall to Story, December 25, 1832. *Proceedings of the Massachusetts Historical Society* (Second Series), XIV, 352–353.

[8] Beveridge, *op. cit.*, IV, 551.

[9] *Cherokee Nation v. Georgia*, 5 Pet. 1 (1831); *Worcester v. Georgia*, 6 Pet. 515 (1832). How bitter Marshall was over President Jackson's refusal to carry out those decisions may be gathered from his characterization of the then governor of Virginia. "You will perceive by the message from our Governor," he writes to Story two years later, "that he is a complete nullifier in the Georgia sense of the term." December 3, 1834. *Proceedings of the Massachusetts Historical Society* (Second Series), XIV, 359.

[10] *Cherokee Nation v. Georgia*, 5 Pet. 1, 16.

term was imposed on anyone who had entered the territory of the
Cherokee Indians without permission from the state.[11] These
laws, Marshall's opinion for the majority declared, "interfere
forcibly with the relations established between the United States
and the Cherokee Nation, the regulation of which, according to
the settled principles of our constitution, are committed exclusively to the government of the Union."[12]

We know from the correspondence between Marshall and
Story that, despite his rapidly failing health, the Chief Justice
was sufficiently agitated over "events" under "the Jacksonians"
to have decided not to resign from the Court in the hope that
Jackson would not be elected to a second term in 1832. For some
reason Marshall thought the Presidential election was due in the
fall of 1831. In those days the Justices lived together in a Washington boardinghouse when the Court was in session. It was while
writing to Story in 1831 to explain why he was not exerting himself more in the matter of boarding arrangements, that Marshall
disclosed his desire to deprive Jackson of the opportunity to
name his successor:

> I am greatly perplexed about our board for the next winter.
> . . . I was unwilling to say any thing for two reasons. Being at any
> rate a bird of passage, whose continuance with you cannot be long,
> I did not chuse to permit my convenience or my wishes to weigh
> a feather in the permanent arrangements of my brethren. But in
> addition, I felt serious doubts, although I did not mention them,
> whether I should be with you at the next term. What I am about
> to say is, of course, in perfect confidence which I would not breathe
> to any other person whatever. I had unaccountably calculated on
> the election of P———t taking place next fall, and had determined
> to make my continuance in office another year dependent on that
> event. You know how much importance I attach to the character
> of the person who is to succeed me, and calculate the influence

[11] *Worcester v. Georgia*, 6 Pet. 515 (1832).

[12] *Ibid.*, p. 561. Georgia's legislation was part of its deliberate policy,
launched in 1828, of compelling the Indians to abandon their lands in the
state and to move beyond the Mississippi. Marshall reminded the country
that Samuel A. Worcester's missionary work among the Cherokees—for which
he was being punished by imprisonment at hard labor in the penitentiary
—was carried on with the blessing of a proclamation issued by a former
President of the United States.

which probabilities on that subject would have on my continuance in office. This, however, is a matter of great delicacy on which I cannot and do not speak. My erroneous calculation of the time of election was corrected as soon as the pressure of official duty was removed from my mind, and I had nearly decided on my course, but recent events produce such real uncertainty respecting the future as to create doubts whether I ought not to await the same chances in the fall of 32 which I had intended to await in the fall of 31. This obliges me to look forward to our quarters for the next winter.[13]

The letter in which Thomas Jefferson speaks of his own election to the Presidency in 1800 as a "revolution" happens to contain a comment which supplies, however unintentionally, a clue to the close link between the political and constitutional battles in the formative era of our history. It therefore also helps to illuminate the chief reason for the fate which Hamilton and Marshall feared they were slated to suffer. Wrote Jefferson to Spencer Roane in 1819:

They [some articles appearing in the *Richmond Enquirer*] contain the true principles of the revolution of 1800, for that was as real a revolution in the principles of our government as that of 1776 was in its form; not affected indeed by the sword, as that, but by the rational and peaceable instrument of reform, the suffrage of the people. The nation declared its will by dismissing functionaries of one principle, and electing those of another, in the two branches, executive and legislative, submitted to their election. Over the judiciary department, the constitution had deprived them of their control. That, therefore, has continued the reprobated system, and although new matter has been occasionally incorporated into the old, yet the leaven of the old mass seems to assimilate to itself the new, and after twenty years confirmation of the federal system by the voice of the nation, declared through the medium of elections, we find the judiciary on every occasion, still driving us into consolidation.[14]

[13] Marshall to Story, June 26, 1831. Charles Warren, "The Story-Marshall Correspondence," *William and Mary College Quarterly,* Second Series, Vol. 21, No. 1 (Jan. 1941), pp. 24–25.
[14] Jefferson to Roane, Sept. 6, 1819. *The Works of Thomas Jefferson,* Ford, ed., XII, 135–136.

If it is at all true, as Ralph Waldo Emerson once said, that "an institution is the lengthened shadow of one man," [15] we need not hesitate to attribute to John Marshall the chief personal responsibility for shaping the Supreme Court into the mighty instrument of government it has come to be. For it was Marshall who succeeded in solidifying the Supreme Court's position as the ultimate constitutional arbiter in the United States. The process by which the Court has been performing this function has come to be known as judicial review.

Throughout the thirty-four years Marshall served as Chief Justice, he was always careful to speak in the name of the Constitution. Judicial power was portrayed as a vehicle for giving expression to the mandates and purposes of the charter of 1787. Yet Marshall denied that the Supreme Court was using its authority to encrust on the Constitution its own subjective views as to what the document allowed or disallowed. Most of the time this central hypothesis of his constitutional philosophy remained implicit, but at least on one occasion it was raised to the level of explicit statement. "Judicial power, as contradistinguished from the power of the laws," he observed in 1824, "has no existence. Courts are the mere instruments of the law, and can will nothing." [16] Thus was Marshall restating Hamilton's familiar theory as to the comparative weakness of the judiciary:

> Whoever attentively considers the different departments of power must perceive, that, in a government in which they are separated from each other, the judiciary, from the nature of its functions, will always be the least dangerous to the political rights of the Constitution; because it will be least in a capacity to annoy or injure them. The Executive not only dispenses the honors, but holds the sword of the community. The legislature not only commands the purse, but prescribes the rules by which the duties and rights of every citizen are to be regulated. The judiciary, on the contrary, has no influence over either the sword or the purse; no direction either of the strength or of the wealth of the society; and can take no active resolution whatever. It may truly be said to have

---

[15] Emerson, "Self-Reliance," in his *Essays*, First and Second Series (Boston and New York: Houghton Mifflin Company, 1883), p. 62.
[16] *Osborne v. United States Bank*, 9 Wheat. 738, 866 (1824).

neither FORCE NOR WILL, but merely judgment; and must ultimately depend upon the aid of the executive arm even for the efficacy of its judgments.[17]

But in one respect this highly mechanistic or "phonographic" theory of the judicial process—as the late Morris R. Cohen once characterized it [18]—would appear to contradict Marshall's own primary justification for the Supreme Court's constitutional function of judicial review. That justification was, after all, that the Court played the important role of "conserving" the principles embodied in the Constitution. The essential contradiction becomes apparent when it is remembered that the great clauses of the Constitution which give rise to public controversy are anything but unambiguous in their meaning. The agency of government which claims the right to impart specific content to these vague generalities is therefore in a strategic position to determine the practical meaning of the whole document.

To explore Marshall's paradoxical attitude toward the Constitution is to do more than merely expose a logical contradiction. Such an analysis may help clarify the unresolved dilemma inherent in the American constitutional tradition. Certainly Marshall would have been pleased with the way Justice Frankfurter expressed the matter soon after coming to the Court: "Judicial exegesis is unavoidable with reference to an organic act like our Constitution, drawn in many particulars with purposed vague-

[17] *The Federalist*, No. 78, p. 490 (Wright, ed.). For an unusually provocative analysis of the relevance of Hamilton's view of the judiciary for the Supreme Court's actual process of adjudication, see Alexander M. Bickel, *The Least Dangerous Branch* (Indianapolis: The Bobbs-Merrill Company, 1962). Professor Bickel's controversial thesis has been subjected to trenchant, but fair-minded, criticism by Professor Gerald Gunther, in his recent article, "The Subtle Vices of the 'Passive Virtues'—A Comment on Principle and Expediency in Judicial Review," 64 *Columbia Law Review* 1 (Jan. 1964).

[18] "The prevailing orthodoxy . . . insists that the duty of the judge is simply to read and obey the statute or the Constitution and that it is no part of his business to make or change the law in any way.This assumes that the framers of a law or constitution can foresee all possible future contingencies and make definite provisions for meeting them, so that the judge can be merely a logical automaton, a sort of phonograph repeating exactly what the law had definitely declared." Cohen, *The Faith of a Liberal* (New York: Henry Holt and Company, 1946), p. 43.

ness so as to leave room for the unfolding future. But the ultimate touchstone of constitutionality is the Constitution itself
and not what we have said about it." [19]

Our constitutional tradition derives from the notion that
those who wield political power in the community are subject to
a law higher than their own will. "Constitutional government
is *par excellence* a government of law," is the way Woodrow Wilson expressed this idea.[20] Defining constitutional government as
"one whose powers have been adapted to the interests of its people and to the maintenance of individual liberty," Wilson went
on to stress the role of the judiciary. "From the very outset of
modern constitutional history," he wrote, "it has invariably been
recognized as one of the essentials of constitutional government
that the individual should be provided with some tribunal to
which he could resort with the confident expectation that he
should find justice there,—not only justice as against other individuals who had disregarded his rights or sought to disregard
them, but also justice against the government itself, a perfect
protection against all violations of law." [21]

Though history has cast them in the role of great antagonists,
belief in the necessity to subject government to restraints is one
article of faith Jefferson and Marshall had in common. The precept is clearly implicit in Jefferson's statement of "self-evident
truths" in the Declaration of Independence—as it is implicit,
ironically, in the rationale behind Marshall's criticism of Jefferson's refusal to honor John Adams' appointment of William

[19] Concurring in *Graves v. New York ex rel. O'Keefe*, 306 U.S. 466, 487,
at 491–492 (1939). A striking example of a less sympathetic view of the relation of the Supreme Court to the Constitution will be found in a widely
discussed recent book: "So, a proper understanding of this ancient document
[the Constitution] points the way to a remedy for all the imperfections in
our government that are attributable to what, we shall see, are the Court's
ill-grounded theories. For it will not be forgotten it is the Constitution, and
not the Supreme Court's accumulated errors about it, which Congress and
the Justices take oath 'to support,' and the President swears he will 'preserve,
protect, and defend.'" William W. Crosskey, *Politics and the Constitution
in the History of the United States* (Chicago: University of Chicago Press,
1953), p. VII (Preface).

[20] Wilson, *Constitutional Government in the United States* (New York:
Columbia University Press, 1908), p. 17.

[21] *Ibid.,* pp. 2, 16–17.

Marbury. Among the "causes" which induced the American colonies to raise the standard of revolt against Great Britain, Jefferson listed first the violation of the principle that "all men" have "certain unalienable rights." Before proceeding to the "long train of abuses and usurpations" with which George III was to be charged, Jefferson presented the political credo of the patriots of '76: "We hold these truths to be self-evident, that all men are created equal, that they are endowed by their Creator with certain unalienable Rights, that among these are Life, Liberty and the pursuit of Happiness. That to secure these rights, Governments are instituted among Men, deriving their just powers from the consent of the governed." [22]

By way of showing how grave an abuse of power Jefferson was guilty of when he declined to deliver William Marbury's commission as a judge, Marshall had remarked: "The government of the United States has been emphatically termed a government of laws, and not of men. It will certainly cease to deserve this high appellation, if the laws furnish no remedy for the violation of a vested right." [23]

In a system of government consisting of coordinate departments—each of which is presumably independent of the other two—the question as to how the requirements of the "higher law" are to be ascertained poses a most perplexing practical as well as philosophical problem. Marshall's solution was quite simple: "It is emphatically the province and duty of the judicial department to say what the law is." [24] But he never did come to grips with the implications of this prerogative for the democratic element of the American polity. It took Justice Gibson of the Pennsylvania Supreme Court just one short forthright sentence to state the most disquieting of these implications: "Every power by which one organ of the government is enabled to control another, or to exert an influence over its acts, is a political power." [25] Ten years later, another Pennsylvanian, in a notable

[22] 1 *The Papers of Thomas Jefferson* 429 (Boyd, ed., 1950).
[23] *Marbury v. Madison,* 1 Cranch 137, 163 (1803).
[24] *Ibid.,* p. 177.
[25] Dissenting in *Eakin v. Raub,* 12 Sergeant and Rowle, 330, 346 (Pennsylvania, 1825).

tribute to the lately departed Chief Justice of the United States, presented the matter in a more sympathetic light:

> The day was to come, and not distant, when laws enacted by the representatives of a free and sovereign people, were to be submitted to a comparison with the Constitution of the nation, and to stand or fall by the decrees of a court, destitute of the smallest portion of political power, and having no independent authority but that of reason. The passions of the people, the interests of the states, and the power of both, were to be controlled and overruled in this name; or if it should be despised and rejected, the only bond of the union that would remain, was to be that which alone remains to nations after reason and law have departed from the earth.[26]

Writing in the same year, Alexis de Tocqueville professed to be mystified by the unique place occupied by the American judiciary. "I am not aware that any nation of the globe," he observed, "has hitherto organized a judicial power in the same manner as the Americans. The judicial organization of the United States is the institution which a stranger has the greatest difficulty in understanding." He went on to describe this phenomenon as follows:

> Whenever a law that the judge holds to be unconstitutional is invoked in a tribunal of the United States, he may refuse to admit it as a rule; this power is the only one peculiar to the American magistrate, but it gives rise to immense political influence. In truth, few laws can escape the searching analysis of the judicial power for any length of time, for there are few that are not prejudicial to some private interest or other, and none that may not be brought before a court of justice by the choice of parties or by the necessity of the case.

De Tocqueville's estimate of the potential impact of the power he was discussing is particularly trenchant: "The power vested in the American courts of justice of pronouncing a statute to be unconstitutional forms one of the most powerful barriers that

[26] Horace Binney, "An Eulogy on the Life and Character of John Marshall," delivered at Philadelphia, September 24, 1835 (Philadelphia: Crissy and Goodman, 1835), pp. 43–44.

have ever been devised against the tyranny of political assemblies." [27]

It is not surprising that one of the best statements of the basic clash between judicial supremacy and popular government should have come from the pen of the patron saint of American democracy. Writing in 1820 to voice his displeasure over recent trends in the Marshall Court, Thomas Jefferson put the matter quite succinctly: "A judiciary independent of a king or executive alone is a good thing; but independence of the will of the nation is a solecism, at least in a republican government." [28]

But it was the conviction that judicial supremacy is fundamentally incompatible with the separation of powers principle which was the recurring theme of Jefferson's quarrel with Marshall. "It should be remembered as an axiom of eternal truth in politics," he wrote to Spencer Roane in 1819, "that whatever power in any government is independent, is absolute also, in theory, only, at first, while the spirit of the people is up, but in practice, as fast as that relaxes." His letter continued, "Independence can be trusted nowhere, but with the people in mass. . . . My construction of the Constitution is very different from that you quote. It is that each department is truly independent of the others, and has an equal right to decide for itself what is the

---

[27] De Tocqueville, *Democracy in America* (New York: Alfred A. Knopf, 1945; Phillips Bradley, ed.), I, 98, 101–102, 103.

[28] Jefferson to Thomas Ritchie, Dec. 25, 1820. *The Works of Thomas Jefferson*, Ford, ed., XII, 178. This is the letter in which is to be found Jefferson's rather unflattering description of the way the Supreme Court functioned under Marshall: "The judiciary of the United States is the subtle corps of sappers and miners constantly working underground to undermine the foundations of our confederated fabric. They are construing our Constitution from a co-ordination of a general and special government to a general and supreme one alone. . . . Having found, from experience, that impeachment is an impracticable thing, a mere scare-crow, they consider themselves secure for life; they skulk from responsibility to public opinion, the only remaining hold on them, under a practice first introduced into England by Lord Mansfield. An opinion is huddled up in conclave, perhaps by a majority of one, delivered as if unanimous, and with the silent acquiescence of lazy or timid associates, by a crafty chief judge, who sophisticates the law to his mind, by the turn of his own reasoning." *Ibid.*, XII, 177–178.

meaning of the Constitution in the cases submitted to its action; and especially, where it is to act ultimately and without appeal." [29] Jefferson's clearest exposition of the view that each department is the "rightful expositor" of the constitutionality of a law is to be found in some sentences he had prepared for inclusion in his first Message to Congress:

> Our country has thought proper to distribute the powers of its Government among three equal and independent authorities, constituting each a check on one or both of the others, in all attempts to impair its Constitution. To make each an effectual check, it must have a right, in cases which arise within the line of its proper functions, where, equally with the others, it acts in the last resort, and without appeal, to decide on the validity of an act according to its judgment and uncontrolled by the opinions of any other department.[30]

How strongly Jefferson believed in this tripartite theory of constitutional interpretation was dramatically demonstrated by his action in pardoning persons convicted under the Alien and Sedition Acts of 1798. On September 11, 1804, Jefferson wrote to Abigail Adams:

> The judges believing the law constitutional, had a right to pass a sentence of fine and imprisonment, because that power was placed in their hands by the constitution. But the Executive, believing the law to be unconstitutional, was bound to remit the execution of it; because that power has been confided to him by the constitution. That instrument meant that its co-ordinate branches should be checks on each other. But the opinion which gives to the judges the right to decide what laws are constitutional, and what not, not only for themselves in their own sphere of ac-

[29] Thomas Jefferson to Spencer Roane, Sept. 6, 1819, *ibid.*, XII, 137.

[30] The preliminary draft of Jefferson's first message to Congress is dated December 8, 1801. Quoted by C. P. Patterson, *The Constitutional Principles of Thomas Jefferson* (Austin: University of Texas Press, 1952), p. 120. Professor Patterson undertakes to argue that Jefferson believed in judicial review, though he is careful to qualify his contention in the following way: "Jefferson's advocacy of judicial review . . . was based upon three important stipulations: First, that the judiciary should be independent; second, that its judges confine themselves 'strictly to their department'; and third, that they should be chosen for their high professional qualifications." *Ibid.*, p. 117.

tion, but for the legislature and executive also in their spheres, would make the judiciary a despotic branch.[31]

Many years later, Jefferson mentioned the same incident in a list of "examples" illustrating what he meant by saying that each department had "an equal right" to determine "the meaning of the Constitution." He also referred to his conduct in the case of *Marbury v. Madison* and to his action in declining to ask the Senate for its advice as to whether or not to submit for ratification a treaty with Britain. Speaking of these events, which had occurred while he was President, Jefferson said: "These are examples of my position, that each of the three departments has equally the right to decide for itself what is its duty under the Constitution, without any regard to what the others may have decided for themselves under a similar question."[32]

Though Jefferson may have placed high social value on the impartial administration of justice by honest and qualified judges, it is equally clear that he would have denied to the judiciary a power to negate the policy decisions of the other branches of the government. The key to his conception of the judicial function is that he would have judges stay within their own "department." In a letter to James Madison urging the importance of adding a bill of rights to the Constitution, Jefferson stated: "In the arguments in favor of a declaration of rights, you omit one which has great weight with me, the legal check which it puts into the hands of the judiciary. This is a body, which if rendered independent, and kept strictly to their own department, merits great confidence for their learning and integrity."[33]

Writing to Madison from Paris two years earlier to convey his opinion of the proposed Constitution, Jefferson said something about the judicial sections of the document which might be seized on as indicating that he believed in judicial review. "I like the negative given to the Executive with a third of either house,

[31] *The Adams-Jefferson Letters*, Lester J. Cappon, ed. (Chapel Hill: University of North Carolina Press, 1959), I, 279.
[32] Jefferson to Roane, Sept. 6, 1819. *The Works of Thomas Jefferson*, Ford, ed., XII, 139.
[33] Jefferson to Madison, March 15, 1789. 14 *The Papers of Thomas Jefferson*, 659 (Boyd, ed., 1958).

though I should have liked it better had the Judiciary been associated for that purpose, or invested with a similar and separate power." [34] There is no evidence, however, that Jefferson repeated this suggestion later on—certainly not after John Marshall began to transform the theory of the judicial veto into a functioning reality. It may be true, as Edmond Cahn has suggested, that "it was not judicial review that he [Jefferson] opposed, but the assumption that its results would be final and beyond further appeal." [35] But is it not equally true that, as conceived of by Marshall, judicial review did come to mean that the *final authority* in the interpretation of the Constitution belonged to the Supreme Court?

Nor did Jefferson believe that the existence of our dual scheme of government necessitated assumption by the Court of an umpiring function. Quite the contrary:

> It has long . . . been my opinion, and I have never shrunk from its expression . . . that the germ of dissolution of our federal government is the federal judiciary; an irresponsible body, (for impeachment is scarcely a scare-crow), working like gravity by night and by day, gaining a little to-day and a little to-morrow, and advancing its noiseless step like a thief, over the field of jurisdiction, until all shall be usurped from the United States, and the government of all be consolidated into one. To this I am opposed; because, when all government, domestic and foreign, in little as well as in great things, shall be drawn to Washington as the center of all power, it will render powerless the checks provided of one government on another, and will become as venal and oppressive as the government from which we separated.[36]

[34] *Ibid.,* 12, 440.

[35] Cahn, "An American Contribution," reprinted in *Supreme Court and Supreme Law,* Cahn, ed. (Bloomington: Indiana University Press, 1954), p. 22. Probably the most candid description of the practical effect of judicial review on the operation of the process of government in the United States was given by Justice Stephen J. Field: "An unconstitutional act is not a law; it confers no rights; it imposes no duties; it affords no protection; it creates no office; it is, in legal contemplation, as inoperative as though it had never been passed." *Norton v. Shelby County,* 118 U.S. 425, 442 (1886).

[36] Jefferson to C. Hammond, Aug. 18, 1821. *The Writings of Thomas Jefferson,* H. A. Washington, ed. (Washington, D.C.: Taylor and Maury, 1854), VII, 216. Some questions posed by Robert G. McCloskey are particularly apt in

The continuing conflict between Jefferson and Marshall concerning the scope of judicial power is a highly instructive lesson in what Max Lerner has called "the basic paradox of American life—the necessity we have been under of squaring majority will with minority rule." [37] For that reason, it is also a significant chapter in the history of the stresses and strains which were bound to afflict the process of making viable a document drafted by men who thought they had found the solution to the age-old problem of governing people without destroying their freedom. The framers of the Constitution were bent on giving America stable and effective government by enlarging central authority, while at the same time subjecting the actual exercise of all governmental power to a variety of restraints—in the form of the guarantee of private rights and departmental checks. Popular government was to be protected against itself through an elaborate system of constitutional limitations.

Appropriately enough, it was the "philosopher" of the Constitution who was one of the first Americans to perceive and to

suggesting the scope of judicial review as conceived of by Marshall: ". . . it was necessary both to confirm and to extend the Court's claim to authority, to transmute 'judicial review' into 'judicial sovereignty.' Granted that it was proper for the Court to adjudge questions of constitutionality, did this imply that the Court's judgment was final? Did it imply that the judges could call the other branches to account even when the question of constitutionality was doubtful? Did it imply the Court would excercise a general supervision over some governmental affairs that fell outside the traditional judicial orbit?" Professor McCloskey concludes that "To Marshall it implied all this, for he was firmly convinced that the more America was guided by judges the happier and more just its system would be." *The American Supreme Court* (Chicago: The University of Chicago Press, 1960), p. 56.

[37] Lerner, "Minority Rule and the Constitutional Tradition," reprinted in his *Ideas Are Weapons* (New York: The Viking Press, 1939), p. 471. Rejecting what he regarded as the false dichotomy often set up between the Constitution and political democracy, Mr. Lerner went on to say in the same article: "The mistake we are all too ready to make is to pose an antithesis between the Constitution as such and the democratic impulse, an antithesis that does not exist. . . . The Constitution, without the accretion of judicial review, could (whatever its origins) have become an instrument of the majority will. The whole animus behind it, despite the system of checks and balances, was a flexible one. It was meant to adapt itself to the changes and chances of the national life. . . . The real antithesis is between the democratic impulse and the judicial power." *Ibid.*, pp. 471–472.

[38] *The National Gazette*, Jan. 19, 1792. Quoted by Saul K. Padover, ed., *The Complete Madison* (New York: Harper & Brothers, 1953), p. 335.

articulate the underlying ambivalence in our national charter. "Every word [of the Constitution] decides a question between power and liberty," observed James Madison in 1792.[38] Speaking of the same dilemma in the decade of the New Deal's struggle with the judiciary, Max Lerner traced its source to the clash of ideas inherent in the century which produced the Constitution:

> The Constitution was born in a century obsessed with the notion of limited powers, a century overhung by the shadows of Locke and Rousseau. Conservative thought clung to the rights of minorities against the tyranny of the majority; and radical theory, such as that of Jefferson and the great European rationalists, took the form of belief in the perfectability of man and the malignancy of government. But the pattern of the century contained a curious inner contradiction in its thought. Its prevailing economic policy was mercantilistic, with all the close and comprehensive controls that the mercantilist state exercised over economic life, and with all its resulting concentration of authority. Its prevailing political thought, however, was atomistic, with its emphasis on individual liberties and governmental dangers. The men who framed the Constitution and ran the government that it created were caught in this contradiction. Their conservative economic interests dictated a strong central mercantilist government; the prevailing political ideas of the time, fortifying their fear of democracy, made them place that government of expanded powers in an intellectual framework of limited powers. Hence, to a large extent, the confusion of the constitutional debates.[39]

In terms of fundamental political as well as legal theory, the closest Marshall ever came to explaining or justifying the "solecism" which troubled Jefferson was when he discussed the nature of the American Constitution. What makes his conception of the Constitution so revealing an intimation of his outlook as a judge is that it reflects his vision of the kind of America he was seeking to mold. Although it is true that Marshall paid all written constitutions the high compliment of calling them "the greatest improvement on political institutions," [40] it was the special qualities he attributed to the American Constitution which be-

[39] Lerner, *op. cit.*, pp. 465–466.
[40] *Marbury v. Madison*, 1 Cranch 137, 178 (1803).

came so essential a part of his apologia for judicial power. A man who wishes "immortality" for a paper document may be assumed to see imperishable values in its purposes. Marshall did not so much glorify the written character of the Constitution as use it as an argument to bolster his case for judicial supremacy.

> A constitution is framed for ages to come, and is designed to approach immortality as nearly as human institutions can approach it. Its course cannot always be tranquil. It is exposed to storms and tempests, and its framers must be unwise statesmen, indeed, if they have not provided it, as far as its nature will permit, with the means of self-preservation from the perils it may be destined to encounter. No government ought to be so defective in its organization as not to contain within itself the means of securing the execution of its own laws against other dangers than those which occur every day. Courts of Justice are the means most usually employed; and it is reasonable to expect that a goverment should repose on its own courts rather than on others. Questions may occur which we would gladly avoid, but we cannot avoid them. All we can do is to exercise our best judgment and conscientiously to perform our duty.[41]

When the time came for Marshall to assert the Supreme Court's right to "control" the other branches of the national government as well as the states and their political subdivisions, he persisted in denying that the Court was exercising power. The Justices were merely discharging their duty of enforcing the Constitution. "Unashamedly I recall the familiar phrase in which he [Marshall] expressed the core of his constitutional philosophy," Felix Frankfurter declared in 1955. After quoting Marshall's assertion—"it is a *constitution* we are expounding" [42]—Justice Frankfurter went on to characterize it as "the single most important utterance in the literature of constitutional law—most important because most comprehensive and comprehending." [43]

[41] *Cohens v. Virginia,* 6 Wheat. 381, 404 (1821).
[42] "In considering this question, then, we must never forget that it is *a constitution* we are expounding." *McCulloch v. Maryland,* 4 Wheat. 316, 407 (1819).
[43] Frankfurter, "John Marshall and the Judicial Function," reprinted in *Government Under Law,* Sutherland, ed., p. 8.

12

"Expounder of the Constitution"

Marshall was not John Adams' first choice to fill the vacancy when Oliver Ellsworth resigned the office of Chief Justice in December of 1800. Adams first nominated John Jay for the post. Jay had served as the first Chief Justice of the United States, but resigned in 1795 to become governor of New York. Writing to inform Jay that he had selected him for "your old station," Adams used the occasion to express his hopes for the future of the American judiciary:

> This is as independent of the inconstancy of the people as it is of the will of a president. In the future adminstration of our country, the firmest security we can have against the effects of visionary schemes or fluctuating theories, will be in a solid judicary; . . . It appeared to me that Providence had thrown in my way an opportunity, not only of marking to the public the spot where, in my opinion, the greatest mass of worth remained collected in one individual, but of furnishing my country with the best security its inhabitants afforded against the increasing dissolution of morals.[1]

It is one of the ironies of Marshall's rather fortuitous appointment as Chief Justice that John Jay refused to return to the Court because he saw no future in it. "I left the bench perfectly convinced," Jay told President Adams, "that under a system so defective it would not obtain the energy, weight, and dignity which are essential to its affording due support to the national government, nor acquire the public confidence and respect

---

[1] President Adams to John Jay, Dec. 19, 1800. *The Correspondence and Public Papers of John Jay*, Henry P. Johnston, ed. (New York: G. P. Putnam's Sons, 1893), IV, 284.

which, as the last resort of the justice of the nation, it should possess." [2] History has surrounded Marshall's judicial career with still another irony. When Jefferson heard that Marshall was being urged by Hamilton to become a candidate for Congress in the election of 1792, he wrote to Madison: "I think nothing better could be done than to make him a judge." [3]

Looking back to Marshall's accomplishments as Chief Justice, John Quincy Adams placed a comment in his diary which is perhaps an even more paradoxical reflection on the circumstances which brought John Marshall to the Supreme Court. Under the date of July 10, 1835 will be found the following entry:

> John Marshall, Chief Justice of the United States, died at Philadelphia last Monday, the 4th instant. He was one of the most eminent men that this country has ever produced. He has had this appointment thirty-five years. It was the last act of my father's administration, and one of the most important services rendered by him to his country. All constitutional governments are flexible things; and as the Supreme Judicial Court is the tribunal of last resort for the construction of the Constitution and the laws, the office of Chief Justice of that court is a station of the highest trust, of the deepest responsibility, and of influence far more extensive than that of the President of the United States. [4]

Something else John Quincy Adams wrote down on the same day may be seen as suggesting a most difficult problem in the assessment of Marshall's stewardship as Chief Justice. We read in the diary:

> John Marshall was a federalist of the Washington school. The Associate Judges from the time of his appointment have generally

[2] *Ibid.*, IV, 285.

[3] "I learn that he [Hamilton] has expressed the strongest desire that Marshall should come in to Congress from Richmond, declaring that there is no man in Virginia whom he wishes so much to see there; and I am told that Marshall has expressed half a mind to come. Hence I conclude that Hamilton has plied him well with flattery and solicitation, and I think nothing better could be done than to make him a judge." Thomas Jefferson to James Madison, June 29, 1792. *The Works of Thomas Jefferson*, Ford, ed., VII, 130.

[4] *Memoirs of John Quincy Adams*, comprising portions of his diary from 1795 to 1848, Charles Francis Adams, ed. (Philadelphia: Lippincott and Co., 1875), IX, 243. John Quincy Adams was mistaken about the date of Marshall's death. The Chief Justice died in Philadelphia on July 6, 1835.

been taken from the democratic, or Jeffersonian party. Not one of them, excepting Story, has been a man of great ability. . . . Marshall, by the ascendancy of his genius, by the amenity of his deportment, and by the imperturbable command of his temper, has given a permanent and systematic character to the decisions of the court, and settled many great constitutional questions favorably to the continuance of the Union. Marshall has cemented the Union which the crafty and quixotic democracy of Jefferson had a perpetual tendency to dissolve. Jefferson hated and dreaded him.[5]

In an age in which powerful forces were pushing the country in an opposite direction, how did it happen that Marshall was able to establish the Supreme Court as the ultimate agency for adapting the Constitution to the requisites of national power? "It may justly be said," Edward S. Corwin has written, "that Marshall's greatest service consisted precisely in the uphill fight which he maintained for years against the trend of his times." [6] Marshall and Jefferson dominated the era as symbols of conflicting constitutional as well as political points of view. The recurring dialogue between them over the place of the judiciary helped to crystallize what is probably the most fundamental and persistent issue concerning the American constitutional tradition. That issue can be expressed in varying ways, but one of the most trenchant statements of it has come from the felicitous pen of Julian P. Boyd. Professor Boyd's formulation deserves to be recalled at some length:

> Both were Virginians. Both had been born within the frontier, though far enough on the outskirts of settlement to feel the challenging winds from the vast wilderness to the westward. Both stemmed from the same distant and progenitive Randolph, deriving from him a consanguinity that neither exhibited in outward expression. Both grew up in the same kind of sturdy, self-reliant home environment, each possessing at its head a stalwart, intelligent, respected leader of the county. Both had been bred to the law under that noble teacher, George Wythe, though his tutelage of Marshall was but a brief and tenuous relationship and that of Jefferson a profound and transforming influence. Both had eagerly embraced the principles of the Revolution and had served the

[5] *Ibid.,* IX, 243–244.
[6] Corwin, *The Twilight of the Supreme Court* (New Haven: Yale University Press, 1934), p. 6.

American cause well, the one distinguishing himself in the field and the other in legislation. Yet out of this remarkable identity of background came one of the mighty opposites of American history. The explanation of this divergence arising from similarity is as baffling as the explanation of genius, but the fact of its existence and of its dynamic influence on this nation is indubitable. Sharing an identity with the heroic conflict between Hamilton and Jefferson, it was both more dramatic in its steady unfolding to its climactic opposition and more incisive in its delineation of the issues.[7]

Any attempt to discover the "explanation" for the divergence between Jefferson and Marshall is bound to take one into the mysterious realm in which human character is shaped. There is some evidence that this "baffling" question intrigued at least one of them. Though Jefferson was the more introspective of the two, it was Marshall who ventured to speculate about the reasons for the particular cast of his own mind. Joseph Story's inference as to the origin of Marshall's ideas supplies a good clue to the intellectual problem posed by Professor Boyd. Said Story in the course of his memorable oration on the life of John Marshall: "It is to this period,—between the close of the war of the Revolution, and the adoption of the present Constitution of the United States,— that we are to refer the gradual development and final establishment of those political opinions and principles, which constituted the basis of all the public actions of his subsequent life." [8]

[7] Boyd, "Thomas Jefferson's Empire of Liberty," 24 *The Virginia Quarterly Review* (Autumn 1948), pp. 538–539. In a rather arresting examination of "Marshall's claims to the title of 'conservative,'" Arthur N. Holcombe suggests that "A good test of the character of Marshall's conservatism is his attitude toward the unquestionably liberal ideas of his third cousin, once removed, and greatest political antagonist, Thomas Jefferson." Professor Holcombe concludes that "Both of these great Virginians and Americans, . . . abhorred extremes, and could not hold for long a political course deviating widely from the natural center, where tradition and reason meet and make the necessary adjustments to the circumstances of the time and the temper of the people." Holcombe, "John Marshall as Politician and Political Theorist," reprinted in *Chief Justice John Marshall: A Reappraisal*, W. Melville Jones, ed., pp. 26, 37.

[8] Story, *A Discourse on the Life, Character and Services of the Honorable John Marshall*, p. 18.

Marshall himself denied that his political philosophy was the product of deliberate reflection or contemplation. "When I recollect," Story quotes him as writing late in life, "the wild and enthusiastic notions with which my political opinions of that day [the Revolution] were tinctured, I am disposed to ascribe my devotion to the Union, and to a government competent to its preservation, at least as much to casual circumstances, as to judgment." Story's quotation from Marshall continues:

> I had grown up at a time when the love of the Union, and the resistance to the claims of Great Britain, were the inseparable inmates of the same bosom; when patriotism and a strong fellow feeling with our suffering fellow-citizens of Boston were identical; when the maxim, "United we stand, divided we fall," was the maxim of every orthodox American. And I had imbibed these sentiments so thoroughly that they constituted a part of my being. I carried them with me into the army, where I found myself associated with brave men from different States, who were risking life and every thing valuable, in a common cause, believed by all to be most precious; and where I was confirmed in the habit of considering America as my country, and Congress as my government.[9]

In the same letter, Marshall speaks of the factors which turned his early "wild and enthusiastic notions" into a more conservative persuasion. "My immediate entrance into the State Legislature," he writes, "opened to my view the causes which had been chiefly instrumental in augmenting those sufferings [the sufferings of the Army]; and the general tendency of State politics convinced me that no safe and permanent remedy could be found, but in a more efficient and better organized general government." He found that "everything was afloat," that principles he regarded as sacred were "brought annually into doubt," and that "we had no safe anchorage ground." The conditions of the country, as he saw them, "gave a high estimation to that article in the Constitution which imposes restrictions on States." [10]

After recalling these autobiographical musings from Marshall, Story went on to explain the impact of his political experi-

---

[9] *Ibid.*, pp. 19–20.
[10] *Ibid.*, p. 28.

ence in the 1780s. There can be little doubt that the Chief Justice would have approved of his colleague's interpretation:

> It was by this course of action in State legislation at this appalling period, that Mr. Marshall was disciplined to the thorough mastery of the true principles of free government. It was here that he learned and practised those profound doctrines of rational, limited, constitutional liberty, from which he never shrunk, and to which he resolutely adhered to the end of his life. It was here that he became enamored, not of a wild and visionary republic, found only in the imaginations of mere enthusiasts as to human perfection, or tricked out in false colors by the selfish, to flatter the prejudices or cheat the vanity of the people; but of that well-balanced republic, adapted to human wants and human infirmities, in which power is to be held in check by countervailing power; and life, liberty, and property are to be secured by a real and substantial independence, as well as division of the legislative, executive, and judicial departments. . . . Yes; his thoughts ever dwelt on the Union, as the first and best of all our earthly hopes.[11]

The profound psychological question Professor Boyd has raised may defy a sure answer, but as applied to Marshall it can serve a very useful purpose. The answer should help shatter the myth that Marshall derived his ideas and attitudes from Alexander Hamilton. However much the two men may have shared a common outlook on the problems of their time, Marshall's intellectual history demonstrates that he did not so much borrow from Hamilton as agree with him. Philosophic affinity is not necessarily the result of imitation.

"While Hamilton's immortal state papers profoundly impressed Marshall," writes Beveridge, "they were not . . . the source of his convictions." [12] Beveridge believed that Marshall revealed "the elements of his Nationalist opinions" in the course of the debates at the Virginia Ratifying Convention of 1788. Moreover, Marshall's labors, in and out of the Virginia legislature, in advocating the program of the Washington administration, his antipathy to the French Revolution, his support of the Jay treaty, and his brief service in Congress [13]—all of these

[11] *Ibid.,* pp. 26–27.
[12] Beveridge, *The Life of John Marshall,* I, 454.
[13] *Ibid.,* vol. I, chs. IX, X, XI, XII; Vol. II, chs. I–IV, X, XI.

efforts and episodes not only afford proof of Marshall's national and conservative slant, but they also show that the point of view was distinctively and consistently his own.

As a yardstick of historical importance, a certain theory advanced by Edmond Cahn is even more helpful than Beveridge's explanation. Though Professor Cahn was refuting the disparaging suggestion that Marshall "borrowed and did not invent" in *Marbury v. Madison*, his hypothesis may be applied to the general question concerning the Chief Justice's originality as an interpreter of the Constitution. "But unless our philosophy of government is to be controlled by the rules of a patent office," Professor Cahn has written, "novelty can hardly be accepted as the sole or decisive test of merit. In point of fact, a mature understanding—far from identifying the important with the novel—would attribute greater value to *Marbury v. Madison* precisely because it formalized and installed political conceptions which had already gained some measure of general support." [14]

The suspicion that Marshall developed his ideas while under the spell of Hamilton apparently goes back to the days when the two men were still active on the stage of national politics. Referring to the debate over Washington's Neutrality Proclamation, Story says:

> On this occasion, Mr. Marshall found himself, much to his regret, arranged on a different side from Mr. Madison. He resolutely maintained the constitutionality, the policy, nay, the duty of issuing the proclamation, by oral harangues, and by elaborate writings. For these opinions he was attacked with great asperity in the newspapers and pamphlets of the day, and designated by way of significant reproach, as the friend and coadjutor of Hamilton, a reproach which at all times he would have counted an honor; but when coupled (as it was) with the name of Washington, he deemed the highest praise. [15]

The striking fact about the important occasions when Marshall found himself championing the administrations of both Washington and Adams is that he usually argued for the constitutionality as well as the policy of the measures under attack. Probably

[14] Cahn, "An American Contribution," reprinted in *Supreme Court and Supreme Law*, Cahn, ed., pp. 1-2.

[15] Story, *op. cit.*, p. 35.

the leading illustrations are his defense of the Proclamation of Neutrality of 1793, the Jay Treaty of 1795, and the action of President John Adams in surrendering Jonathan Robbins to the British government to be tried for murder allegedly committed on a British warship. Concerning Marshall's speech in Congress vindicating the Chief Executive's right to turn Robbins over to the British, Story observes that it "placed him at once in the first rank of constitutional statesmen." [16]

According to Joseph Story, then, the true measure of Marshall's stature as "constitutional statesman" was clearly evident as early as the first crucial decade under the Constitution. Its hallmark was Marshall's success in vindicating assertions of national authority not only in terms of constitutional sanction, but also in terms of desirable public policy. And later, while speaking of Marshall's contributions as Chief Justice, Story suggests that there was a common source of inspiration for Marshall's service to the nation in both periods of his career:

> He [Marshall] was in the original, genuine sense of the word, a Federalist—a Federalist of the good old school, of which Washington was the acknowledged head, and in which he lived and died. . . . He boldly, frankly, and honestly avowed himself, through evil report and good report, the disciple, the friend, and the admirer of Washington and his political principles. . . . When, under extraordinary excitements in critical times, others, with whom he had acted, despaired of the Republic, and were willing to yield it up to a stern necessity, he resisted the impulse, he clung to the Union, and nailed its colors to the mast of the Constitution.[17]

One can be sure that for John Marshall the transfer from the hectic arena of political conflict and public debate to the more serene forum of constitutional arbitration was a perfectly natural and easy transition. Marshall took the essentially amorphous character of the judicial article and turned it into a mandate for enabling judges to speak in the name of the Constitution while subjecting the other governmental organs to their will. A comment by Edward S. Corwin conveys a cardinal truth about the relation between the Supreme Court and the Constitution:

[16] *Ibid.,* p. 44.
[17] *Ibid.,* pp. 57–58.

"No part of the Constitution has realized the hopes of its framers more brilliantly than Article III, where the judicial power of the United States is defined and organized, and no part has shown itself to be more adaptable to the developing needs of a growing nation. Nor is the reason obscure: no part came from the hands of the framers in more fragmentary shape or left more to the discretion of Congress and the Court." [18]

But perhaps even more important than the largely undefined character of the provisions which confer the "judicial power of the United States" is the generality of the language in which the great clauses of the Constitution are couched. Since the vagueness and sweep of these clauses invited definition or interpretation, the tribunal which claimed the right of authoritative exposition was bound to assume a strategic and unique position in the constitutional system. Their very ambiguity made it possible, moreover, for the conflicting forces in American society to invoke the Constitution in defense of their respective interests.

"It is a commonplace that the great divisive contests in American history," writes Paul A. Freund, "have been played out across the boards, as it were, of the Supreme Court. There, as in the sublimation of a morality play, have passed in review before a tribunal of authoritative critics the dramatic conflicts over slavery, the contest between land and water transportation, the struggle of industrial competition against the forces of concentration, the clashing interests of workers, consumers and investors, and the claims of dissenting groups and individuals." This comment by Professor Freund was made with reference to the Supreme Court's special role as "umpire" of the federal system and led him to raise a rather important question: "A federal system presupposes diversity and must cope with corresponding tensions. Does it assume also a judiciary vested with the role of arbiter?" [19]

Indeed, the appeal to the Constitution is almost as old as the document itself. It is sometimes forgotten that the issue of unconstitutionality became a weapon in the conflict over public policy even before the doctrine of judicial review had been enunciated by

[18] Corwin, *John Marshall and the Constitution*, p. 12.
[19] Freund, "Umpiring the Federal System," 54 *Columbia Law Review* 561 (1954).

Marshall. " 'Unconstitutionality' vied with 'liberty' as the popular rallying cry," is the way John C. Miller has aptly described the strategy of the opposition to Hamilton's measures in the early 1790s.[20] Like other Federalists, Hamilton came to be greatly irritated by the resort to this technique, as his anonymous letters in defense of the Jay Treaty reveal.[21]

"Why were Americans soon ascribing to the Constitution," another perceptive historian has asked, "a finality which none of the framers had claimed for it?" Among the factors making for the "apotheosis" or "cult" of the Constitution, he singled out for special emphasis what he calls "the silences" of the Constitution:

> When, therefore, assumption and the bank came up as party measures under the Constitution, it was possible alike for those who advocated and those who opposed these controversial measures, while bitterly contending with one another, to appeal to the same document in defense of their respective positions. Again the large majority of the framers were certainly opposed to universal manhood suffrage, but their attitude toward it was not betrayed in the document which they drafted.[22]

It is these same "silences" of the Constitution which furnish one of the major clues to the significance of both John Marshall and Alexander Hamilton as architects of American statecraft. Without indulging in mere eulogy, what can one say about the way in which Hamilton and Marshall used the rare historic opportunity that time and circumstance afforded them? Something a distinguished lawyer of the last century said with Marshall

[20] Miller, *Alexander Hamilton: Portrait in Paradox*, p. 296.

[21] "It is only to know the vanity and vindictiveness of human nature, to be convinced, that while this generation lasts there will always exist among us men irreconcilable to our present national Constitution; embittered in their animosity in proportion to the success of its operations, and the disappointment of their inauspicious predictions. It is a material inference from this, that such men will watch, with lynx's eyes, for opportunities of discrediting the proceedings of the government, and will display a hostile and malignant zeal upon every occasion, where they think there are any prepossessions of the community to favor their enterprises. A Treaty with Great Britain was too fruitful an occasion not to call forth all their activity." Hamilton, "Camillus," No. 1, July 22, 1795. *Works*, Lodge, ed., IV, 371.

[22] Robert L. Schuyler, *The Constitution of the United States*, pp. 201, 204–205.

in mind is an equally valid measure of Hamilton's achievement: "The test of historical greatness—the sort of greatness that becomes important in future history—is not great ability merely. It is great ability combined with great opportunity, greatly employed." [23]

Certainly neither Hamilton nor Marshall can be accused by posterity of having been unconcerned with the future direction of the country's development. On the contrary, their special claim to importance in the evolution of the United States as a great nation derives precisely from the fact that they quite consciously set themselves the task of helping to bring it to fruition. Sharing a common intuitive vision of America's future grandeur, each of them assumed the responsibility for fashioning the necessary instruments, intellectual and practical, for realizing the high goals they had in view. They also shared the conviction that the government established by the Constitution was "clothed with powers competent to calling forth the resources of the community," as Hamilton phrased it.[24]

The problem of achieving effective government was linked, in the minds of both Marshall and Hamilton, with the necessity of pursuing policies which would build strength and influence for the Union. Ironically, it is this preoccupation with national power which is the source of their reputation for political conservatism and at the same time the reason for their significance for the twentieth century. What Louis M. Hacker has said about the lasting impact of Hamilton's "public program" is substantially true also of Marshall: "Hamilton was a statesman whose policies remained the staples of American government long after his personal retirement—indeed, his defeat—and which continue to furnish guidance for our contemporary world." [25] Perhaps

[23] Edward J. Phelps, "Chief Justice Marshall and the Constitutional Law of his Time," An address before the American Bar Association, Saratoga, Aug. 21, 1879, p. 5.

[24] The words will be found in Hamilton's "Report on the Public Credit," Jan. 14, 1790, *Papers of Alexander Hamilton*, VI, 69.

[25] Hacker, *Alexander Hamilton in the American Tradition* (New York: McGraw-Hill Book Co., Inc., 1957), p. 19 (Introduction). For an interesting resumé of the attempt by recent writers on American conservatism to deny to Hamilton a place in the "conservative tradition," see Professor Hacker's Epilogue to this book, pp. 247–256.

some might wish to add the qualification voiced, appropriately enough, by Jefferson's biographer. Conceding that Hamilton enunciated "principles of liberal construction which have echoed and re-echoed through the generations," Dumas Malone has observed that "It is fortunate, however, that these can be applied in behalf of more popular interests than Hamilton himself gave thought to, as they have been since his day." [26]

In her recent attempt to correct the "distortion" of Hamilton which was apparent in the bicentennial celebration of his birth, Adrienne Koch charges that an effort was made "to take him forcibly beyond his human scope." She digresses long enough from her analysis of "Hamilton and the Pursuit of Power" to give us one of the clearest statements of the chief reason for Hamilton's importance for the century of the common man. Professor Koch writes:

> Of the five men [Franklin, Jefferson, Adams, Madison, and Hamilton] we are discussing, Hamilton had the sharpest vision of an infant nation's need to acquire national strength, both economic and military. In stressing this and providing a program for the deliberate encouragement of productive and capital strength in the United States, he was—as we now see—a reliable prophet of the mightiest industrial economy the world has yet produced. And there is no wisdom in belittling the contribution of a richly productive economy to the basic welfare of the people as a whole. This is certainly one of the foremost virtues of a democratic society, that it can offer most of its people freedom from the grinding misery of a subhuman struggle for bare life. The direction of Hamilton's thought to this constructive end was good fortune for this nation.[27]

Similarly, it is possible to explain Marshall's meaning for today without incurring the serious intellectual hazard of tearing ideas from the soil in which they were nurtured. A sense of history is the best safeguard against confusing constitutional tactics with an identity of purpose. The fact that Marshall's broad views of national authority supplied a basis for federal control of the

[26] Malone, *Jefferson and the Rights of Man* (Boston: Little, Brown and Company, 1951), p. 346.

[27] Koch, *Power, Morals, and the Founding Fathers* (Ithaca: Great Seal Books, 1961), pp. 51, 57–58.

American economy, for instance, is no reason for assuming that
he would have approved of the objectives which may have inspired such legislation.

It is necessary to bear in mind that the economic, political, and
constitutional outlook of both Marshall and Hamilton evolved
under the pressure of events and was not the product of abstract
reasoning. They were not political philosophers in the classical
sense of the term. In today's vocabulary, we would probably say
that they were conservative in their attitude toward the economic
process—as regards property, business, and finance—and liberal
in their interpretation of constitutional language. It is certainly
conceivable that had they lived at a time of vigorous governmental activity in behalf of social welfare, they might have been
less bold and imaginative in the use of the art of interpretation.
But seen against the background of the great epoch to which they
belong, Marshall and Hamilton may be included among those
builders of a nation whose contribution is continuously adaptable
to the changing purposes of the society meant to be served. David
Hume might well have installed them in his pantheon of law-
givers: "Of all men, that distinguish themselves by memorable
achievements, the first place of honour seems due to Legislators
and founders of states, who transmit a system of laws and institutions to secure the peace, happiness, and liberty of future generations." [28]

A year after he had resigned from Washington's Cabinet,
Hamilton argued a case before the Supreme Court which stands
as a suggestive bridge to the important work of constitutional
exegesis shortly to be initiated by Marshall. Appointed by the
Attorney General as special counsel in the case, he appeared to
defend the constitutionality of the tax on carriages which Congress had adopted on his recommendation in 1794. In the course
of addressing himself to the main issue in the case—whether the
levy was to be treated as a "direct" or "indirect" tax—Hamilton
made a remark which may be said to foreshadow Marshall's
method in construing the Constitution. Said Hamilton: "What
is the distinction between direct and indirect taxes? It is a matter
of regret that terms so uncertain and vague in so important a

[28] Hume, *Essays, Moral Political and Literary,* I, 127.

point are to be found in the Constitution. We shall seek in vain for any antecedent settled legal meaning to the respective terms —there is none." [29]

To Marshall the presence of "uncertain and vague" phrases in the Constitution was not so much "a matter of regret" as an opportunity and a challenge. Unencumbered by prior decisions or the views of legal authorities, he could give free rein to his fertile imagination and, in the process of doing so, proclaim constitutional principles expressive of his deepest convictions. Speaking as one whose experience and philosophy made him sure of the meaning and mission of the Constitution for America, Marshall succeeded in placing the Supreme Court's imprimatur upon a conception of the document which made it appear that there could be no other interpretation. He cemented the tradition of looking to the Constitution itself as the source of the power to deal with problems which could not have been foreseen by the Nation's founders.

Yet what Vernon Louis Parrington termed "constitutional centralization" [30] is not the only facet of Hamilton's theory of government to which Marshall also subscribed. No less significant, at least from the point of view of the future of constitutional law, was the great importance they attached to the protection of minority rights, particularly private property. Both of them anticipated—even before the Constitution was launched—that courts would come to serve as a shield against what Marshall was to refer to, late in life, as "the tyranny of majorities." [31] As subsequent events were to prove, acceptance of the notion that the judiciary was the guardian of constitutional limitations upon governmental power became the cornerstone of judicial review itself.

In the early decades of the nineteenth century, the most significant of the judicially developed weapons against legislation infringing property rights was the idea which Edward S. Corwin

[29] Brief in *Hylton v. United States,* 3 Dallas 171 (1796). See Richard B. Morris, *Alexander Hamilton and the Founding of the Nation,* p. 254.
[30] Parrington, *Main Currents in American Thought* (New York: Harcourt, Brace and Company, 1927), I, 306.
[31] John Marshall to Edward Everett, June 19, 1832. (*Proceedings of the Massachusetts Historical Society.*)

long ago "baptized" as the doctrine of vested rights—"the most prolific single source of constitutional limitations of any concept of American constitutional law." Its rationale, it would seem, was the assumption that *"the effect of legislation on existing property rights was a primary test of its validity;* for if these were essentially impaired then some clear constitutional justification must be found for the legislation or it must succumb to judicial condemnation." [32] The assimilation of the theory of vested rights into "due process" was the logical precursor of the jurisprudence which became dominant toward the end of the century, when due process of law began to be applied to the substance of legislation. In the field of industrial relations, the new course of decisions was justified with the aid of the doctrine of "liberty of contract" as the test of the constitutionality of governmental regulation.

It is thus clear that Marshall's contract clause opinions rested on a concept which is at the root of one of the most important principles of American constitutional law. But a closer look at the occasions on which Marshall manifested his solicitude for the rights of property will show that this predilection was basically related to the Chief Justice's other great constitutional concern. He was seeking to reverse a trend which he regarded as due to the abuse of their power by state legislatures. Benjamin F. Wright's fine summary of the way in which economic and political factors converged to shape Marshall's constitutional theory in these cases has obvious relevance for his stewardship as Chief Justice:

> It is safe to assert that the contract clause as the Framers thought of it was a very different thing from the clause at the end of Marshall's years on the Supreme Court. No one can be sure how important a place in American constitutional law and economic history the clause would have had if Jefferson, rather than Adams, had appointed a Chief Justice in 1801. . . . The Court with a Republican Chief Justice probably would have given a broader meaning to the clause than was foreseen in 1787. It might have held that public contracts as well as contracts between private persons come within the scope of the clause. But it is doubtful whether a Jeffersonian would have been so thoroughly imbued with the

[32] Corwin, *Liberty Against Government* (Baton Rouge: Louisiana State University Press, 1948), p. 72.

Hamiltonian distrust of legislative interferences with the rights of private property. And it is unlikely that an appointee of Jefferson's would have ruled against so many acts passed by Republican legislatures. Consequently it seems reasonable to believe that the work of writing into the texture of the Constitution the tenets of Hamiltonian economic theory depended upon the chance of an appointment to the judicial post which before 1801 had been of little significance.[33]

But it is not particular legal doctrines or economic dogmas which make Marshall's labors as the "great Chief Justice" pertinent for us today. American society has changed so radically and the nature and dimensions of the problems confronting the Supreme Court are so vastly different from those of Marshall's day, that what might be called his "case law" should not be expected to be always directly applicable. Marshall's significance must be sought elsewhere—in his spacious conception of the Constitution and in the realm of broad principle.

We are living in an age which has seen the Supreme Court gradually veering away from the property bias and becoming increasingly concerned with the protection of personal rights deemed to be essential to liberty and equality. In the dramatic struggle for civil rights, Americans are looking to the federal government for the removal of barriers to their freedom and independence. Our political leaders have an opportunity to develop a national policy on human rights and to place it on as firm a constitutional footing as the basis for federal action in the fields of economic control and public welfare has come to be. Should this happen, no small debt will be due to John Marshall for having cultivated a national outlook on matters which seemed to so many of his contemporaries to be of only local importance.

The effort to take the measure of Marshall's achievement goes back to the closing years of his service on the Court. Each generation has naturally found its own special reason for turning to him for inspiration and guidance. Yet on one thing all the interpreters have agreed. They have accepted Joseph Story's conclusion concerning the one domain in which Marshall made his permanent contribution as a judge. Said Justice Story:

[33] Wright, *The Contract Clause of the Constitution*, p. 27.

But his peculiar triumph was in the exposition of constitutional law. It was here that he stood confessedly without a rival, whether we regard his thorough knowledge of our civil and political history, his admirable powers of illustration and generalization, his scrupulous integrity and exactness in interpretation, or his consummate skill in moulding his own genius into its elements as if they had constituted the exclusive study of his life. His proudest epitaph may be written in a single line—Here lies the Expounder of the Constitution of the United States.[34]

Story, who had served on the Supreme Court with Marshall for nearly twenty-four years, was here repeating sentiments which he had expressed much more ardently when he dedicated his *Commentaries on the Constitution* to his chief in 1833. The dedication is in the form of a letter and reads in part as follows:

Sir,

I ask the favor of dedicating this work to you. I know not to whom it could with so much propriety be dedicated as to one whose youth was engaged in the arduous enterprises of the Revolution, whose manhood assisted in framing and supporting the national Constitution, and whose maturer years have been devoted to the task of unfolding its powers and illustrating its principles. When, indeed, I look back upon your judicial labors during a period of thirty-two years, it is difficult to suppress astonishment at their extent and variety, and the exact learning, the profound reasoning, and the solid principles which they everywhere display. Other judges have attained an elevated reputation by similar labors, in a single department of jurisprudence. But in one department (it need scarcely be said that I allude to that of constitutional law), the common consent of your countrymen has admitted you to stand without a rival. Posterity will assuredly confirm, by its deliberate award, what the present age has approved as an act of undisputed justice. Your expositions of constitutional law enjoy a rare and extraordinary authority. They constitute a monument of fame far beyond the ordinary memorials of political and military glory. They are destined to enlighten, instruct, and convince future generations, and can scarcely perish but with the memory of the Constitution itself.[35]

[34] Story, *A Discourse on the Life, Character, and Services of the Honorable John Marshall*, pp. 70–71.
[35] Story, *Commentaries on the Constitution of the United States*, vol. I, p. III.

The outpouring of homage to Marshall which was evoked by the centenary of his selection as Chief Justice was a long series of echoes of Story's prophetic words. Typical is the statement by the scholarly and perceptive James Bradley Thayer: "In the field of constitutional law, especially in one department of it, that relating to the national Constitution, he [Marshall] was pre-eminent,—first, with no one second." [36] But in our own time, no one has expressed more succinctly or in more tangible terms, than has Justice Frankfurter, the subtle and ramifying effects of Marshall's constitutional thought:

> When Marshall came to the Supreme Court, the Constitution was still essentially a virgin document. By a few opinions—a mere handful—he gave institutional direction to the inert ideas of a paper scheme of government. Such an achievement demanded an undimmed vision of the union of States as a Nation and the determination of an uncompromising devotion to such insight. Equally indispensable was the power to formulate views expressing this outlook with the persuasiveness of compelling simplicity.
>
> It is shallow to deny that general ideas have influence or to minimize their importance. Marshall's ideas, diffused in all sorts of ways, especially through the influence of the legal profession, have become the presuppositions of our political institutions. He released an enduring spirit, a mode of approach for generations of judges charged with the awesome duty of subjecting the conduct of government and the claims of individual rights to the touchstone of a written document, binding the Government and safeguarding such rights.[37]

As long as the American people will continue to respect the Constitution as the fundamental "law of the land" and the Supreme Court as its legitimate interpreter, John Marshall's con-

[36] Thayer, *John Marshall*, pp. 56–57. Thayer also suggested that one of the principal factors responsible for the growth of the Court's power and prestige under Marshall's leadership was his success in putting an end to *seriatim* opinions—the former practice of having each member of the Court announce his opinion in every case. The fact that for ten years the Chief Justice "alone" spoke for the Court created an impression which "seemed, all of a sudden, to give to the judicial department a unity like that of the executive, to concentrate the whole force of that department in its chief, and to reduce the side justices to a sort of Cabinet of advisers." *Ibid.*, pp. 54–55.

[37] Frankfurter, "John Marshall and the Judicial Function," in *Of Law and Men*, pp. 4–5.

tributions as Chief Justice are bound to be valued by them. The reason is clear and significant. He succeeded in projecting the Supreme Court as a vital forum for the amicable adjustment of the deep conflicts which permeate American society. If the Supreme Court has become "the greatest Court in the world," as Justice Black recently characterized it,[38] John Marshall helped to make it so. Its tragic failure to avert our major constitutional crisis only served to confirm his memorable admonition in *McCulloch v. Maryland.* Did he not there warn that questions of power between the nation and the states "must be decided peacefully or remain a source of hostile legislation, perhaps of hostility of a still more serious nature." [39] The function of judicial arbitration contemplated by Marshall is altogether consistent with Lincoln's ringing declaration in his first Inaugural Address: "A majority held in restraint by constitutional checks and limitations, and always changing easily with deliberate changes of popular opinions and sentiments, is the only true sovereign of a free people." [40]

History, so often a useful synonym for the vast panorama of ideas and events which shaped an institution, has a way of ignoring the logic of origins and ideology. The judicial veto may have been conceived of by both Hamilton and Marshall as a necessary brake on popular government. In actual practice, the process of constitutional interpretation in which the Supreme Court has been engaged has come to serve the interests of an ever-expanding American democracy. This paradox, if such indeed it be, is in itself an important key to the understanding of the complex system of government ordained by the Constitution of the United States.

[38] "Justice Black and First Amendment 'Absolutes': A Public Interview," conducted by Professor Edmond Cahn before the biennial convention of the American Jewish Congress, April 14, 1962. Reprinted in *One Man's Stand for Freedom*, Irving Dilliard, ed. (New York: Alfred A. Knopf, 1963), p. 482.

[39] 4 Wheat. 316, 400–401 (1819).

[40] March 4, 1861. *Messages and Papers of the Presidents,* Richardson, ed., VI, 9.

Index